TRUE STORIES OF THE PARAS

The Red Devils at War

ROBIN HUNTER

Also by Robin Hunter

TRUE STORIES OF THE SAS
TRUE STORIES OF THE FOREIGN LEGION
TRUE STORIES OF THE SBS

First published in Great Britain by
Virgin Publishing
Thames Wharf Studios
Rainville Road
London W6 9HT

A catalogue record for this book is available from the
British Library.

ISBN 0 7535 0301 8

Typeset by TW Typesetting, Plymouth, Devon
Printed and bound in Great Britain by
Mackays of Chatham PLC

CONTENTS

ACKNOWLEDGEMENTS

This book could not have been written without the help of a great many Parachute Regiment soldiers and various military institutions. Thanks therefore to the Airborne Forces Museum, Aldershot, and the Editor of *Pegasus*, the Airborne Forces magazine; to the staff of the Imperial War Museum, and the National Army Museum, London; the School of Army Flying, Middle Wallop, and the Assault into Normandy Trust, especially to Keith Howell, who recorded the story of 6th Airborne on D-Day.

Among Airborne soldiers, my thanks to the late General 'Shan' Hackett for his account of the Arnhem battle; to the late Brigadier Joe Starling, for his tales of Northern Ireland and Aden; to Lt-Colonel CC Norbury MBE MC for his account of Operation *Varsity*, the Rhine Crossing of 1945; to Hugh Clarke of the 2nd Ox and Bucks Light Infantry, 6th Airlanding Brigade, 6th Airborne; to Tom Godwin of 1 and 3 Para, in Aden and Cyprus; to Ernie Price of 12 Para; to Roy Howard of the Glider Pilot Regiment; to James Wallwark, also of the Glider Pilot Regiment; to David Wood, of the Ox and Bucks Light Infantry, 6th Airlanding Brigade; to Bill Elvin, 7 Para; to George Price and SF Capon, 9 Para; to Dennis Milborne for his account of 5 Parachute Brigade at Semarang; and indeed to all those who contributed the personal accounts in the following pages. This is their story, and I commend it to you.

INTRODUCTION:
THE PARACHUTE COURSE

'Knowledge dispels Fear'

Motto of the RAF Parachute School

This is a book about parachute soldiers, but principally about
those who served, or are serving, in the Parachute Regiment
of the British Army, a regiment that has established an
outstanding battlefield record since it was created in 1940, in
the early months of the Second World War.

During that war the Regiment expanded to two full
divisions, the 1st and 6th Airborne Divisions, and came to
include many battalions and a large contingent of airborne
soldiers who flew into battle in gliders. It also included
gunners, sappers, signallers, and medical staff, all of them
parachutists, all qualified to wear the red beret and the
coveted airborne wings. Theirs is a thrilling story and the
following pages contain many accounts from men who
served in the Parachute Regiment at that time and whose
courage and determination in some terrible battles gave
that Regiment its unique style and very special *esprit de
corps.* That spirit comes in part from the shared experience
that all parachute soldiers must endure, that of leaping
into hundreds of feet of damn-all from a transport aircraft,
and trusting life to an assembly of silk and nylon cord
called a parachute.

Every parachute soldier, from private to general,

without exception, has to do this several times before he can 'put-up' his parachute wings, and do it to order thereafter; whatever anyone may say later, the experience of parachute jumping is not for the faint-hearted. This shared experience binds parachute soldiers together and creates that tremendous *camaraderie* that all Airborne soldiers share. It also sorts out the men from the boys but, given a little nerve and guts, anyone can do it – though anyone who has done it and says he has never been scared of jumping is a liar. You can get used to it, and you can even get to like it, but anyone with any imagination at all will find it something of a strain, especially in the 'hanging-about' period before the aircraft takes off.

However, the reader of this book should realise at the start that the parachute is only a means to an end. The object of military parachuting – the only object of parachuting – is to put a fully organised infantry section, platoon, battalion, brigade or division, on the ground, behind the enemy lines, fully equipped and ready to fight. Military parachuting is not a sport but a way to get to battle, nothing more. Once the parachute soldier is on the ground he is an infantryman, gunner or sapper or signaller, and the last thing parachuting should do is scatter these well-trained and valuable men all over the countryside, though, as we shall see in later chapters, that all too often happened.

Nor are parachute assaults all that frequent. The Second World War saw less than a dozen airborne landings, by parachute and glider, and the Parachute Regiment history reveals only one occasion since the Second World War – at Suez in 1956 – when the Regiment actually parachuted into battle. Most of the Parachute Regiment's formidable reputation has been gained in infantry battles, but parachuting defines the parachute soldier, so it might be as well to describe parachuting now, as background to what follows.

The first step towards what the RAF Parachute Jumping Instructors (PJIs) used to call 'The Second Greatest Thrill', is to volunteer. All parachute soldiers, in all armies which have such troops, are volunteers, and no soldier is dragooned out the aircraft door. In the British Army a Parachute Regiment volunteer will spend some time – several months at least – on normal basic and infantry training before he is sent on to the Parachute School. This training is completed by a spell in P Company, where the regimental recruit will be joined by young officers fresh out of Sandhurst who want to be commissioned into the Parachute Regiment, and by officers and men from other arms, who either want to do the parachute course or are destined for a role in the parachute support units – the sappers, gunners, signallers, etc. P Company training is hard, virtually a commando course, and only those who complete it successfully can go on to the relative joys at the RAF Parachute School.

The first surprise for the airborne recruit here is that the Parachute School is run by officers and NCOs from the RAF Physical Training Branch. These gentlemen are all extremely fit, many having amassed a formidable total of parachute jumps, a 1,000 plus not being at all uncommon. They are arguably the finest instructors in the Service and they certainly possess the unique gift of inspiring confidence, both in the parachute itself and in the training, that moves the recruit inexorably towards that wide-open doorway on an aircraft high in the sky. Parachuting *is* unnatural. As someone once said, only a lunatic would jump out of a perfectly safe aircraft, and for most people the idea of 'dicing with death in the skies' is not one they care to entertain. The great knack of the PJIs is to make this behaviour seem perfectly normal.

They do this with an air of unruffled calm and by breaking the whole business into easily digestible fragments. Training begins in the hangar – using full-scale models or actual fuselages – where the recruit learns to fall and roll out the shock of the landing, to move up to the door of the aircraft without stumbling, to fit and check the parachute correctly and to exit the aircraft with force and precision, punching through the slipstream and away from the aircraft. All this has to be learnt with and without equipment, for as the training progresses the recruit is supplied with a weapons container and two 'skyhooks', quick-release devices with which to attach the weapons container to the parachute harness. He is also supplied with a reserve parachute . . . just in case.

This training is enjoyable and physical. After a few hours of landing and rolling the stomach muscles are screaming for a rest and most recruits get out of bed on the second and third mornings of the course by pulling themselves upright by their hair or rolling out on to the floor. The stress is not only physical, for as an exit and landing aid the recruit has to endure 'The Fan'; The Fan is just that, a flat-bladed fan, attached to a steel cable which is attached in turn to a parachute harness. The recruit climbs to a platform about thirty feet above the concrete floor of the hangar, dons the harness and, on the command 'Go!', hurls himself off the platform in the approved parachuting manner.

Men who have done hundreds of jumps have been known to quail at The Fan. There is a second of falling, then the cable takes up the slack, the fan whirls, offering air resistance to slow the descent, and the landing on the mats below is usually quite gentle. The Fan though is a cold-blooded device and you have to have a great deal of faith in your instructors to believe that it will actually work and that you will not land up with a brace of broken legs or paraplegic. As the days go by, more and more such devices are introduced and the recruit learns – or is programmed – to hurl himself out of the door on the word 'Go', to follow the correct mid-air drill, to look for problems with the parachute rigging lines and correct them, to release the weapons container, assess his drift over the ground and then land and roll correctly. And then comes the first real jump.

There are those – and this writer is among them – who regard the first parachute jump as little more than the logical end of a trial period. By the time you get there you are so keyed-up and trained that you go out the door without thinking about it. The one that tightens the bowels is the *second* jump, when the novelty has worn off and you know – more or less – what to expect. I can recall shaking with fear before the second jump, and if anyone is going to refuse this is often when they do it.

Until 1996 the first two jumps were made at 800 feet from a cage dangling below a captive barrage balloon; one jump was made out the door, the other through a hole in the floor. The balloon has now been replaced by a helicopter, but the process is otherwise the same. Four or five recruits file into the cage or helicopter and are taken up to 800 feet. If all is well and the wind is not too strong, they are called forward one at a time by the PJI, who positions them in the door and, with a shriek of 'GO!', slaps them on the shoulder – and out they go.

There is not much sensation of falling. Those who keep their eyes open after they have dropped – which is advisable – will see their feet come up as they pass 100 feet, and then there is a tug on the shoulders and the parachute – wonderful creation that it is – has opened. You are going to live, and only shouts from below, where another PJI is monitoring your descent, prevents you from enjoying the view and the delights of floating down gently to the earth below. You land, hopefully without breaking anything, roll out the shock in the approved manner and feel like a god. Then you have to do it again.

The training continues. You move on to aircraft and drop out in ever increasing numbers, first in 'slow pairs', two at a time as the aircraft crosses the drop zone (DZ) at a few hundred feet – for the lower and slower the drop the less the troops will be dispersed on the ground. You jump in fives and tens, racketing down the fuselage as fast as you can, hurling yourself out the door on the heels of the man ahead. You jump in full plane-loads, maybe a hundred at a time, where the air is full of parachutes and dangling weapons containers. You jump with full equipment and then with equipment at night, when only the thud of the weapons container, hitting the ground, lets you know that *terra firma* is coming up fast. If you are a Royal Marine or in the SBS you will even jump into the sea. The standard parachute course consists of eight jumps, and by the time that is over – which, because of wind and weather considerations can take several weeks –

the recruit knows all he needs to know about military parachuting.

Finally, the parachute course is over and the time arrives for the big moment, the event that most parachute soldiers have been waiting or training for ever since the idea of joining a parachute unit entered their heads. With the rest of the course you parade in front of the transport aircraft, and the course officer, or some visiting bigwig, comes along the line and presents you with those much-coveted Parachute wings. With them comes a warning. Up to now you could have refused to jump and no hard feelings; you leave the course and return to your unit or are transferred to some other non-parachuting post. You may feel low, but you have done no wrong.

Once a parachute soldier 'puts-up his wings', however, all that changes. Refuse to jump now and you face a court martial for refusing to obey an order. But few parachute soldiers think of that in the euphoria of the moment. The main thing now is to get to the tailor and get those wings sewn on to your tunic. You have made it: you are parachute qualified, a member of an elite. And the pleasing fact is that you are. Parachute soldiers are an elite; those who wear the wings today are the latest in a line of hard-fighting soldiers that have long since earned the reputation of being ranked among the finest soldiers on earth; fierce in battle, relentless in attack, resolute in defence, an enemy to beware of.

It might be worth mentioning that I did not serve in the Parachute Regiment. I saw my service in the Royal Marines Commandos. I did the parachute course, much as described above, and have many friends in the Parachute Regiment, especially in 3 Para, which soldiered alongside my unit in Cyprus, many years ago. Since then a myth has grown up, and been spread by the media, that Parachute soldiers and Royal Marines do not get on, but I have found no evidence of this – quite the contrary. Major-General Julian Thompson, who had 2 and 3 Para under command in the Falklands War, told me once that he 'could not think of better men to go to war with'. This is their story, and, as a Royal Marine, I commend it to you.

6

1

EARLY DAYS:
1940–41

*'We are inclining to the view that dropping troops by
parachute is a clumsy and obsolescent method.'*

Report of the Air Staff to Prime Minister
Winston Churchill, 12 August 1940

When the British Air Staff sent that depressing note to the
Prime Minister shortly after the Dunkirk evacuation in
June 1940, the idea that Britain should even have airborne
forces had been in existence for less than three months.
The Air Staff were not actually against the idea of
parachute forces but they felt that far better results would
be obtained by creating glider forces. This view may have
been influenced by the fact that gliders, though without
engines, were at least aircraft, while parachute soldiers
were a little betwixt and between; soldiers certainly and
therefore Army, but soldiers who came from the skies and
needed the RAF to get them into battle. All in all, the
RAF felt that glider-borne troops were more useful, and
had the advantage that they would not be scattered all
over the landscape on landing. Besides, the Germans, who
currently knew a lot more about parachute warfare than
the British, had placed all their parachute and glider
forces under the Luftwaffe, and the RAF might well end
up having the same responsibility.

In this they had a point, for all the airborne units of the

Second World War, British, United States and German, had a glider element and the airborne divisions always contained a glider brigade. For the airborne operations of the day the glider was essential, for a glider could carry heavy stores, ammunition, radio equipment, jeeps, guns, even light tanks. Besides, the glider was capable of landing men in formed-up bodies of platoon strength – thirty men – and therefore were particularly useful for *coups de main* attacks, sudden attacks against particularly important objectives or strongpoints, as the 6th Airborne Division were to demonstrate when they sent Major John Howard's glider-borne troops of the Oxfordshire and Buckinghamshire Light Infantry, the 'Ox and Bucks', against the Caen Canal and Orne River bridges on D-Day, 1944. Though this book concentrates on parachute operations, and gliders went out of use at the end of the Second World War, it has to be remembered that for a long while the term 'airborne forces' included glider troops.

The Germans had used both parachute and glider forces in their blitzkrieg offensives since the start of the war in September 1939, and after the British had been bundled out of France via Dunkirk in June 1940, it seemed sensible to create parachute and commando forces in the UK: raiding forces who could harass the enemy-occupied coast of Europe and develop techniques for the inevitable invasion necessary to return to the Continent and win the war. To this end, in June 1940, Winston Churchill ordered the creation of Commando units – 'men of the hunter class' – and a corps of at least 5,000 paratroopers. Two months later and not much had been done: the prime minister wanted to know why; hence the memorandum from the Air Staff of 12 August.

The initial call for volunteers had attracted plenty of men and some 500 were now 'in training', but the difficulties were formidable. Two officers, an RAF squadron leader, Louis Strange, DSO, MC, DFC – a man who, as these decorations indicate, had seen service in the Royal Flying Corps during the Great War – and from the

Army, a Major JF Rock of the Royal Engineers, had been ordered to set up a parachute training school, and they had set up shop at Ringway Airport in Manchester. Major Rock recalls that they found it 'impossible to get any information as to policy or task'.

The idea seemed to be that Squadron Leader Strange would handle the parachute training side of the problem while Major Rock would be responsible for working out how a parachute battalion should be used. These officers were given no guidance nor were they told what to do, but were simply obliged to do their best and create a course that would produce trained paratroops. As staff they had some Army and RAF Physical Training Instructors (PTIs) and an eight-man packing team from the RAF's own parachute section, a group usually employed packing parachutes for aircrew. This newly formed unit did not enjoy a great deal of support from the Air Ministry, who had the Battle of Britain to fight and a whole range of problems to overcome, and which regarded this call for paratroops as a most unwelcome additional task.

Parachute troops were not new. The Germans had been training parachute soldiers for some years and German parachute battalions were an integral part of the *Luftwaffe*, not the *Wehrmacht*. Russia had much larger parachute forces and had used them in action in Central Asia as far back as 1929, and the Russians had demonstrated their airborne capability in large-scale army exercises in 1936. A senior British Officer, General Wavell, who attended these exercises, commented that if he had not seen these parachute descents – which put a full battalion plus equipment, machine guns and artillery on the ground inside half an hour – he would not have believed it possible. The British, as so often, paid no attention to this activity overseas, and now had to start from scratch with their backs already pressed against the wall.

The first thing to be done was to rough out a training programme, find some parachutes and some suitable aircraft. Parachutes were a major problem, for the only ones available were the aircrew type, which were opened in freefall by pulling a rip-cord. As for aircraft, the two types available were a bomber, the Whitley, and a large transport aircraft, the Bombay. Parachutes and aircraft were assembled at Ringway where the parachute school now had a name, the Central Landing School, and a programme prepared for the first volunteers. A notice was also distributed to the troops training in the surrounding area, telling them that, although a German invasion was indeed imminent, any paratroops seen descending around Manchester were almost certainly on our side and should not be shot at.

The first volunteers, two 'Fighting Troops', about 150 men, all of No. 2 Commando, arrived at Ringway on 9 July. This unit, which later became the 1st Battalion, the Parachute Regiment, had been recruited as a Commando and the men still wore their own regimental badges and berets. They were fit and willing and very anxious to get their training over and done with, for they were hungry for action. They wanted to get to grips with the enemy which was why they had volunteered for Commando and Airborne training. First though, they had to learn to parachute, and at least in the early days, to pack their own parachutes. This task was later taken on by women parachute packers who, apart from the reminder that 'A man's life will depend on every parachute you pack' hanging over the packing benches, were allowed to make a parachute descent themselves, just to see what it was like and drive home the importance of correct packing. All that lay in the future though when the first volunteers reached Ringway in 1940.

The method then chosen to introduce men to parachuting was known as the 'pull-off method', a hair-raising process which had been used to train skydivers and pre-war aircrew volunteers. In peacetime this activity normally took place from a slow biplane; the volunteer would climb out of the open cockpit on to the wing, make his way out along it, clinging to the struts, until he was well clear of the tail. Then, clinging on grimly with one hand, he would pull the rip-cord of the parachute. The parachute would then whisk out and develop – or deploy – and the volunteer would be jerked off the wing and into space. The theory was that if the parachute failed to deploy, but just swirled about in the slipstream like mum's washing, the volunteer could climb back into the aircraft and have another go later.

For the new recruits at Ringway this method had been refined somewhat, using the Whitley bomber. About ten volunteers at a time would climb in to the Whitley and sit on the floor while the aircraft took off and climbed to 1,000 feet. Then, one by one, they were summoned forward to the jumping platform at the rear of the aircraft, a position created by removing the rear gun turret. They crawled under a bar, turned and hung on to it; by now they were effectively outside the aircraft and exposed to the full force of the slipstream. Then, at a signal from the instructor they would let go with one hand, pull the rip-cord of their parachute and be whisked off. It sounds terrifying, and it was, but amazingly enough, there was no shortage of men willing to do it.

The 'pull-off' method was also extremely dangerous and the first military parachuting fatality took place a few days later when a Commando volunteer, Driver Smith of the Royal Army Service Corps, fell to his death with an undeployed canopy. Driver Smith was the first but by no means the last soldier to die from the effects of a 'Roman Candle' the then-popular name for what happened when the parachute leaves its bag but refuses to fill with air, and streams above the parachutist like a candle in the wind as he falls at terminal velocity – about 120 mph – to earth.

This first fatality occurred after only 135 descents and led to an investigation and further parachute trials, during which three dummies 'Roman Candled' in full view of the anxious volunteers. Morale plummeted and only revived when technicians from the Irving Parachute Company and the GQ Parachute Company rapidly produced a combined version of the military parachute known as the 'X' Type, a model that was both safe and effective and which stayed in service with Britain's airborne forces for the next 25 years.

The 'X' Type did away with the rip-cord. The parachute was pulled from its bag and deployed by the use of a static line fixed to a point inside the aircraft. As the parachutist fell, the static line and a long 'strop' inside the parachute allowed the parachutist to get well clear of the aircraft before the static line pulled out first the strop, then the harness lift webs, then the rigging lines to the canopy and finally the canopy itself, thus eliminating the risk of entanglement. Men also got entangled on the tail wheel of the Whitley aircraft, though this problem was solved by fitting a spat over the wheel. Before the trials were completed, however, another parachutist, Trooper Watts of the Royal Horse Guards 'Roman Candled' and fell to earth before the horrified eyes of his comrades.

After the introduction of the 'X' Type, parachuting became much safer, but there were still a number of problems to solve before it could become an effective means of sending soldiers into battle. To begin with, jumping was too slow; sending the men out one at a time from an aircraft travelling at 100 miles an hour scattered them widely. So the rear exit was abandoned for a slightly faster method, the men dropping through a hole in the fuselage of the Whitley aircraft.

For this, the men were grouped on either side of the hole and, on a given command, one man swung his legs into the hole and when the Green ('Go') light flashed, went out, keeping as straight as possible. The second man, on the opposite side, did likewise and fell away, their places being immediately taken by the follow-up men who came shuffling down the fuselage on their behinds to take position at the edge of the hole. By this means about ten men could get out of the aircraft in about thirty seconds – but they were still scattered over a quarter of a mile or more of ground. Nor was it without risk; many men were knocked unconscious or lost teeth after smashing their faces on the far side of the hole – an event known as 'ringing the bell' and parachutes still had a tendency to get caught on the tail wheel of the bomber as it went past. There was also another fatality when the snap hook connecting Corporal Carter's static line to the aircraft twisted loose and he fell to his death, the parachute still in its pack. The answer to the twin problems of speed of exit and safety was seen to be some means to jump out a door cut in the side of the aircraft, and using the Bombay transport aircraft seemed the ideal solution . . . except that the RAF needed the Bombays to move stores and men about their airfields and had none to spare for parachute training.

By the end of September 1940, three months after Ringway opened for business, things were not going well. Some 330 men had entered training, of whom thirty had refused to jump at some stage, twenty had been badly injured and two had been killed. Since most of the men had only done two jumps these statistics were alarming, and since the men were of high quality, keen and willing to learn, the problem clearly lay with the training and equipment. While a solution was being sought training continued and by the end of 1940 the first parachute battalion, formerly known as No. 2 Commando and now known as No. 11 Special Air Service Battalion, was formed up and anxious for battle. Another No. 2 Commando was formed for seaborne operations and made its name at the St Nazaire raid in 1943.

No. 11 SAS Battalion was given a chance to show what it could do in November 1940, when it was tasked to jump before an audience of VIPs assembled on Salisbury Plain. Fifty volunteers duly jumped, many thunderflashes were let off, smoke grenades were used in quantity and when the dust settled a staff car was seen to be missing, purloined by B Troop of the SAS battalion and used for a lightning raid against the 'enemy' bridge at Shrewton. This display of initiative went down very well until it was discovered that the missing staff car belonged to the guest of honour, Crown Prince Olaf of Norway.

Soon after this exercise the 11th SAS Battalion formed a Glider Wing and shortly after that sent a number of troops to attack the Tragino Aqueduct in Italy, a raid which will be described in the next chapter. So, slowly, the parachute arm developed, solving its problems as it went along.

Meanwhile, the Central Landing School had gained another officer, Wing-Commander Maurice Newnham DFC, a man who was to revolutionise parachute training. Newnham had been a fighter pilot in the Great War and wanted an active role in this one, and although his task at Ringway was to run the administration, he was soon involved in finding a solution to the high drop-out and injury rate suffered by volunteers in training.

Matters came to a head in April 1941 when Winston Churchill visited the school and was shown a 'mass' parachute jump by twenty volunteers. It had been decided that the prime minister would find it more interesting if he had a radio link to the aircraft and could hear all that was going on. Unfortunately, the first thing he heard was the commanding officer telling the pilot to take off and the pilot replying that he was not yet ready to do so as . . . 'five of the paratroopers have fainted'.

On his return to Downing Street Churchill sent out one of his famous 'Action this Day' memos, demanding a complete overhaul of parachute training, and reminding the Chiefs of Staff that a year before he had asked for 5,000 paratroops . . . and where were they? There was then a considerable amount of discussion, culminating in a firm promise by the Chiefs of Staff that there would be two parachute brigades and one airlanding (glider) brigade, in existence and fully trained by May 1942. So much for the promise, but how was it to be kept? The man chosen to deliver on the chiefs' promise was Wing-Commander Newnham, and in July 1941 he handed over his office files and took full charge of parachute training at Ringway.

Newnham had had plenty of time to think about the problems of his new post and his first decision was that parachute training must be made more comprehensible and far less frightening. Both ends could, he believed, be more easily achieved if the entire process was broken down into its component parts and as far as possible organised as a 'drill'. Those unfamiliar with the military world may not appreciate that the great aim of soldiering is to reduce life to a series of successful painless drills – or routines. A soldier who can get a good routine going is a happy soldier and a drill is simply another word for a successful routine.

Newnham set about this task, and had soon developed a number of routine drills that remain as the basis of parachute training to this day. He also realised that some gentler method had to be developed in order to get the men used to parachuting and in instructing them in landing drills while they were in the air. The answer he settled on involved training jumps from a small cage, suspended below a static balloon. The advantage of balloon jumping was that it was not only safer than jumping from an aircraft but the men could be 'talked-down' by instructors on the ground, shouting directions at them through loud hailers. The disadvantage was that balloon jumping, whether through the door or through a hole in the floor, was a remarkably cold-blooded business. Without the aid of the aircraft slipstream the parachutist falls sheer for about 200 feet before the canopy deploys, and most parachutists will admit that they much prefer the noise and bustle of an aircraft drop, to the cold calm of a balloon descent. Even so, as a training aid the balloon was unrivalled, certainly by the Whitley and Bombay aircraft, and balloon jumping soon became part of the standard parachute course.

Newnham had not yet made a parachute jump, but he believed in leading from the front and made his first descent in July 1941, a day or two after taking up his appointment. This was from a balloon, and Newnham ordered that from now on the volunteers' first two drops should be from a balloon cage. Before long more than 5,000 balloon jumps were being made at Ringway every month, most of them early in the morning or in the early evening when the air was still. The number of accidents fell dramatically and when the men went on to do their aircraft jumps they knew what to expect, having a good grasp of parachute handling and steering techniques. As a result the refusal and accident rate fell sharply.

Among the volunteers, was George Price, who went for parachute training in 1943:

My old pal Bill Worley and I volunteered for the Paras in August 1943. In a very short time indeed we were sent to Hardwick Hall near Chesterfield for selective training, where in three weeks we developed muscles we didn't know we had. Everything we did had to be done at the double. If we were caught walking, no matter where to, we were for the high jump. The hardest part was the ten-mile route march – run a mile, walk a mile, in full battle order. At the end of it our socks were covered in blood. It was a really tough course and a good many of the lads were RTU'd [Returned To Unit], but Bill and I got through and were duly graded as A1+.

From Hardwick Hall we were sent to Ringway near Manchester, where we did our parachute training. The hangar we used looked more like a circus: we rolled, tumbled, and jumped from heights on to mats. Then came the dreaded balloon drops. I can still hear the shout: 'Up 800 – four men dropping' We did two daytime drops and one night drop from the balloon. After that came the real thing, from a hole in the floor of a Whitley bomber. It was pretty good fun really and we enjoyed it, especially the extra shilling (5p) a day after we got our parachute wings. That was a lot of money sixty years ago, when a pint of beer was only a few pence.

In September 1943 we were posted to the 12th [Yorkshire] Parachute Battalion, which was originally the 9th Battalion, the Green Howards, and consisted mainly of Northerners. This was a bit strange for Bill and me, he being a Londoner and me coming from Slough. We had quite a dialect problem for a while, but we soon got used to it, which was just as well because I eventually married a lass from the North.

The training was very hard. We did many exercises, including being dropped in Wales and having to mock-fight our way back to Larkhill. I think in all I must have done about twenty jumps from various types of aircraft: Halifax, Albemarle, Stirling and the American Dakota – the C47. We once had a visit from General Montgomery while we were digging a slit trench, and he asked us what we were doing. I thought that was a bit daft, coming from him.

George Price jumped into France on D-Day, and this story will pick him up again later.

Two further developments occurred in late 1941. The first was the appointment of Brigadier Richard 'Windy' Gale, to command the newly formed, four-battalion-strong 1st Parachute Brigade. The second was the establishment of a permanent cadre of RAF PJIs as the parachute instructing staff at Ringway. There were some Army PJIs who served as instructors with the parachute units, but all the basic training on the parachute course was handled from then on by the RAF, who handled it superbly. They worked out new methods handling problems in the air, especially a method of 'kicking out the twists', when a parachute rigging lines became entangled, and 'steering' the parachute by spilling air from the canopy by pulling down on the front or rear lift webs. They also improved methods of landing, by introducing the 'para-roll', in which the parachutist rolled over on to his side on landing to absorb the shock of hitting the ground. All these steps made parachuting safer, and in November 1941 the RAF PJIs trained the men of the newly formed 2nd and 3rd Battalions of the Parachute Regiment (2 and 3 Para), running a full course for over 1,000 men, with only twelve men injured, two refusals . . . and none killed.

Brigadier Gale had no time for the 'tough-guy' image that was then being promulgated about Airborne and Commando soldiers. He maintained that a parachute battalion was merely an infantry battalion that made its way to the battle by air and once it was on the ground it would act and fight like a normal infantry unit. Thanks to the quality of the men – all volunteers – and the demands of parachute training, a parachute battalion never was exactly a 'normal' unit, but Gale insisted on a high standard of training, turnout and discipline in the units of his brigade. The first unit – the already formed No. 11 Special Air Service Battalion – fell short of his high standards and was promptly disbanded, but the majority of the men soon found a second home in the 1st Parachute Battalion – 1 Para – which formed in September 1941, under the command of Lt-Colonel EE Down, a fierce disciplinarian – known to his men as 'Dracula' Down – who soon tamed the wilder spirits and whipped his unit into superb shape. It has been said that in the early days everyone in the battalion 'hated Colonel Down . . . but there came a time when we would have gone to the ends of the earth for him and not from fear but from affection'.

In September 1941 the 1st Parachute Battalion, now a first-class and well-trained infantry unit, was ordered to Hardwick Hall, near Chesterfield in Derbyshire, to join up with the other units of the now forming 1st Parachute Brigade. This brigade was to form part of an Airborne division, 1st Airborne, a formation under the command of Major-General Frederick 'Boy' Browning, DSO, a Guardsman and a man who became known later as the 'Father of British Airborne Forces'. The early days were now coming to an end as this division formed and trained and took its place in the Order of Battle.

By now, at the end of 1941, fifteen months after the order to form an airborne force had been issued, the training at Ringway was getting well into its stride, with hundreds of troops going through the parachute course every month. A pattern had developed, but military parachuting was still a new activity and problems continued to surface. The winter of 1941–42 saw some grim times; in one two-month period five men fell to their deaths with unopened parachutes and in February 1942 two men were killed and 48 injured, most of the latter by landing on frozen-hard ground. Newnham decided to demonstrate that, in spite of all this, matters were going well and led the instructors on a demonstration drop. This did not go well or greatly impress the assembled soldiery, for Newnham and three of his team were injured and had to be carried off the DZ on stretchers.

Even so, the training went ahead, not just on the purely parachuting side but also on the military side, where all the techniques for waging this new kind of warfare – airborne warfare – had to be worked out. Some of the lessons came from the enemy, after the Germans launched a successful airborne invasion of Crete in 1941. This was something of a Pyrric victory for the German parachute units, for though they eventually took their objectives, the Cretan airfields, and so allowed more troops and heavy equipment to be flown in and overwhelm the British and New Zealand troops defending the island, their losses were so severe that the Germans never again launched an airborne attack.

Part of the German success on Crete was due to airpower, especially close air support from Stuka dive-bombers and ground-strafing fighters to which the defending troops had no answer. One lesson the defenders did learn and pass back to the British airborne planners, was that an airborne attack must be strongly supported, for the troops themselves could not hold out for long without fresh supplies of men and ammunition and prompt support from tanks and artillery. This lesson was to be reinforced again and again in the years ahead and a lot of brave men died before it was finally learnt.

In March 1942 the 1st Brigade of British Airborne soldiers left Hardwick and went to join other units of the British Army at Bulford Camp on Salisbury Plain. Up to now none of the 'heavy infantry' troops had seen much of these Airborne soldiers. Those who volunteered and were accepted were kept in training and on trial exercises and there were still not many of them. Those who failed to get accepted returned to their parent units bearing tall tales of the horrors of parachuting and the great demands made on the would-be Airborne soldier. As a result, the Army at large regarded the Airborne soldier as either a superman or a gangster.

These impressions, both incorrect, did not last long once the paratroopers and the other soldiers had a chance to look each other over. The Airborne commanders had no time or use for hard cases and 'professional heroes', and those who joined expecting adulation and glamorous badges were soon sorted out and sent away again. It is fair to say that some soldiers played up to their public image, but not for long. Every soldier likes to go to battle in his own chosen way; the infantryman does not fancy the role of the tankman and the tank trooper wonders what it must be like to fight without the protection of armour plate, while everyone has respect for the sappers, clearing minefields ahead of the advancing troops. And then there are the other services: the Royal Air Force where you can get shot down in flames and the Royal Navy where, apart from being chronically seasick, there is always the chance of being drowned.

All in all therefore, the parachute soldier was happy in the role he had elected to play and had plenty of respect for those who served in other branches of the Service; and if the parachute soldiers got a bit of extra pay and attracted more girls, well, that was the fortune of war. The Airborne soldier did not look much different from any other kind of soldier and when you got right down to it, after a few seconds in the air, they became infantrymen; they came from every corner of the United Kingdom, and if there was a slight imbalance in favour of Scotsmen, Welshmen and Cockneys, the same could be said of most Special Force units. There were four battalions of the new Parachute Regiment in the 1st Parachute Brigade and the only way of telling one from the other was by their shoulder lanyards; green for the 1st Battalion, yellow for the 2nd Battalion, red for the 3rd Battalion and black for the 4th Battalion.

What did make an impression to the outside observer

was the abundance of headgear, and the great display of regimental badges. One parachute battalion contained men from over forty different corps and regiments of the British Army and while all wore khaki, all retained their regimental badges and head-dress, from Guardsmen's 'cheese-cutter' caps to Highland infantry bonnets and Tank Corps berets. The same held true of the Commandos and their solution was to adopt a common head-dress, the green beret, in a lighter green than that favoured by the Light Infantry battalions. General Browning, himself a Guardsman, did not care for this strange collection of headgear and decreed that his men should also have some distinctive form of head-dress. A number of berets were collected, each in a different colour, and the Chief of the Imperial General Staff, General Alanbrooke, was asked to choose one for the parachute soldiers. Alanbrooke hummed and hawed over the choice and in the end, unable to make up his mind he asked a private soldier what he thought. The man said that he preferred the red beret and so the choice was made. The red beret is now worn by parachute soldiers in all the armies of the world, and when the 1st Parachute Brigade wore it into action in North Africa in 1943 the Germans soon noticed it, and having experienced the quality of the troops who wore it, gave them a name they would cherish; the 'Roten Teufel' – the Red Devils.

2

FIRST BLOOD: THE TRAGINO AQUEDUCT AND THE BRUNEVAL RAID, 1941–42

'What happened to us afterwards did not matter very much as the job was done.'

Major TAG Pritchard on the Tragino Raid, 1941

The first two parachute operations of the war were raids, not airborne assaults. Parachute raids are not often mounted, for while it is easy – or at least relatively easy – to get the men to their assault area, it is much harder to get them back again after the raid is over. This point is amply demonstrated by the two operations covered in this chapter, the attack on the Tragino Aqueduct in Italy and the Bruneval Raid on the coast of France. The Tragino operation took place in February 1941, even while all the initial parachute training was going on, and it therefore became the first British parachute operation of the war.

Seven months after the creation of airborne units, it was high time that some paratroop soldiers went into action. It was also necessary that they should do so, and quickly, for most of the soldiers had volunteered for airborne forces on the understanding that it would swiftly lead them to the battlefield. When the prospect of action started to recede, the number of volunteers declined and a significant number of trained men asked to go back to their parent units. A unit left out of action for too long goes stale and for all these reasons when the call came for a strike against the Italian mainland, the 11th Special Air Service Battalion was called on for the task and took it on with alacrity.

Getting bored troops into action was not the main object of this operation, however. Destroying the aqueduct also had a strategic purpose, for Italian troops destined for the campaign in North Africa were being shipped across the Mediterranean from the ports of Taranto and Brindisi, two towns which relied for their water supply on the Tragino Aqueduct. If this aqueduct could be cut, the flow of troops would have to be reduced. The plan called for six Whitley bombers, loaded with paratroops, to fly from Malta and drop a sabotage party close to the aqueduct. They would take a large quantity of explosives and damage the aqueduct to such an extent that rapid repair would be impossible. Once the aqueduct had been destroyed the party would escape overland to the mouth of the River Sele – a distance as the crow flies of about fifty miles, but on foot a good deal further across some very rugged and mountainous terrain. They would then be taken off by a submarine, HMS/M *Triumph*. The party was to be commanded by Major Pritchard, an officer of the Royal Welch Fusiliers, while the sabotage team came from parachute-trained, Royal Engineer volunteers under a Captain Daly, Royal Engineers (RE).

The dropping aircraft were supplied by 91 Squadron from RAF Bomber Command which was then commanded by Wing-Commander Willie Tait, an officer who was later to command the famous 617 'Dam Busters' Squadron. This was the first parachute operation launched from Britain and everyone had a lot to learn, not least the bomber crews, who were more used to dropping bombs than men and needed careful training before they became accustomed to flying at 600 feet and as slowly as possible. Flying that low and that slow made the aircraft vulnerable to anti-aircraft fire – flak – but the lower the aircraft could fly and the slower speed they could manage while dropping the paratroopers, the closer the men would be when they landed on the ground.

The training took place at Tatton Park, near Ringway, using a 'mock-up' of the aqueduct. This training took another fatality when Lance-Sergeant Dennis parachuted into an ice-covered lake and drowned before he could be rescued. High winds ruined the dress rehearsal but otherwise all went well, and on 1 February 1941, Lieutenant Anthony Deane-Drummond, an officer who was to make his mark in Airborne operations later in the war, flew out with the advance party to Malta, taking with him the explosives and other specialised equipment.

A week later, on 7 February, the rest of the party followed in six Whitley bombers. Among those taking part were two Italian anti-Fascists, Private Nastri and Private Picchi. Both were already serving in the British Army and had volunteered to come along as guides and interpreters. These men took a great risk; before the war Picchi had been the banqueting manager at the Savoy Hotel and on the outbreak of war had helped to found the Free Italy Movement in London; his name was known to the Italian Fascists, and although he changed his name he did not look remotely British. His colleague, Private Nastri had lived in London so long he spoke English with a Cockney accent, but if either man was detected they could anticipate an early meeting with a firing squad.

After final briefings and a complete equipment check, the raiders took off from Luqa Airfield, Malta, on the evening of 10 February and at 2130 hours, Deane-Drummond's 'stick' of paratroopers jumped into the dark over Italy. Deane-Drummond jumped last, in order to see where his men were landing, a practice other airborne commanders were to follow; all went well and only one man was injured, breaking his ankle on landing.

At first it appeared that the entire drop had gone very well, but then it transpired that not all the paratroopers had arrived on the main DZ and that one complete plane load was missing. Deane-Drummond and his men had landed within a few hundred yards of the aqueduct and the next four aircraft had dropped their parachutists with equal accuracy. Only the sixth aircraft had gone amiss, dropping its men and their weapons' containers in the next valley – and this was tragic, because the men included Captain Daly and his sappers and those containers held most of the explosives necessary to destroy the aqueduct. At this stage of the war paratroopers did not drop with their weapons or equipment, other than side arms, grenades and perhaps a sub-machine gun, a Sten, shoved under their chest harness. Everything else was dropped separately in cylindrical weapons' containers carried down by coloured parachutes, which then had to be collected and their loads distributed. This always led to delay or, as now, ran the risk that vital items of equipment failed to arrive on the main force DZ.

There was nothing to be done about it now and Captain Pritchard sought out Second-Lieutenant Patterson, RE, who had landed near the aqueduct and told him to do his best with the explosives they had. By now a number of local peasants had turned up and were standing about, chatting to the paratroopers, and with their willing assistance the explosives were humped up the mountain to the foot of the aqueduct. Matters became even more difficult when Patterson examined the aqueduct and found that instead of being of brick, as described in the intelligence summaries, it was actually built of reinforced concrete. Here again, there was nothing to be done about it, so Patterson pressed on, and piled all his 800 pounds of explosive around one of the abutments. At 0030 hours the charge was fired and to everyone's great satisfaction part of the aqueduct collapsed, sending a torrent of water into the valley below.

So far the paratroopers had been undetected for the aqueduct had not been guarded. After the explosions however, the whole countryside woke up and search parties were soon combing the hills, calling in the *carabineri* and the Italian Army. The paratroopers had to leave behind the man with the broken ankle, and he was placed in the care of a local farmer while the rest struck out for the mouth of the Sele. They had four days to make the rendezvous and, before leaving the aqueduct, destroyed or buried all their heavy equipment and spare kit. In the hope of avoiding detection they marched by night and lay up by day but found it difficult to make any sort of time over the mountains in the dark. When they came down to lower slopes, hoping to make better time, they became caught up in a maze of small fields, stone walls and ploughed ground and were soon detected.

It is unlikely that these men ever stood any real chance of evading the enemy. The whole countryside was on the look out for them by now and on the third day Pritchard and Deane-Drummond's party was detected by a party of children. Some children hung about, staring at the soldiers, while others ran to fetch their families. When their mothers came up, followed by a party of soldiers, Pritchard ordered the troops to surrender, rather than risk a fire-fight which might kill women and children. This act of charity did not do the British soldiers much good; the women and children stoned and spat at them as they surrendered their weapons and were marched away. Eventually, all the parties were picked up, only Lieutenant Daly's team getting anywhere near the Sele. Of the two Italians, Picchi was soon identified, taken away, tortured, and shot, but Private Nastri, who managed to conceal his nationality, was sent off to prison as a British soldier and survived the war. At first the Italians threatened to shoot the entire party, but after a few days of interrogation – and very little food – the parachutists were transferred to a prison camp.

Deane-Drummond only stayed a prisoner for a year and a half. In December 1941 he staged his first escape and got as far as the Swiss frontier before he was recaptured. Six months later, in June 1942, he tried again, reached Switzerland and got back to Britain with help from the French *Maquis* escape line to Spain and Gibraltar. As for the Tragino Aqueduct, that was soon repaired, and the raid had at best a marginal effect on the movement of

26

troops to North Africa. What it did do was thoroughly alarm the Italians ... and give a great fillip to the morale of the Airborne soldiers mustering in England.

The next parachute operation was also a raid, and the plan also involved a parachute landing behind enemy lines and subsequent extraction by sea. Unlike the Tragino raid, the next operation, to seize vital parts from the Bruneval radar station, went very well. Small-scale raids like this were not really part of the paratroops' operational role, but in early 1942 the RAF had a problem that they thought the new parachute forces might help to solve. RAF bombers raiding Germany were being detected on their way to France by a radar system known as *Freya*, which could pick up bombers as soon as they took off from their bases in England. These bombers were tracked on *Freya* until they crossed the French or Dutch coasts and then handed over to another system known as *Wurzburg*, which was accurate enough to home on to individual bombers. This was just one stage in the electronic battle that the Germans and the Allies would wage throughout the war, and in 1942 – thanks to *Wurzburg* – the Germans were then winning.

British scientists had begun to deal with *Freya* but were very anxious to get their hands on a *Wurzburg* set and find out how to jam it. Aware of this, the Germans kept the *Wurzburg* stations carefully concealed and heavily guarded, but one was eventually detected close to the French coast, in the village of Bruneval, ten miles north of Le Havre. The task presented to the parachute troops was to raid the Bruneval radar station, capture the *Wurzburg* set, or at least let an RAF technician examine it, and bring either the set or the information back to Britain. This task went first to Vice-Admiral Louis Mountbatten, commander-in-chief at Combined Operations HQ who delegated it to Brigadier 'Windy' Gale of the 1st Parachute Brigade. Gale duly passed it on to the newly formed 2nd Parachute Battalion, and the battalion adjutant, Captain John Frost of the Cameronians (Scottish Rifles), was placed in charge of the operation.

He chose men from C Company, a company largely composed of Scotsmen, to do the job and it was this company, 'Jock' Company, that brought the Parachute Regiment its first battle honour.

Frost had not yet completed his parachute course when this task was laid before him, for he had injured himself on his second jump and ended up in hospital. He therefore rushed back to Ringway and completed the rest of his course in five days and rejoined C Company at Tilshead. Training commenced around Devizes on the Wiltshire Downs, though at this stage Frost did not know he was training for an actual operation. The cover story put out by Major-General Browning, now commanding the 1st Airborne Division, and Brigadier Gale, commanding the 1st Parachute Brigade, was that 'Jock' Company were simply to lay on a top-class exercise for the War Office brass, probably on the Isle of Wight, though, as a little encouragement, the men were told that if they tried hard and put on a good show they would be allowed to carry out a real raid some time later.

This was a good ruse and it worked; the men flung themselves into the training with great enthusiasm and the cover story remained intact. Eventually Frost was told the real task – to land on the coast of France and bring back parts of a secret German radar – and with this knowledge he was able to plan the actual raid and beat off a large number of unwanted suggestions from his superior officers.

The final plan was not unlike the one drawn up for the Tragino operation, but Frost was more than a little annoyed when he was told that the plan for the operation would be drawn up by Airborne Division HQ; all he had to do was obey orders and carry out the plan as directed. This was not only most unwise, it was contrary to accepted military practice. In most modern armies the officer charged with an operation is also charged with planning it, subject to whatever limitation in men, transport and support are inflicted on him by his superiors. Having drawn up a plan, he then submits it for their approval, but unless there is any real objection that plan will be adopted, subject perhaps to a little tinkering. The idea that people not actually involved in making the attack should presume to dictate how it should be made was most unusual, and Frost protested strongly but to no avail.

The company was divided into four parties, each with a separate task, and they were joined by sappers and an RAF technician, Flight-Sergeant Cox, a radar expert, who would examine the *Wurzburg* and if possible remove some vital parts for inspection in the UK. Flight-Sergeant Cox was the key man in the entire operation and one of the main tasks of the party charged with seizing the *Wurzburg* station was both his protection and that of a party of men from the Parachute Field Squadron, who had to dismantle any parts of the *Wurzburg* that looked interesting. The raiders would be flown to France by twelve RAF bombers of 51 Squadron, commanded by Wing-Commander Percy 'Pick' Pickard, DFC, a man who had recently starred in an RAF-sponsored film, *Target for Tonight*. Pickard was to be killed in February 1944, shot down while leading a low-level Mosquito attack on Amiens Prison. Pickard was a most experienced pilot and his men trained hard, aiming to drop Frost and his men virtually on top of the Bruneval radar site. Like the RAF crews charged with dropping the 11 SAS men on the Tragino Aqueduct, Pickard and his men had never dropped paratroopers before.

Since the cover story – that all this preparation was for a high level demonstration to senior officers – was still in place, it was possible to stage a number of rehearsals, some on Salisbury Plain, where the company were dropped by Pickard's squadron and made a full assault in the hills north of Pewsey Vale in Wiltshire, where the terrain somewhat resembled the coast of Normandy near Le Havre. These rehearsals went smoothly, and the company then moved on to practise with the Royal Navy, where matters did not go well at all, since the Navy coxswains could not find the right beach in broad daylight, even on the English coast. After a little more practice and liaison with the assault landing ship HMS *Prince Albert*, which would provide the landing craft and pick up the men from the beach before dawn, a full dress rehearsal was held. This went totally wrong from the start; the paratroopers landed on the right DZ but their weapons' containers were dropped ten miles away. The men had just been issued with a new weapon, the Sten sub-machine gun, but this alone would not be sufficient to subdue the Germans at Bruneval, and they needed the equipment in those containers. Matters did not improve; the landing craft failed to find the right beach yet again, and when the troops attempted to move up the coast to find them, they wandered into a minefield. Another rehearsal seemed advisable, and that too went wrong, with the landing craft running aground some distance offshore.

None of this was very surprising. Indeed, the object of having rehearsals is to find out if the plan will work and put things right before the actual operation. Even so, the inability of the naval crews to find the right beach was an additional worry for Frost as he waited for the weather to clear. By now he knew this was no demonstration but the real thing, though he had to keep this information to himself. After the drop and a – one hoped – successful attack, the raiders and their *Wurzburg* booty would withdraw down the nearby cliffs and be picked up by the Royal Navy in assault boats. This was a small but complete Combined Operation, involving the Army, Navy and Air Force and it was apparent that unless everyone played their part correctly, and the whole operation was endowed with a large amount of luck, it could all end in disaster.

Meantime, more information was coming in, either from RAF photo-reconnaissance aircraft or from agents of the French *Maquis*. It gradually became apparent that the Bruneval radar station was closely guarded, with a full company of German troops in the immediate vicinity, and about thirty soldiers, technicians and guards, at the site itself. Those not on duty were billeted at a nearby farm some 300 yards from the radar site and finally there was

30

a German platoon in Bruneval village. This gave the enemy about 400 men to oppose 'Jock' Company and it would take a careful plan to cope with them.

The final plan called for a three-phase attack, which had to be carried out and completed during the hours of darkness. The drop would take place as soon after dark as possible; the radar station would be attacked and taken and the men withdrawn to a nearby beach, which would be held by a protection party. As the first of the main force arrived, this party would call in the landing craft from the *Prince Albert*, which would close with the French coast after dark, and these landing craft would take the men back to the assault ship which would then proceed at best speed for the south coast of England. Air cover would be provided at dawn, but it was clearly not desirable to be hanging about off the French coast when daylight came and the Luftwaffe arrived to investigate.

Clearly, the first objective was to secure the line of retreat, so forty men, the 'Nelson' party were tasked, under Lieutenant Charteris, to drop and clear the beach defences and hold the exit routes. The second wave comprised the main force under Captain Frost, and consisted of three platoons, 'Jellicoe', 'Hardy' and 'Drake', about ninety men in all. They were to escort Flight-Sergeant Cox and the sappers to the radar site, fight their way in and hold it while Cox did his work. They would then get him back to the beach after the job was done. The final party, 'Rodney' was the reserve force, consisting of thirty men who would be used to counter-attack any enemy interference and cover the withdrawal to the beach. This plan was studied for days on a model and rehearsed time and again on the ground. The DZ for all these parties was a large field about half a mile east of the radar station, and on 24 February 1942, just a year after the Tragino operation, 'Jock' Company was ready to go. Then came a delay caused by bad weather.

As with the D-Day operation two and a half years later, the timing of the Bruneval raid was largely dictated by the tides. If the landing craft were to get in and pick up the raiders they had only a limited number of days when the tides were suitable – the 24th February and the three succeeding days. If the operation could not be carried out by Thursday 27 February, it would have to be postponed for an entire month – and then the same problem might arise again. Keeping an operation on hold like this is not easy, not least from the point of view of security. By now all the men knew what was going on and there was a risk that someone would be indiscreet, mention the fact to another soldier in another unit and the news would spread. Tilshead Camp was in the heart of a military area and the parachutists were not kept apart from the other units; nor could they be separated now or rumours would certainly get around that the Airborne lads were up to something.

Besides all that, nerves were starting to fray at the edges, not least at Battalion HQ. Thursday passed and it was starting to look hopeless, but then the Royal Navy decreed that they could *just* manage to get in and pick up the force, if the raiders went in that night. Suddenly, it all came right. The weather moderated, the winds dropped and at teatime on Friday 28 February 1942, the raid was on again. The soldiers were briefed and given their individual tasks and just after dark the men marched out to their aircraft, played on their way by the warlike rant of bagpipes. The C Company piper, Piper Ewing, played on until the last man was embarked; then handed his pipes to another soldier, and pulled on his parachute. Like the rest of 'Jock' Company, Piper Ewing was going on the raid. At 2230 hours the first aircraft took off and Pickard's squadron were on their way to France.

The Whitleys were not good parachute aircraft, cramped and cold, but the men were so glad to be under way at last that spirits were high as they flew across Southern England and out across the Channel, the men singing and telling jokes; the liveliest man in the party being Flight-Sergeant Cox, who sang two songs by popular request and followed them up with a number of jokes. It was a clear, frosty night, with bright moonlight, and before long the French coast was in sight, the floor hatch was prised open, revealing the sea rushing past a few hundred feet below, and a great gale of icy wind swept through the fuselage. The men shuffled into their parachuting positions, and on the green light Frost led them out through the hatch.

As Pickard had promised, the drop of the main party, including Frost and Flight-Sergeant Cox went well. The men got out fast, the formation was tight and as Frost landed – in a foot of snow – he saw the parachutes of the last group – the 'Rodney' party – start to blossom in the sky. Frost did not know it at that time but two aircraft had got lost and the 'Nelson' party, tasked to seize and hold the beach for the withdrawal had not arrived on the DZ.

Charteris and his men should have been dropped in the right spot as they were in Pickard's aircraft and the one directly behind it. In the event they came down about a mile south east of Bruneval and in wooded country. Luck was with them, however, for they were able to guess where Bruneval was by watching other aircraft fly in to the main DZ, and Charteris, obeying the Airborne rule of getting on with the job in spite of the snags, formed his men up and led them at a steady trot around Bruneval, heading west to the beach. This took them through the houses on the outskirts of the village where they bumped into a German patrol. One of the Germans managed to tack himself on to the end of the parachute section, where he was detected and shot down, after which the paratroopers overran a machine gun post and took up a defensive position on the chalk cliffs above the beach. So far, so good; now they had to let Frost know that they were in position . . . but they could not raise him on their radio, or make that vital contact with the Naval landing craft which should by now have been somewhere off-shore.

Back on the main DZ, Frost was getting on with his attack; his problem was to get on with the main job, to find and take the radar installation. Frost led his men at a steady trot towards the villa and, much to his surprise, found the door open and the Germans apparently absent.

The soldiers cleared the house, killing the only German they found, a man who was sniping from a top window at the sappers now entering the *Wurzburg* installation. The Germans manning the radar installation had been taken by surprise and overwhelmed, and Flight-Sergeant Cox was soon at work, examing the *Wurzburg* radar, taking notes and removing parts for later inspection in England.

Frost had meanwhile deployed his men around the buildings and was trying to contact the other parties and get a grip on the overall situation. This was not easy as his radios also did not work; those familiar with military matters will not find this surprising, for it is a fact of military life that *the radios never work*. That the Germans were starting to react was both expected and inevitable, and the sound of firing was now coming from the area of La Presbytere and bullets were starting to glance off the walls of the radar building and the villa. It was clearly time to go, and since Cox now had all he needed there was no reason to delay. The problem was how to give the withdrawal signal without radio.

By now the situation was noisy, with plenty of fire and flares, and tracer bouncing about off the frozen ground, but the plan was working well and everything was under control. Well-trained and well-led soldiers can usually be trusted to make a success of a workable plan, and will not find the odd glitch or error too upsetting. Constant practice and regular exercises give soldiers plenty of experience in coping with the unexpected and none of the paratroopers were too surprised to find that matters were not going exactly to plan. In fact, after all the problems in training, most were pleasantly surprised to find that all the main parts of the operation were going remarkably well; the drop had been fairly accurate, the enemy position taken, the object of the raid achieved and the enemy now had to be held off while the troops withdrew to the beach and were taken off. The only problem was a failure of communications – the blasted radios.

Frost rounded up his troops and sent them packing towards the beach, losing his company sergeant-major,

Sergeant-Major Strachan, who was hit in the stomach by machine gun fire but who was taken along with the rest. When they reached the beach they found Charteris and his men fighting for its possession with a pillbox which overlooked the main withdrawal area, while a burst of firing from the villa area gave notice that the Germans were putting in a counter-attack and would soon be on their heels. Frost led an attack which knocked out the pillbox, then linked up with Charteris and put the men into a defensive ring around the beach, determined to fight it out if the landing craft did not come in.

Since the radios still refused to function, light signals from Verys flares were sent up and, after a delay which seemed interminable, landing craft were seen coming in to the beach. These craft had been offshore all the time, unable to close the coast because two or three enemy E-boats – fast patrol craft – were cruising about, attracted by the sound of firing on shore. When they finally cleared off, the landing craft homed in on the Verys lights and were soon grounding on the shingle just offshore. There was then some confusion as the Bren gunners on the landing craft began to fire on the cliff top, in the mistaken belief that they were helping the paratroops withdraw. Coming under 'friendly fire' at such a time was the last thing Frost and his men needed and a few shouts and curses taught the *matelots* the error of their ways. The soldiers then waded or swam out to the landing craft and by 0400 hours, still well under the cover of darkness, they were on their way home, well content. The entire operation, from take off to reembarkation had taken just five hours; the RAF were delighted with the information obtained and a great many useful lessons were learnt. Meanwhile there was a successful operation to celebrate. The operation had cost two killed, six wounded and six missing. Frost and Lieutenant Charteris were awarded the MC, Flight-Sergeant Cox got a very well-earned Military Medal, and CSM Strachan, who had been brought back to England, and was soon back with the company got the Croix de Guerre.

Frost's subsequent report pointed out the necessity for

reliable radios and for a better system of control on the ground. One of his points was that a set plan rarely worked on an airborne operation and some elements of flexibility had to be built into it, since matters would always go awry to some degree. The same is true of all military operations, but a parachute unit has to cope with some additional problems, not least when they are dropped behind the enemy lines and beyond the reach of immediate resupply or reinforcement. These points were valid and were to be stressed yet again two and a half years later when John Frost, by now a Lt-Colonel and commanding 2 Para, found himself tasked with taking and holding the bridge at Arnhem.

3

THE RED DEVILS, AFRICA, 1942–43

*'Now they call you the Red Devils . . . such distinctions
given by the enemy are seldom won in battle except by the
finest fighting troops.'*

General Sir Frederick Browning, commander,
1st Airborne Division, signal to the
1st Parachute Brigade, 1943

One of the problems faced by all the special units in the
Second World War was getting permission to send their
men into action. Special force units, Commandos and
Parachute units to name but two, are raised, trained and
equipped for special tasks. This special treatment and
training does not always endear these troops or their
commanders to the powers-that-be, who often do not
know what to do with these units and tend to regard
them, at least for a while, as a nuisance. Besides, such
special units are not always suited by equipment, training
or temperament to the normal roles and duties required
of standard infantry units in battle.

This is not to say that they are not often called on to
act as 'heavy' infantry units, or that they do not do
extremely well when tasked to do so – as we shall see in
the course of this chapter – but the planners cannot always
find a use for a special unit in their operational plans and
therefore fail to make the best use of special force talents

and fighting abilities. The task of getting their men into action in a suitable role therefore devolved on to their commanders, who had to 'sell' the idea of using parachute or commando units to the army or area commanders responsible for a particular campaign. At the end of 1942, this task fell on General Browning, the elegant and aggressive commander of the British 1st Airborne Division.

Browning's chance to press the claims of this new formation arose when he was informed that the US forces destined for Operation *Torch* – formerly Operation *Gymnast* – the Anglo-American invasion of North Africa in November 1942, would contain just one US parachute unit, the 2nd Battalion of the US 503rd Parachute Infantry Regiment (2/503 PIR). This struck Browning as less than adequate for the North African terrain, with its vast distances between objectives, which seemed to offer endless opportunities for airborne troops, who could seize and hold vital objectives well ahead of the advancing Allied armies until the main force came up, or generally harass the enemy by sudden strikes behind the lines. Browning lobbied effectively and, as a result, the British 1st Parachute Brigade was duly sent to North Africa and placed under the command of General Anderson's British First Army, which would form the British contribution to the western end of the North African campaign. This force would be under the overall command of the US general, Dwight D. Eisenhower, whose Anglo-American armies would advance east from Algeria and Morocco to meet General Montgomery's Eighth Army coming west from Egypt and Libya, across the Western Desert.

This attachment to Operation *Torch* also brought British Airborne troops the benefit of US transport aircraft in the shape of the C47 transport or parachute aircraft, a type better known to the British in later years as the 'Dakota' – of which the civil version or DC3, is still flying in parts of the world, sixty years later. The Dakota was to prove the great parachuting aircraft of the Second World War, capable of carrying twenty fully-equipped men and allowing them to jump like gentlemen – out of the door. A group of C47s arrived in Britain in the summer of 1942 and were attached to the 1st Airborne Division for training.

Once again there were fatalities, still more examples to prove that parachuting in the early days was fraught with risk. The first jumps were made by Lt-Colonel Hill's 2nd Parachute Battalion and after the first stick had jumped over Netheravon airfield one man was seen to be hooked up on the tail wheel. It transpired that the static line and strop used on the British 'X' type parachute was too short for use with the C47 and would have to be lengthened. This was duly done and Lt-Colonel Hill led the men out on the next jump . . . and all went well.

This was followed by a full battalion jump from transport aircraft of the US Army Air Force (USAAF) and though most of the men landed without injury there were four deaths; two men became entangled and fell without their parachutes opening, one man was killed when the snap hook connecting his static line to the aircraft twisted free – a fault everyone had believed cured – and one man's parachute suffered a 'Roman Candle'. This unexpected number of fatalities on a single jump put a stop to all parachuting until the problems had been investigated. Most of the brigade therefore still had to do a drop from a C47 when they sailed for the Mediterranean in the late summer of 1942.

There was also another potential problem. Many of the American pilots had come over to the UK early because they were experienced civilian pilots, called up for war duties and fully capable of flying a two-engine transport aircraft and navigating their way to a drop zone – in peace time, or on exercise. What they had not had time to grasp was that an operational jump, flying across a defended area at low height and slow speed was not the same thing at all. Parachute aircraft were vulnerable to everything from rifle bullets to anti-aircraft fire, and the pilots were about to discover that this could make their job a very hazardous task indeed.

The 1st Parachute Brigade mustered in Algiers, where a good time was had by all, pending orders committing them to the battle in North Africa, where the German Afrika Korps, though sandwiched between the British Eighth Army advancing from El Alamein and the Americans and British pushing east from Algeria, were still fighting fiercely. The first task of the British First Army was to take the city of Tunis, some 500 miles east of their front line. Tunisia was then held by Vichy French troops – Vichy France, under Marshal Petain was allied to Nazi Germany, but after the *Torch* landings Vichy support for the German cause had begun to waver. It therefore seemed more than likely that a German parachute unit would be sent to seize Tunis airfield unless the British got their first. The first proposal was that 1st Parachute Brigade should drop on Tunis airfield and hang on to it until First Army came up. This was a hopeful plan, to say the least, and was soon dropped in favour of something less ambitious after the Germans deployed fighter aircraft on their forward airfields, to forestall just such a thrust by Allied transport aircraft into Tunisia.

The next proposal was for a drop on the airfield at Bone, 380 miles in front of First Army. This also seemed a very reckless plan, but when Lt-Colonel Pine-Coffin's 3rd Parachute Battalion arrived at the Maison Blanche airfield on 11 November 1942, they were told to prepare themselves for an immediate operation against the town and airfield at Bone. This airfield was currently held by the Vichy French troops and – as at Tunis – it was considered necessary to get British troops on the Bone airfield before the Germans arrived and took it over.

At 0600 hours on 12 November 1942, 3 Para took off from Algiers and two hours later parachuted on to Bone airfield. The drop was from a very low level, less than 500 feet, but the men were still widely scattered and many of their weapons' containers were lost. Even so, with the help of No. 6 (Army) Commando, under Lt-Colonel Mills-Roberts, Bone airfield was held until First Army came up and took the town and port. While 3 Para were thus engaged, the other two battalions of the brigade, 1 and 2 Para arrived in the Mediterranean by sea. Lt-Colonel Hill's 1 Para were promptly tasked to capture El Aouina, the airfield at Tunis, or, if the Germans had got there first, the airfield at Setif. The Germans did get to Tunis first and the battalion therefore disembarked at Algiers and marched to the nearby airfield at Maison Blanche to await further orders.

These orders arrived the next day, after the battalion had spent a solid 24 hours without sleep getting their kit and parachutes off the ship. Hill's new orders were for the battalion to mount an operation the following day into the country around Beja, fifty miles west of Tunis. When Hill protested that his battalion had just got off the ship and needed more time to get organised and accustomed to the climate and terrain, he was told to stop arguing and get on with it. Specifically, he had to prevent more German ground forces crossing the Beja region and getting to Tunis. As an aid to this end he had to convince the wavering Vichy French forces of General Darlan to come off the fence and join the winning – Allied – side in the defence of that city. He was also to harass the enemy wherever they were found, and see if the airstrip at Souk el Arba was in a fit state to receive Allied fighters.

Any one of these tasks would have been enough for one lightly equipped force of parachute infantry but there were a few snags as well. To begin with, there were no maps of the Beja area, other than a pre-war motoring map. The USAAF transport pilots, though eager and willing to help, had never dropped parachutists before and their aircraft lacked both a means to communicate with the parachutists they were carrying and the means to communicate between aircraft in the air.

Hill's solution to this problem was pragmatic. He would sit alongside the pilot in the lead aircraft and map-read the way to the DZ, using the motoring map. When it appeared he would go back into the body of the aircraft, hook up and jump out. His men would follow him and, seeing them jump, all the other paratroopers in all the other aircraft would do likewise, following their colonel to the ground. Unfortunately, the transport aircraft were intercepted by German fighters and although US Lightning fighters drove the German aircraft off, the weather deteriorated and the transport aircraft carrying the parachutists were forced to turn back. The return of 1 Para did not go down at all well with General Anderson, the First Army commander, who did not seem to grasp that parachute operations are weather dependent. He ordered Hill to try again next day . . . and land at all costs.

The following day, somewhat refreshed by a good night's sleep, 1 Para took off again; this time the drop went off as planned, with only one man being killed. French trucks were seized and the entire battalion, all 525 of them, moved on Beja, which was found to be garrisoned by a full brigade of Vichy French troops. Hill managed to convince the French commanders that his battalion was actually a light brigade, by marching his men around the town several times, sometimes in their red berets, sometimes in steel helmets, always with their heavy weapons – mortars and Vickers machine guns – prominently displayed.

This ploy succeeded, and the French moved out, leaving the battalion to take over their trenches and prepared positions just as German aircraft began to bomb the town. Bombing continued sporadically all day and the following morning a patrol of German armoured cars came into the town, cruised about the streets for a while, and were ambushed by S Company on the way out. The battalion succeeded in knocking out four German armoured cars and capturing another four, and the sight of these captured armoured cars – and their captured crews – was another step towards getting the French to join in the fight. After a day or two of talk, the Germans attacked the French positions around Medjez el Bab, the French resisted and, with British assistance, drove the Germans off. The French commander then declared for the Allies and the third of Lt-Colonel Hill's tasks had been successfully completed. He now had to find the enemy units, which lay somewhere between Beja and Bizerta, and make their life as uncomfortable as possible.

A leading role in this task was taken by Major Alastair 'Jock' Pearson, the second-in-command of 1 Para and a man born for war. Pearson was a pre-war, Territorial officer who rose in four years to become an outstanding fighting soldier, winning four DSOs as well as the MC and who – according to those who knew him – richly deserved the Victoria Cross for his leadership and gallantry in the field. Pearson was to win his first DSO and the MC in the fighting around Medjez el Bab and another DSO later in the campaign. The battalion held on to the positions at Medjez el Bab for ten days until First Army came up, then withdrew into Army reserve at Algiers for a rest and a long-overdue chance to get properly organised after marching off the ship and into battle. This respite did not last long.

Meanwhile what of Lt-Colonel John Frost's 2 Para? Like 1 Para, they had landed at Algiers but while 1 Para were instantly handed various tasks by the Army command, 2 Para had to hang about for a few days, anxious not to miss all the fun, until Colonel Frost was given rather too much to do. His first task was to prepare for a drop on Sousse, but after he had made an aerial reconnaissance of the proposed DZ, been shot at by the US 503 PRI – by mistake – and returned to Algiers, he was told to forget Sousse and take a look at Enfidaville, with a view to a drop there.

Frost duly flew off for another reconnaissance and came back to learn that the Enfidaville drop was now off and the new plan was to drop at Pont du Fahs airfield and destroy any enemy aircraft there, then march to Depienne airfield and do the same again, and finally to attack the airfield at Oudna on the outskirts of Tunis, after which – with any luck – the battalion would link up with First Army, which would be rushing east to join them. This amounted to a five-day raid behind the enemy lines and everything the battalion needed, from ammunition and food to water and radio batteries, would have to be carried in the packs of the officers and men.

It sounded a trifle risky, and matters did not improve. On 29 November the battalion duly emplaned for the drop on Pont du Fahs but, as the aircraft engines were warming up, another message arrived, cancelling the Pont du Fahs drop, and telling Frost to drop instead at Depienne and carry out the original plan from there. It does not seem to have occurred to anyone at First Army HQ that this might present 2 Para with problems – like the fact that no orders had been issued for such a drop, no time scale prepared, no DZ chosen, no arrangements for support or supply at this new location. It says a great deal for the training and resilience of the battalion and its commander that, after a quick run round the airfield, to tell the company commanders that there had been a slight change of plan, the battalion took off, Frost flying in the cockpit of the lead aircraft, having decided to select the new DZ from the air.

Fortunately, these C47 aircraft did have radio contact between one another and when Frost decided to jump on to Depienne airfield, a message was passed to the other aircraft, advising his men to follow the colonel's parachute and close on the sound of his hunting horn when they reached the ground. This they duly did, but since the men had not been briefed and the terrain was not what they had expected, some confusion inevitably ensued. Fortunately, the Germans were absent and the only problem was the presence of Tunisian locals, who were not above looting containers and, if given the chance, would rob or kill the wounded. These had to be chased away with rifle fire at regular intervals and, after a disturbed night, better news arrived with the dawn when three armoured cars came up: the advance guard of First Army.

Thus encouraged, the battalion, less some men left behind to care for the wounded, set out for Oudna, humping all they needed in their packs; air supply had not yet arrived in North Africa and all they would need they had to carry – the total weight per man coming to around 60 kilos, about 130 pounds; a great weight to hump over the rugged mountainous terrain. Still they pressed on, at best speed, and came to their reward at dawn on the following day when they crested a ridge and saw before them, just ten miles away, the white buildings of the city of Tunis.

The battalion came down on to the coastal plain and marched hard for Oudna airstrip, which they found lightly garrisoned but not being used by the Luftwaffe. This did not mean that the Germans were anxious to give it up, and hardly had the paratroops taken it, in the early afternoon, than the Germans put in a counter-attack, in company strength supported by five Mark IV tanks and ground-strafing from Messerschmitt fighters. This attack was beaten off, but two hours later the airfield was dive-bombed by Stukas. This attack went on for some time and forced Frost to make a decision.

The task of 2 Para was essentially a raid, to take the airfield and destroy any aircraft and installations. They destroyed what they could but there were no aircraft – and if the Germans came on again, in greater strength, he might be hard pressed to repel them on the open ground of the airfield. He therefore withdrew the battalion to some high ground to the west and they were still there on the following morning when news arrived at battalion HQ that armoured cars and tanks, bearing First Army yellow recognition panels, were approaching their position. This turned out to be German armour, using yellow panels picked up on the DZ at Depienne; after a skirmish and a brief exchange of fire, the Germans sent in a British prisoner to tell the paratroopers that they were completely surrounded and were advised to surrender as soon as possible.

Frost was just digesting this message and working out a peremptory reply when a radio signal, the first and only one received during the entire operation, told him that the armoured thrust First Army had been going to launch to join up with him that day had been postponed – 2 Para were finally on their own.

They were also in a very tricky situation; the advanced elements of First Army were, at best, some thirty or forty miles to the west, while the main German base at Tunis was just over the hill and buzzing like an angry hive; German troops, armour and artillery, now surrounded the battalion position while the paratroopers only had the weapons in their hands and the ammo in their pouches to repel any attack. The only thing to do was break out – or surrender – and since the latter course of action lacked appeal, Frost told his men to destroy every spare item of equipment, lighten their loads as much as possible and stand by for a rapid withdrawal west as soon as it got dark; this would mean leaving the wounded and the RAMC officers and men who had volunteered to stay behind and look after them.

Meanwhile, to keep the Germans occupied, fighting patrols went out, destroying a couple of German tanks. Then the battalion pulled out, trudging under fire back to the Sidi Bou position, five miles from the airfield, where they dug in to await the assault. The Germans were well aware what Frost was up to and pressed hard on the heels of the battalion, putting in strong attacks backed by tanks, aircraft and artillery fire; fortunately the German fighters got confused and came in to strafe their own infantry advancing over open ground and this caused delay.

The battalion held on all day at Sidi Bou, breaking away at night, this time in company sized groups, leaving their wounded behind again with some fit volunteers to keep the Tunisians away and look after them until the Germans arrived. It is one of the happier aspects of the desert war in North Africa that both sides took great care of each other's wounded and each side knew that they could safely leave their wounded behind, if need be.

During the night the battalion split up; at dawn Frost only had his HQ and B Company to hand. He chose to lay up in a farm where he was joined later that day by A Company – both of these companies being much reduced by the actions of the previous four days. During the day, inevitably, the Germans came up and surrounded the farm, subjecting the silent garrison to sporadic mortar barrages but without putting in an assault until dusk, when they came surging in only to be driven back with loss by a hail of rifle and machine gun fire. This was the battalion's last effort for the soldiers were almost out of ammunition, so as the Germans vanished into the darkness, the paratroopers ran after them and kept on going, charging through the enemy lines and breaking out into open country. Those who made it rallied to Frost's hunting horn and at dawn, after another exhausting march, the remnants of 2 Para marched into Medjez el Bab.

The battalion had been fighting its way back for five days, from 29 December until 3 January. They had covered over forty miles, fought a battle every day, usually against superior numbers and tanks, and got back entirely due to their own efforts – and the steady leadership of Lt-Colonel Frost. The cost had been high; sixteen officers and 250 men had been lost but some came trickling in later having evaded capture, including fifty men who fought their way back and came in a body.

Even after this First Army debacle, there was no rest for the battalion. First they were employed manning the defences of Mejez el Bab and only after a week were they finally relieved and sent back to regroup and muster men. As reinforcements they were offered a group of 200 Royal Artillery gunners who, though at first not too happy to find themselves serving as infantry, soon took to their new role, many of them volunteering to do the parachute course at the first opportunity and stay on with 2 Para.

This raid on the Tunis airfield was the last parachute operation carried out by the 1st Parachute Brigade in North Africa. From now on the brigade would fight as 'heavy' infantry, and as a first operation they were tasked to support the 1st Guards Brigade in the action to take a German position known as Longstop Hill; in the event they were not needed, for the attack on Longstop Hill was beaten back with loss and First Army, instead of advancing on Tunis, went on to the defensive in order to stem the renewed German attack. In this a role was quickly found for the Parachute Brigade, which spent the winter in the mud and snow of the Tunisian mountains. For much of the time the various battalions and companies were serving with, or acting in support of other brigades and battalions and by doing so the reputation of the airborne troops as first-class fighting soldiers was soon widely spread among the ranks of First Army – and among their German opponents.

In January 1943, the 3rd Battalion was attached to the 36th Infantry Brigade and used in the attack on a position called Green Hill. One company, under Major Terrell, attached to the 4th Buffs, got to the top of the hill – the only troops to do so – but were forced off again at dawn. The next night another attack went in, this time with two companies of 3 Para and two companies of the Buffs; again the paratroopers got to the top of the hill where they were counter-attacked by strong German forces and having run out of ammunition, were again driven off. This fighting greatly reduced the battalion strength and in early January, 1 and 3 Para were pulled back to Algiers, partly for a rest, partly to prepare for another parachute operation, which was later cancelled.

In early February, the full brigade was sent out to the right flank and ordered to send out fighting patrols and do all they could to keep the Germans on their front occupied on and around the Jebel Mansour. This fighting went on for most of the winter and the depleted ranks of the battalions were thinned still more; by early March, 3 Para had only seven officers left and had lost nearly 200 men; the other battalions were similarly reduced. The brigade still hung on, and on 5 March they were moved from the right flank of First Army all the way across to the left or coastal flank at Tamara, where the 1st Parachute Battalion was expected to take over a position previously held with some difficulty by a 1,000 strong Guards battalion. The officer in charge, Alastair Pearson, knew that the only thing to do was carry out an aggressive defence and, having discovered that the Germans had no taste for night fighting, ordered his men to make attacks night after night, and deny the Germans all rest and any

chance to counter-attack. This aggressive, flexible defence
worked well, even though the troops opposed to the
paratroopers were also Airborne, German parachute
engineers fighting as infantry and backed by at least four
crack German regiments, who attacked Pearson's positions regularly, often having to be driven out with the
bayonet.

One of these attacks is memorable for more than its
ferocity. The Germans had attacked in great strength and
on this occasion had succeeded in breaking through the
outposts and getting as far as battalion HQ. Matters might
have gone badly for 1 Para but at the crux of the battle
the parachute cooks, signallers, drivers and storemen
came storming into action with the bayonet, driving the
Germans out and stemming their attack with the
battalion's promptly adopted war cry, *'Whoa, Mahommed'*
a shout normally employed to halt Arab *gharri* drivers.

For his leadership and tenacity in the fighting around
Tamara, Jock Pearson was given the second of his four
DSOs. The Parachute Regiment has won its share of
Victoria Crosses, but it remains a mystery why men like
Pearson and Frost, though regularly decorated, were
never given the ultimate decoration which they clearly
earned, not once but several times.

The German attacks on First Army continued with
ever-mounting strength, many of their attacks falling on
the 1st Parachute Brigade positions. In mid-March an
entire division was sent in against the brigade and only an
error by Stukas of the Luftwaffe, which dive-bombed the
tanks of the advancing 10 Panzer Division prevented the
German tanks over running 2 Para's lines. Finally, on 21
March 1943, after three months in the line, the brigade
went into its final North African battle at Sidi Bou Della,
a position known to the parachute battalions as 'The
Bowler Hat'. It was taken by 3 Para, but they were driven
off at dawn next day, after running out of ammunition.
Pearson's 1 Para were then ordered to retake it and
Pearson told the corps commander bluntly that, while he
could take it, he could not hold it, as his troops were

exhausted. As a result, 3 Para was tasked to support Pearson's attack which went in that night and went well, though it soon became an extended struggle against the redoubtable *Oberst* Witzig and his parachute engineers.

The final assault started on the night of 27–28 March and was a full Parachute Brigade 'show' with 1 and 2 Para leading and 3 Para in reserve. Led by a Tunisian Arab who had been bribed with cigarettes, 1 Para succeeded in hitting the enemy position at a point were the German and Italian lines met. As expected, the Italians fled at the first shots, but Witzig's paratroopers did not give up so easily, slamming in a series of counter-attacks against 2 Para, which only held its position with difficulty and at the cost of heavy casualties. When they were down to about one company, John Frost ordered the survivors to fix bayonets and charge, an assault that drove the enemy back – and they kept going back until they had retreated about twenty miles.

The 1st Parachute Brigade had now been in continuous action for nearly two months and this latest thrust had put them well ahead of the brigades that should have been covering their flanks. In mid-April, the brigade were finally relieved and went back to Algiers for a well-earned rest.

There was also time to count the cost. It is fair to say that First Army did not know how to use the Parachute Brigade and failed to give its airborne operations the support and back-up they needed. Since Airborne troops were new to the Order of Battle, there may be some excuse for this, but the units were used again and again as heavy infantry although the parachute battalions were forty per cent smaller than heavy infantry battalions and lacked an adequate transport scale and heavy equipment. The 2 Para War Diary comments that 'it [the battalion] had fought as infantry with none of the amenities that an infantry battalion expects, bren gun carriers, anti tank guns and transport'. That the brigade did so outstandingly well speaks volumes for the quality of the men, the skill of the officers, and the training and guts of all concerned.

The brigade had suffered some 1,700 casualties – about seventy per cent, across the brigade as a whole – and served on every sector of the Tunisian front. The War Diary of 2 Para for April 1943 records that the battalion had come out of battle with 14 officers and 346 men, having gone in with 24 officers and 588 men, and had taken on 230 replacements at various stage in the fighting; to put it another way, 24 officers and 810 men had gone in and more than eighty per cent of that number had been killed or wounded before the battalion came out. The War Diary goes on to add that since the 2 Para drop at Depienne, five months before, the battalion had spent exactly *six days* out of the line – there were no weekends off in that kind of war.

They had taken over 3,500 prisoners, killed a great many Germans, often in hand-to-hand fighting, and earned a great deal of respect, not least from the Germans, who were increasingly wary of engaging the *'Roten Teufel'* – the Red Devils – in battle. They also paid the 1st Parachute Brigade a great tribute when the battle was over. At one stage in its journey, the train carrying the paratroopers to Algiers went past a prison camp full of German POWs; the British soldiers were leaning out of the windows and when the Germans saw their red berets they ran in their hundreds to the wire, waving and cheering their former opponents as they passed on their way to a short but well-earned rest.

4

SICILY AND ITALY, 1943

'The password is "Desert Rats"; the answer is "Kill Italians".'

Allied orders for the invasion of Sicily, 1943

While the 1st Parachute Brigade was making a mark in Tunisia, the 1st Airborne Division was expanding in the United Kingdom. The 2nd and 3rd Parachute Brigades were now in training in England, and Brigadier 'Shan' Hackett's 4th Parachute Brigade was forming and training in Egypt. Hackett was a cavalry officer, who had been badly burned in the tank fighting in 1942 and been posted to Middle East HQ as the officer in overall charge of Special Forces. There were then a considerable number of these in the Middle East Command, ranging from Captain David Stirling's SAS to the Long Range Desert Group and the exotically named Popski's Private Army. Hackett got on well with these irregular soldiers, but he hankered for a fighting command himself and when the 4th Parachute Brigade formed he obtained the post of brigadier.

Recruited largely in the Middle East and trained in Palestine and Cyprus, the 4th Parachute Brigade included one unusual formation, the 156th Parachute Battalion, which had been raised from British forces in India by Lt-Colonel Lindsay, the man who had made the first ever 'pull-off' descent from the back of a Whitley bomber in the autumn of 1940. The 156th Parachute Battalion was still commanded by Lindsay when it arrived in the Canal Zone to provide the nucleus of 'Shan' Hackett's new brigade.

The other two battalions were raised by a slightly different method, but one that became common among parachute battalions as the war progressed. The decision was made to take a regular, heavy infantry battalion, in this case the 2nd Battalion The Royal Sussex Regiment, and turn it over to the airborne role as the 10th Battalion, The Parachute Regiment. This proposal did not go down at all well with the Sussex soldiers, and less than 100 volunteered to parachute and stay with the new battalion – hence the call for volunteers. Fortunately, enough arrived to fill out 10 Para, and form the final battalion, 11 Para. Once formed, this brigade – less 11 Para – was sent west in June 1943, to join up with the other brigades of the 1st Airborne Division in Tunisia, where they were preparing to take part in the invasion of Sicily and the Italian mainland.

The other airborne expansion – and a significant one – was the formation of the Airlanding Brigade. This brigade flew into battle in gliders towed by bomber aircraft of the RAF or transport aircraft from the USAAF. The gliders were either the American *Waco*, or the much larger British *Horsa*, both of which were in service with the 1st Airlanding Brigade of the 1st Airborne Division when it assembled in North Africa for the invasion of Sicily. The airlanding, glider-borne troops, wore the red beret and the winged Pegasus arm badge, but not the parachute wings, which remained the mark of the qualified parachutist. Nevertheless, these glider soldiers were recognised as full members of the Airborne Division, and an integral part of the Airborne family.

When tasked for Sicily, 1st Airborne Division, now commanded by Major-General Hopkinson, a glider soldier, consisted of three brigades, 1st and 2nd Parachute Brigades, commanded by Brigadiers Lathbury and Down, and the 1st Airlanding Brigade commanded by Brigadier 'Pip' Hicks. Their task in Sicily, Operation *Fustian*, the Airborne part of the entire landing, code-named Operation *Husky*, was to make three airborne assaults ahead of the amphibious landing and to seize and hold certain vital points, usually bridges, ahead of the advancing XIII Corps of General Montgomery's Eighth Army. Those of 2 Para who had taken part in the landings and fighting around Tunis, heard of this familiar-sounding plan with a certain amount of anxiety.

The Airlanding Brigade were to land near Syracuse and take the port and the bridge at Ponte Grande. The 2nd Brigade were to take the port of Augusta and the vital road bridge outside the town and, finally, the 1st Brigade were to take the equally vital Primasole Bridge which carried the road from Primasole to Catania over the Simeto River. In short, the main task of the division was to take three bridges and so ensure the rapid advance north of XIII Corps – a task not unlike that with which three Airborne *Divisions* would be charged with a year later, on the road to Arnhem. This point is worth noting now and remembering later, for Sicily gave the 1st Airborne Division some practical experience in taking and holding bridges.

The first snag encountered by the staff planning this phase of the operation was that there were not enough aircraft to carry the entire division to its dropping and landing zones (LZs) in one lift. This was a great pity, for it greatly reduced the possibility of surprise. Nothing could be done about it and it was finally decided to drop the Airlanding Brigade first, at Syracuse, and the other two brigades on the following two nights – in short it would take the 1st Airborne Division three full days to get to Sicily. Training for the operation commenced at once, in early May 1943, and in the next two months the two parachute brigades completed nearly 9,000 parachute jumps, for the loss of two men killed and about 100 injured, mostly from landing hard on stony ground – itself a useful preparation for the tumbled and rocky terrain of Italy.

It was at this time that 2 Para invented the 'weapons' container', by which a parachutist could land attached to his personal weapon, be it a rifle, Bren Light Machine Gun (LMG), or the various component parts of a Vickers Medium Machine Gun or a 3-inch mortar. These early models of the weapons' container were later developed into a larger type which would be attached to the individual's parachute harness with two hooks – inevitably known as 'skyhooks'. When these were released the container fell to the end of twenty feet of rope and dangled there, well out of the way, until the ground came up to meet it.

The invasion began on the night of 9 July 1943, when Brigadier Hicks's Airlanding Brigade flew into Syracuse – and hit another snag. Because of the shortage of transport aircraft, and the fear that too many would be lost to German coastal flak batteries, the towing aircraft had been instructed to cast loose their gliders well away from the coast. This fatal decision was compounded by the guns of the Allied Fleet now closing on the landing beaches. The Royal and US Navies were always nervous of overflying aircraft and promptly opened fire on the aircraft and gliders passing overhead.

Apart from causing losses from 'friendly fire' this barrage disrupted the parachute and glider approach to the cast-off position. As a result, 1st Airlanding Brigade took heavy casualties even before the first shot was fired. Seventy-eight of the 144 gliders landed in the sea, some a considerable distance offshore; more than 250 soldiers were drowned and a great deal of heavy equipment was lost. Those dumped in the water included the brigade commander, Brigadier Hicks, who had to swim for two miles before he got ashore, arriving without his equipment and his boots.

Even those gliders who made it to land were affected by this naval error. A glider landing is at best a controlled crash, and the olive trees and low stone walls of Sicily took a heavy toll of the gliders which had been driven from their LZs and forced to land where they could. Losses among the glider pilots were particularly severe; 61 gliders made it over Sicily, but they were cast off all over the place and well scattered on the ground; of the 288 sergeant pilots of the Glider Pilot Regiment who took part in this operation, 101 were lost, several being killed when their gliders crashed on landing.

The landing phase was a shambles, but good troops can still work wonders and those who got ashore soon got a grip on the situation, and thrust directly at the Ponte Grande bridge which was in British hands by first light – though it was lightly held since only eighty men of the tasked battalion, the 2nd South Staffs, turned up to hold it. They still managed to defend the bridge until they ran out of ammunition, but then the survivors were overrun by the enemy before any XIII Corps troops arrived. Advance units of the corps finally showed up in the afternoon and retook the bridge before dark. The rest of the Airlanding Brigade, operating in small parties, mixed platoons or alone, infiltrated into Syracuse and ranged about the surrounding country, shooting up the enemy wherever they were found and, by disrupting the enemy defence, managed to play a useful part in overcoming XIII Corps' initial objectives and allowing a rapid advance towards Catania . . . and Primasole.

This advance scuppered the intended drop of the 2nd Parachute Brigade at Augusta, for as they went out to board their aircraft that night word arrived that the Augusta bridge was already in British hands, having been taken by No. 3 Commando. The brigade was then sent, cursing furiously, into divisional reserve and the spotlight switched to 1st Parachute Brigade which was to carry out Operation *Marston*, the landing and capture of the bridge at Primasole. The troops would be carried in 105 C47s of the US Troop Carrier Command and eleven Albermarles of the RAF. The Albermarles were not popular, for they could carry only ten parachutists and these men had to drop through a hatch in the floor. The heavy equipment, anti-tank guns and engineers' stores would be carried in nineteen *Waco* and *Horsa* gliders towed by the RAF.

Here again, the basic plan was flawed. Regular air reconnaissance had revealed a thickening of German air defences around Primasole, and although ground-attack aircraft from Malta had bombed and strafed these positions several times in the days before the landing, the plan did not call for the paratroopers to have air cover after first light. This was a flaw in an otherwise sound plan, for it left the brigade without any support until and unless XIII Corps came up quickly.

The way to take a bridge is to seize both ends at once *and hold on*. The brigade plan therefore called for Alastair Pearson's 1 Para to land as close as possible to their objective and take the bridge. Meanwhile 2 Para, under John Frost, would block the road to the south towards Augusta while 3 Para blocked it to the north, towards Catania. All three battalions, with eight anti-tank guns landed by glider, would then dig in to hang on to what they had until XIII Corps arrived, which it had promised to do soon after daylight. It should be appreciated that this was now the *third day* of the invasion, and the Germans, never slow to react, were now well into their stride, and advancing from every quarter to stem the invasion and throw it back into the sea. A single parachute brigade, out on its own ahead of the main force, was too good a target to ignore.

The 1st Parachute Brigade took off at dusk on 13 July – Brigadier Lathbury's birthday. The pilots and commanders of the USAAF transport aircraft taking them to Sicily, with rapidly developing experience and considerable confidence, assured them that they would be dropped on time, and on the correct DZ; this hopeful pledge was not to be honoured.

Lt-Colonel John Frost, his HQ and most of A Company did indeed land close to their objectives, but the rest of 2 Para were either scattered widely aross the surrounding countryside or taken back to Africa by USAAF pilots who shied away from the sheets of gunfire put up by the Allied invasion fleet offshore, which was clearly still nervous of aircraft overhead. Poor navigation resulted in other aircraft failing to find the DZ and many of those pilots who did cross the coast were dismayed by ground fire and hurled their aircraft all over the sky – an action which had the effect of hurling their passengers all over the aircraft, and greatly disrupted the drop. The result was a disaster; less than 300 of the brigade actually landed in Sicily and more than one third – some 600 men, or thirty plane loads – never even had the chance to do so, for their pilots took them back to base in North Africa. The final result was that of the 1,800 men who took off from North Africa only 295 reported at the bridge after the drops.

John Frost, charged with blocking the road south of Primasole with his entire battalion, had just 100 men for the task; however, being paratroopers, they got on with it and took two of their positions; the third turned out to be held by German paratroopers, who refused to budge, and so the two groups went to ground and prepared to fight it out.

Meanwhile, 1 Para, tasked to actually take the Primasole Bridge, had similar problems and were also widely scattered in the drop. The first man jumped at 2230 hours and four hours later only fifty men had arrived at Primasole Bridge, where they were taken under command by Captain Rann. Rann and his men duly took the bridge, capturing two Italian half tracks and 50 Italian soldiers in the process. As the night wore on more men trickled in, each with a tale to tell, none stranger than that of Alastair Pearson.

Pearson's aircraft had both a USAAF pilot and a trained USAAF navigator, and here again, they assured Pearson that they would land him and his men, on time and on the right spot. All went well until they crossed the anchored ships of the invasion fleet and met with anti-aircraft fire, at which point the pilot took violent evasive action and then told Pearson that he was not flying any closer to that inferno ashore and turned the aircraft away from Sicily.

He said it to the wrong man. Pearson drew and cocked

his revolver and told the pilot to turn back towards the DZ. This move apparently backfired when the American pointed out that if Pearson pulled the trigger, who would fly the aircraft? No problem, said Pearson; it just so happened that the ranks of 1 Para included a washed-out RAF aircrew trainee who had failed his pilot's course and transferred to the Airborne. This man was called forward and, in response to Pearson's question, said that he could certainly fly the aircraft but could not land it – which again was no problem; apart from the crew, everyone else on board intended to land by parachute anyway. Stymied, the USAAF pilot turned back, but crossed the DZ in a dive and at well over dropping speed. All the parachutists jumped but half of them were killed, either hitting the ground before their parachutes could open or swinging violently into the ground. Other men, in other aircraft had similar, if less dramatic, encounters with their aircrew.

By dawn there were around 250 of 1 Para at the Primasole Bridge, with three anti-tank guns and a certain amount of heavy weapons, mortars and medium machine-guns. However, they had no radios and were unable to contact the other battalions or brigade HQ other than by runner. Brigadier Lathbury had come up to the bridge with part of his headquarters but their radio was only suitable for the brigade 'net' and he was unable to contact XIII Corps and tell them that, while the bridge was in British hands, it was only held by a couple of scratch companies, and unless the corps came up quickly it could not be held. If the enemy brought up tanks it would be even more difficult since only three of the anti-tank guns had arrived – their glider drop had been abysmal – and they were also short of ammunition.

Hard as it is to imagine, the drop of 3 Para, north of the bridge, was the worst of all. By dawn, only sixty men of the battalion had appeared on the road and all these were sent to join 1 Para at the Primasole Bridge since there were not enough of them to make a blocking force. Soon after dawn the enemy started probing forward and soon had the bridge and its defenders under fire. One bright moment came when the naval Forward Observation Officer (FOO) with 2 Para managed to make radio contact with the fleet and the reputation of the Royal Navy improved mightily when six-inch shells from a cruiser began to pound the German positions around the battalion perimeter.

Fighting went on all day and since it was impossible to entrench on the rocky ground, casualties mounted, 2 Para, such as it was, sustaining forty men killed and as many injured in the first hours of the battle. Attacks were also coming in down the road from Catania, where a platoon of 3 Para were in position. The first attack was beaten back but the Germans then sent in a full battalion and by mid-afternoon the paratroopers had been forced across the bridge and on to the south bank of the river. The Germans then crossed the river on either flank and began to box them in, though they could not get to the bridge and destroy it, for the paratroopers kept up under steady fire on the bridge approaches.

By now, Lathbury's HQ had managed to get a message through to the British 4th Armoured Brigade of XIII Corps, and just had time to tell them that they had the bridge and were holding on when the 'net' went dead; poor radio communications were to be the bane of airborne operations for much of the war, and the link here was never re-established. Getting some support up was critical, for the German troops surrounding the position had now worked out that the paratroopers were few in number and in shallow trenches, or in stone sangars constructed from stone walls, and were pounding these positions with mortars.

An infantry attack was inevitable and it duly came in the early afternoon, when the Germans put in two company-sized attacks, backed by artillery and tank fire, against the platoon of 3 Para on the north bank of the river. These were driven off but were probably just probes, for at 1600 hours the enemy put in a full battalion attack, again with tank and artillery support. This was too much for the paratrooper resources and by 1700 hours, both 1 and 3 Para – or those few men who represented those battalions – had been withdrawn south of the bridge, where they set up another perimeter and hung on grimly, denying the enemy the use of the bridge. The perimeter was inherently indefensible, for the enemy had enough troops to hold the paratroopers in position while sending others away to where they could cross the river in safety and come in against the paratroopers' flank.

The position around the Primasole Bridge was becoming untenable. Brigadier Lathbury was out of touch with 2 Para, south of the bridge, and out of contact with XIII Corps; he was also running out of ammunition, men and medical supplies, and was faced with an enemy growing in strength and increasingly aggressive. In fact, the position was not as bad as the current situation suggested, for advance armoured elements of XIII Corps were now only two miles south of the bridge. Not knowing this, Lathbury ordered 1 and 3 Para to withdraw and link up with 2 Para on their ridge to the south. At this Alastair Pearson raised an objection, stating that in his experience the Germans were not keen on fighting at night and it would be as well to hang on where they are, at least until dawn and see if XIII Corps finally turned up; if not it would still be possible to slip away before first light.

Lathbury did not agree and ordered that the withdrawal should begin as soon as it got dark. Then came some good news, for just after 1900 hours the first tanks of the 44th Royal Tank Regiment rolled into their perimeter, more arrived later, together with a company of the Durham Light Infantry, which reached 2 Para's position just as the first of the men from 1 and 3 Para came filtering back; encouraged by the tanks and the Durhams it was now decided to hang on to the bridge and await events, and this they did, keeping the Germans off during the hours of darkness by firing across the bridge on fixed lines. During that time the rest of the Durhams came up and at dawn they tried to attack across the bridge, a venture that was bloodily repulsed by the Germans. This did not deter the commander of the 4th Armoured Brigade, who came on the scene as the Durhams were driven back and announced that they must try again. This aroused the ire of Alastair Pearson who first asked the brigade commander if he really wanted to have the battalion wiped out? If not, he, Pearson, could personally guarantee to take the bridge with the minimum of casualties.

Pearson and his batman took the Durham's CO and two company commanders off to the flank, to a point where the river was shallow enough to wade. There the Durham's commander was told to take his battalion across and attack the bridge from the flank; this they did, but took another pounding when the Germans discovered them clustered around the bridge next morning. The Durhams held on, and by mid-morning the Primasole Bridge was intact and firmly in British hands, and the 1st Parachute Brigade was withdrawn, first back to Syracuse and then back to North Africa, to link up again with those disgruntled men who had not had a chance to join in the battle.

Primasole was a fine example of the Airborne's fighting spirit, but a complete shambles from the operational point of view. John Frost was not the only one to wonder how long it would be before one of these half-cocked operations resulted in a major disaster. There was an internal inquiry and it was agreed that the division must land, if not in one lift, at least on the same day. Also, that they must have air support to compensate for their lack of artillery and heavy weapons, and that the land element must show greater urgency in getting up to join them. Above all, they must have their own, fully committed and trained air transport element, to ensure that the troops and gliders were dropped on time, at the right height and in the right place. Frost's enquiry showed that only 30 of the 116 aircraft carrying the two parachute brigades dropped their passengers on or close to the right DZ.

Other lessons had been learnt. Since weapons' containers still went astray, it was decided that all paratroopers should become proficient in using German weapons, so that they could, if necessary, equip themselves from enemy dead and prisoners. A force of parachute 'Pathfinders' should be created, to drop ahead of the main body, to find and mark the right DZs for the main force to land on. It was also decided that a medical unit should go in early and carry doctors and surgeons ready and able to operate on wounded men, even as the battle was in hand; it was not enough for the First Aid men to keep the men alive, if possible, sometimes for days, until proper medical care arrived with the ground troops. These were sensible ideas, the fruit of hard won experience, but although the USAAF aircrew attended the talks and vowed to do better, no one from the Airborne Division HQ deigned to turn up.

Perhaps as a result of this official indifference, two vital lessons were not learnt, with dire results when the 1st Airborne Division next went into battle; first, it was not grasped that an Airborne Division was not equipped to hold a position indefinitely, or until the ground forces got around to relieving it; getting up to the airborne perimeter was, or at least should have been, an essential, maybe even *the* essential part of the entire assault plan. While airborne troops could take a position – a fact they had demonstrated in North Africa and now again in Sicily – they could not hold it for long against strong and determined opposition of the kind handed out by the Germans. Secondly, if they were to hold out, then they must have support from ground attack aircraft.

It was clear by now that the enemy tactic for eliminating an airborne bridgehead was to drive right into the heart of it, using infantry, tanks, artillery and air support. The paratroopers had little answer to this tactic except to draw on their fighting ability, skill and guts; these Second World War parachute soldiers were superb fighting men, but proper support from the rest of the Army and the Tactical Air Force would have made them even more successful.

Back in North Africa, 1st Airborne Division took up the

now familiar tasks of retraining, re-equipping and absorbing replacements. As the weeks went past, more and more men came trickling back from Sicily, where they had made their way back to the Allied lines. These included the Captain Dover, the adjutant of 2 Para, who had been dropped no less than 25 miles from the correct DZ and landed close to the glowing crater of Mount Etna, an active volcano. Dover rounded up the four other men from his stick of twelve and although two of these soon disappeared, Dover and a brigade HQ signaller, Corporal Wilson, made their way across country for the next month, hiding by day, moving by night, annoying the Germans whenever the chance presented itself, by sniping, ambushing transport, and cutting telephone wires, before they eventually reached the British lines.

Before long, more parachute operations were being planned. Hackett's 4th Parachute Brigade, which had not been used in Sicily, was tasked to make a drop in support of the landings on the Italian mainland at Salerno, but this task was then delegated to a battalion of the US 82nd Airborne Division. Then several operations which sound little short of suicide were proposed, namely that the 4th Parachute Brigades' battalions should drop in the North of Italy and hold the mountain passes to prevent German reinforcements entering Italy after the Italians surrendered.

This scheme was soon dropped, but the 4th Brigade was finally employed to make a seaborne landing at Taranto, and the brigade duly sailed from Bizerta in early September, 1944. While at sea they saw the wonderful sight of the entire Italian battlefleet sailing south to surrender to the Allies and anchor under the guns of the island fortress of Malta. The Taranto landing went well, except for one tragic incident when the fast minelayer, HMS *Abdiel* struck a mine and some 130 men of the 6th Parachute Battalion, one of the 2nd Brigade's battalions, were drowned.

As far as the Airborne were concerned, the rest of the Italian campaign lasted just over a week. The men of 1st

Division entered Naples and pushed on from there to the airfield at Foggia, for the loss of less than 100 men, killed, wounded and missing, a small total compared to their losses on other, much smaller operations. One of the casualties was Major-General Hopkinson who was replaced by Major-General Down, the officer who had formerly commanded the 2nd Parachute Brigade. Down was a well regarded officer in Airborne Forces but he did not command 1st Airborne for long.

At the end of the year he was sent to India to raise the 44th (Indian) Airborne Division and was replaced by Major-General Urquhart. The 1st Airborne Division returned to the UK at the end of 1943, leaving behind the 2nd Parachute Brigade. The division that arrived in England was the same as the one that was to drop on Arnhem nine months later, consisting of the 1st and 4th Parachute Brigades, commanded by Brigadiers Gerald Lathbury and 'Shan' Hackett respectively, and the 1st Airlanding Brigade commanded by Brigadier 'Pip' Hicks. They would stay in England, training hard, while their sister formation, 6th Airborne won glory in Normandy.

5

OPERATION *OVERLORD*, 6 June 1944

'Finally, gentlemen, do not be surprised if chaos reigns; it undoubtedly will.'

Brigadier James Hill, 3 Parachute Brigade,
pre-D-Day briefing, 1944

The 6th Airborne Division formed in England in May 1943, specifically for Operation *Overlord*, the forthcoming invasion of Europe. Like the 1st Parachute Division, it consisted of two parachute and one glider (Airlanding) brigades, and some of the most experienced officers in Airborne forces came back to the UK from North Africa and Italy to take command of the battalions and brigades. James Hill took command of the 3rd Parachute Brigade, while Lt-Colonel Alastair Pearson took command of the newly formed 8 Para; the other two battalions in this brigade being the Canadian Parachute Battalion, and 9 Para which was first commanded by that veteran parachute officer, Lt-Colonel John Lindsay, but when he fell out with Brigadier Hill and left to take command of the 2nd Battalion, The Gordon Highlanders, the post fell to Lt-Colonel Terence Otway of the Royal Ulster Rifles.

The 5th Parachute Brigade was commanded by Brigadier Nigel Poett, who had under command 7 Para and two new battalions, 12 Para, formerly the 10th Green Howard's, a Yorkshire battalion and, to keep the trans-Pennine balance, 13 Para, formerly the 2nd/4th South Lancashire Regiment. These last were 'made-over' infantry battalions, but anyone who did not wish to go parachuting voted with his feet and left for more pedestrian climes. More volunteers arrived and these battalions were soon indistinguishable from the all-volunteer Parachute Regiment battalions of the 1st Parachute Division.

The 6th Airlanding Brigade was another new formation, and consisted of the 2nd Oxfordshire and Buckinghamshire Light Infantry, the 1st Royal Ulster Rifles and the 12th Battalion The Devonshire Regiment, under the command of Brigadier Hugh Kindersley. These glider battalions were 25 per cent larger than a parachute battalion, numbering 800 to 1,000 men, and their *Horsa* gliders were capable of carrying field artillery, jeeps and even light tanks, as well as engineer stores and large quantities of ammunition. For the airborne operations of the time, gliders were vital, and they had the other advantage that unlike the parachute, which inevitably delivered scattered contingents widely, the glider could deliver compact bodies of fighting soldiers to particular spots on the ground – if the navigation of the towing aircraft so permitted.

When General Montgomery, the field-commander for D-Day and much of the Normandy campaign, took his first look at the initial plan, the outline of what would become the plan for the D-Day invasion, Operation *Overlord*, in January 1944, his first impression was that the chosen thirty-mile invasion front along the bay of the Seine was too narrow. If the armies landed there they stood a good chance of being boxed in, and he therefore decided to widen his front by an extra twenty miles, putting it across the River Orne at Ouistreham in the east and on to the Cotentin Peninsula in the west. His seaborne forces would land on five beaches, *Omaha* and *Utah*, for the US divisions, *Gold* and *Sword* for the British and *Juno* for the Canadians.

The flanks of this seaborne invasion would be held by

three airborne divisions, landing ahead of the seaborne forces. Two US divisions, the 82nd ('All American') and the 101st ('Screaming Eagles') would land in the Cotentin, south of Cherbourg and secure *Utah* Beach. The British 6th Airborne Division would land east of the River Orne and seize the Caen Canal and Orne bridges at Benouville, and the Ranville heights, just east of the Orne, which gave artillery observation over the *Sword* and *Juno* beaches to the west. They would also seize the heavy gun battery at Merville which overlooked these beaches, and hold these positions east of the Orne against all odds, until they were joined by Brigadier Lord Lovat's 1st Commando Brigade, landing on *Sword* beach and marching to their assistance.

Their tasks having been allocated to the division, Major-General Richard Gale had then to allocate them to the various battalions and brigades . . . and immediately there was a snag, the old one, that there would not be enough aircraft available to permit the entire division to go in at one time. Fortunately, this problem was reduced slightly when two RAF transport groups, Nos 38 and 46, were allocated to the division, but when the various aircraft had been allocated there was still not enough aircraft to carry the whole division in one lift, but they could at least land on the same day.

The allocation of objectives depended on Gale's appreciation of the priorities, and he decided that these were first to seize the bridges over the Caen Canal and the River Orne at Benouville and to knock out the Merville battery. To get these bridges intact was vital, for they gave access from the beaches to the Ranville heights. This called for a sudden strike, a *coup de main*, to take these bridges before the defending Germans could destroy them. The task was allocated to a company of the Ox and Bucks in the Airlanding Brigade, which would fly in by glider, land beside the bridges and – given a large amount of luck – seize them before the defenders knew what was happening. The command of this party went to Major John Howard. This party would be reinforced by men of the 5th Parachute Brigade, landing north of Ranville, though the brigade would also be responsible for finding, marking and holding the glider LZ's where divisional headquarters and the vital anti-tank guns could land two hours after the parachute drop. H-Hour for this, the first action of the invasion, was to be midnight on 5–6 June 1944 – D-Day.

For the actual capture of the bridges, John Howard had under command a glider force of 180 men from the 2nd Ox and Bucks Light Infantry and from 249 Field Company Royal Engineers. Major Howard's plan was to land his glider force beside the bridges, but his plan appeared to suffer a setback some days before the invasion when anti-invasion posts – see below – suddenly sprouted in the fields around the bridges. Fortunately, his glider pilots – members of the Glider Pilot Regiment – were not a bit disconcerted as they considered they could run the glider wings against these posts and slow their landing speed.

The Glider Pilot Regiment was a regiment of undaunted sergeants, all capable of flying gliders and joining in the subsequent infantry fighting. Sergeant James Wallwork and his co-pilot, Sergeant John Ainsworth, were flying the first glider to land, and with the other five crews they started training for the operation in March 1944, at Netheravon in Wiltshire.

'No word as to why, in the usual Glider Pilot style,' recalls Sergeant Wallwork, 'but on arrival we were addressed by Colonel George Chatterton who pointed out a couple of broad, white-tape triangles marked out on the airfield. Not very big, but in his judgement, big enough. "You will be towed," said the colonel, "at one-minute intervals to 4,000 feet, and you will release three miles away, at a point decided by your tug. Numbers one, two and three will land in this one and four, five and six in the other, from a left-hand circuit. Now, hop off for lunch. Take-off 1300 hours." So that is what we did, and all six crews landed within the taped-off areas ... our first practice for D-Day.'

69

Another of these glider pilots involved was Staff Sergeant Roy Howard:

For the next phase, a formation of trees close to the east side of Netheravon airfield had been selected. Each day the six chosen glider crews, three from B Squadron and three from C Squadron, were towed to the same height and course and pull-off point, to simulate the operation's requirements, of which we still knew nothing. Three gliders would land in two very small fields. RAF ground crews then had to get the *Horsas* back to Netheravon airfield and service them, but we could only do one of these so-called 'Deadstick' landings each day.

We found out later that the operation required the three gliders attacking the river bridge to shed height as quickly as possible, whereas the three gliders attacking the canal bridge were to carry out a longer and more orthodox approach. Our three gliders had only about half the distance to fly, although from the same height, 6,000 feet, and in order to lose so much height in sufficient time, we had to apply full flap as soon as we released. As soon as we cast off, our Halifax tugs were to continue and drop bombs on Caen.

By this time we were training at night. At first, with a few lights on the ground, but as our landings became more precise these were removed and we were told to do spot-on landings, in these small fields with no lights or aids of any kind. At first I thought that it could not be done, but after one or two hairy missions we found that it could. In all we practised our 'Deadstick' routine 42 times, so we should have been – and were – bloody good at it by June 1944.

While the glider troops were seizing the bridges, the 3rd Parachute Brigade would land on the higher ground east of Ranville. The 9th Battalion would seize the Merville Battery and destroy the guns while a detachment of sappers under Major Rosclere would speed by jeep to the

River Dives and destroy the bridges at Troarn and Bures, to seal off the drop zones and the Ranville heights from attack from the east. This need, to hold the Orne and Caen Canal bridges and destroy those over the River Dives, may require some explanation. Rivers are ideal defence lines and bridges are therefore vital to both defenders and attackers; by destroying the bridges over the Dives, the Airborne prevented the Germans gaining easy access to their lines for a counter-attack against the landing and drop zones; by seizing the ones at Benouville intact, the Airborne secured their supply line, or line of retreat if need be back to the landing beaches, and provided the seaborne forces with easy access to the ground east of the Canal and the Orne. Once their various tasks at Benouville, Merville and the Dives had been carried out, all the Airborne and Commando troops would march on Ranville and hold the wooded ridge from Breville to the Bois de Bavant.

The balance of the Airlanding Brigade, less Howard's party, would land south of Ouistreham on the evening of D-Day – and many D-Day veterans still remember the inspiring sight this made, as hundreds of gliders swept in to land. The glider-borne troops would then cross the bridges at Benouville and join the rest of the division on the Ranville heights. Important places here were the villages of Ranville – where the D-Day cemetery now contains many Airborne soldiers killed in the D-Day and Normandy battles – as well as the villages of Bas de Ranville and Herouvillette.

Gale was well aware that a lot could go wrong on this operation and certain adjustments and alternative plans had to be laid. Brigadier Nigel Poett took Howard's party under command and, as a back-up force in case of need, had 7 Para take a number of inflatable dinghies so that, whatever happened, his men could still cross the river and canal and get to Ranville.

Though the precise targets were not revealed below commanding officer level until a month before D-Day, once these tasks had been allocated, the battalions began to train hard and rehearse their individual roles. Lt-Colonel Terence Otway, tasked to take the Merville battery with 9 Para, had the War Office purchase some suitable land near Newbury and had it bulldozed into a replica of the battery, against which his battalion carried out dozens of trial attacks.

Though none of the D-Day tasks were easy, 9 Para certainly had one of the most difficult and vital. The guns of the Merville Battery could dominate the seaborne landing area for twenty miles and since the guns were sunk in reinforced concrete bastions, impervious to air attack, the only way to knock out the guns was by a direct assault. Unfortunately the Germans were well aware of this. The Merville Battery was surrounded by minefields and thick belts of barbed wire, all overlooked by machine guns and field artillery, and the defences were manned by two companies of infantry.

To cover all eventualities, Otway prepared an elaborate plan, beginning with an attack on the battery by 100 RAF heavy bombers dropping 1,000-pound bombs. As the dust settled, there would be a *coup de main* attack by three gliders, full of troops from 9 Para, which would crash-land directly on the battery and attempt to take it by storm; this party would consist of sixty men from 9 Para and a platoon of sappers carrying demolition charges. This attack would trigger an assault by the main body of the battalion which, having landed on a DZ half a mile away, should by then be lying-up outside the German wire. This would be cut with bangalore torpedoes and the paratroopers would storm through to seize the casements and reinforce the *coup de main* party. The main party would carry ladders for crossing the outer ditches and be supported by anti-tank guns, all supplied by glider. When the battery had been seized and the guns destroyed, the battalion would move off and join the rest of the brigade, occupying the villages of Le Plein and Sallenelles, extending the Airborne Division line north from Bavant and Breville.

Meanwhile 7 Para went off to Devon and practised crossing the River Exe and the Weir Canal, these waterways standing in for the Orne and the Caen Canal. Alastair Pearson, commanding 8 Para, knowing that his men would have to fight in the woods of the Bois de Bavant, took them off Salisbury Plain, and found a wood where the battalion spent two weeks training hard in close-quarter fighting, using live ammunition.

By mid-May most of the plans had been worked out and were being endlessly rehearsed, but those who have followed the other operations in this book will have spotted the chronic and inherent snags of airborne operations. First of all there were the Germans, an opponent never to be taken lightly, and one rarely overwhelmed by surprise. The paratroopers could rely on a swift reaction and strong counter-attacks as soon as their presence was established and their objective divined.

The Normandy front was held by various divisions of the German Seventh Army and the Normandy defences had been greatly improved in recent months since Field-Marshal Erwin Rommel had taken over command of Army Group West, the forces manning Hitler's Atlantic Wall. Mines had been laid in profusion, fresh units drafted in and ordered to prepare and man strong, defensive positions. Rommel was determined to defeat the forthcoming invasion on the first day – 'the longest day', as he called it. His men were to dig in on the beaches and possible landing grounds and get stuck in as soon as the Allied forces appeared.

Rommel's strategy was sound but it had been hindered by two factors: the attitude of Adolf Hitler, who did not believe the Allies would land in Normandy at all, and General Gyer von Scheppenburg, who commanded the panzer (tank) forces on the Channel Coast. Von Scheppenburg believed that since the front was so long and the Allies so strong, a landing simply could not be prevented. He therefore intended to keep the vital panzer divisions concentrated, some distance from the beaches, ready to move in force against the Allied bridgehead as soon as it had been recognised as the real thing and not a diversion.

This was not a bad plan either. Rommel saw the thinking behind it, but totally disagreed with it, given the conditions at the time. The Allies would have complete air superiority over the battlefield and Rommel believed that the tanks would be attacked by rocket-firing fighter-bombers as soon as they moved, and would be destroyed long before they reached the landing areas; he therefore wanted the panzer divisions well forward, close to the Normandy beaches – and in the event he was right. The argument between these two positions was still going on when the Allies came ashore, but Rommel had wrung one concession from Von Scheppenberg. Two panzer divisions, 21 Panzer and the 12 (SS) Panzer Division ('*Hitler Jugend*') were moved up close to the Normandy beaches and in close reserve lay another formidable force, Panzer Lehr. The word *lehr* means training, but Panzer Lehr was no training formation. This strong division was the demonstration division for the German panzer forces and therefore had the best tanks and anti-tank guns, the most experienced officers and the pick of the men.

Equally formidable, though in a different way was 12 SS Panzer. This division was full of young soldiers, just called to regular service from five years service in the Hitler Youth – the *Hitler Jugend*. Most of the men in 12 SS were very young – the average age was just eighteen and many were seventeen; all were fervent supporters of Hitler, strongly imbued with Nazi ideology and determined to fight to the last man to defend the Reich. They were also quite ruthless: shooting prisoners, killing wounded and devastating French villages suspected of supporting the *Maquis* or the Allied cause was common behaviour from the men of 12 SS.

These young men of 12 SS were shooting Canadian prisoners on the afternoon of D-Day, and before long 12 SS men were being shot out of hand by the Canadians and other Allied troops who happened to capture them; the animosity between the invaders and 12 SS veterans continues to this day. While many Allied veterans have made firm friends among the German soldiers they fought against in Normandy, no one has a good word to say for the men of 12 SS – though all admit they were formidable fighters.

Two of three panzer divisions, 12 SS Panzer and 21 Panzer were mustered on the left flank of the invasion area, along the Bay of the Seine, in an ideal position to drive into the side of the Allied forces and roll them up. The only thing to stop them until the seaborne troops were firmly ashore was the 6th Airborne Division, and its supporting 1st Commando Brigade, a force ill-equipped to fight off a strong attack by tank forces.

Nor was German reaction the only worry. The Germans were well aware that the invasion was coming, a good notion of where it might fall, and no doubts that it would be accompanied by parachute and glider landings. Therefore, in the months before June, the flat land along the Normandy coast had been studded with stout posts – nicknamed – Rommel's asparagus – posts which could destroy a landing glider, tear off its wings or crush the fuselage and the men inside.

These sprawling plantations had soon been detected by air reconnaissance but another hazard had passed undetected. The Germans had dammed the local streams and rivers and broken the banks to flood the fields to the east of the Orne, especially along the Dives valley, which was now flooded to a depth of several feet, a potential death trap for any heavily-loaded parachutist. Even worse, weed had grown up and spread rapidly over the surface of the water, concealing the existence of the flooded areas to surveying aircraft – and many of those paratroopers who fell here were to drown in these hidden waters.

Secrecy was vital to the success of the invasion, and it was only at the end of May 1944, barely a week before the intended date of the landing that the glider crews met their passengers. Sergeant Roy Howard remembers it well: 'On 28 May we met our passengers, Major Howard and his Ox and Bucks Light Infantry – or in my case Lieutenant Fox and his platoon of men. Then followed the most intensive briefing on the military side of the operation, greatly aided by an elaborate sand-table model. This showed every detail of the terrain with all the trees, and of course, the river and canal with its bridges, though we did not know where it actually was until about two days before D-Day.'

Lieutenant David Wood, one of John Howard's platoon commanders, also recalls the briefings. 'The company was increased to six platoons by the addition of two from B Company and moved into a sealed camp on 27 May 1944. The officers were briefed on 28 May and the men on 30 May. We had a marvellous model on which every house, slit trench and even tree in the landing zone was shown. We even knew the name of the English speaking café proprietor near the canal bridge, Monsieur Gondree. We were not told where the bridges actually were but an issue of French francs in our escape kit gave us a clue to the country concerned.'

Bad weather delayed the start of the D-Day operation, forcing a change from 5 June to 6 June but when the weather moderated, on the morning of 5 June, the order to go was given. Out in the Channel the storm-tossed landing ships and warships turned again towards the French coast and that night as they closed on the beaches, the drone of a thousand aircraft engines announced that somewhere overhead the three airborne divisions were being flown in to start the decisive battle of the Second World War – the Allied invasion of German-occupied Western Europe.

Like most other airborne operations that night, Major Howard's task did not go entirely to plan. Of the six gliders, four landed on target, close to the canal and river bridges. One landed half a mile away, and one beside a totally different river, eight miles away. There were still enough men at Benouville to do the job as James Wallwork describes:

We took off at 2245 hours through low cloud and into the clear at 6,000 feet over the Channel, avoiding the Navy – that most trigger-happy Service – who had done their best to shoot us down on our way to Sicily the year before. The troops, encouraged by Major Howard, sang and thank heavens, none was airsick. We were right on time and dead on target, thanks to our tug crew; we saw the French coast with plenty of time to get set and then, five, four, three, two one, Cheers! Cast off! That's when the singing stopped. We came in on the final leg at ninety miles per hour and touched down, crashing through several fences in the process and coming to a final stop halfway up the river embankment.

We made an awful lot of noise but it seemed not to have bothered the German sentries who perhaps thought that part of a shot-down bomber had landed. Exactly one minute later No. 2 arrived, followed by No. 3. There was only one casualty on landing, the Bren gunner in No. 2 glider was thrown out and drowned in the pond in our field. Johnnie and I revived in a few minutes and I managed to crawl free of the debris, but it required two of us to drag Johnnie out. Nothing was broken except an ankle and a badly sprained pair of knees for Johnnie. The medic took him to the ditch which had been designated the regimental aid post. That was the last I saw of him until back in the squadron several weeks later. I had taken a header through the Perspex nose and was bleeding from a head cut. Blood had congealed quickly in my right eye socket and I thought all night that I had only one eye left.

Glider pilot Sergeant Roy Howard, whose troops were tasked for the Orne bridge, also had a successful crossing.

We cast off at 1,200 feet and there below us the canal and river lay like silver, instantly recognisable. Orchards and woods lay as darker patches on a dark and foreign soil. I thought that it all looked so exactly like the sand-table model that I had the strange feeling I had been there before. I took off the flaps for a moment to slow our headlong descent and put them back on as we shot towards the line of trees over which I had to pass, not by fifty feet or we should overshoot and be crushed as we hit the embankment which I knew was at the end of our field.

I had to just miss and scrape over the tree-tops as we deployed the parachute brake specially fitted to the rear of the glider in order to shorten our landing run to the minimum. Up with the nose and then the heavy rumble of the main wheels as we touched down a few minutes after midnight, close to the river bridge. 'You are in the right place, sir,' I shouted to Lieutenant Fox and with a drumming and crash of army boots, he and his men disappeared into the night.

It was only much later that we learned that Number Four had undershot by some 400 yards, while due to the tug navigator's error, another had landed miles away, and the lads were busy capturing a bridge on the wrong river. Realising their error they later fought their way through the night to our bridge, an astonishing feat of skill and determination.

Major John Howard's *coup de main* was completely successful. As their gliders came to a crashing halt, the men scrambled out and charged for their bridges. A white phosphorus grenade was thrown at the pill-box guarding the Canal bridge approaches, followed by a grenade through a gun port. The German NCO in charge did manage to get off a burst of machine-gun fire, killing Lieutenant Brotheridge, the first British soldier to die on D-Day, who now lies buried in the church cemetery at Ranville. The bridge was in Allied hands within minutes, the Royal Engineers searching for and dismantling its demolition charges.

David Wood and his men were in glider No. 3.

Quite suddenly, the pilot shouted, 'Christ! There's the bridge,' and we were descending for a rough and bumpy landing at about 90 mph with the skids throwing up sparks from flints in the ground. We thought they were rounds of tracer and that we were already under fire. The impact of landing broke the glider's back and I was thrown through the side. I collected myself and my canvas bucket full of primed grenades – all still intact, which says something for the boys who designed the safety factor in those grenades, and pushed on across the road to clear the inner defences.

The enemy had by this time come to life and Don Brotheridge was killed as he led his platoon on the far side of the Canal bridge. We were all a bit dazed but acted more or less automatically. There was a good deal too much firing and shouting, which is fairly typical of troops in action for the first time. I heard the success signals 'Ham and Jam' on the radio before being sent for by my company commander. As I went towards him in the dark I was hit in the leg by a burst of fire, which also caught my platoon sergeant and my runner. I regret to say there were no heroics, although I had heard about folk who can run around on only one leg. I found I simply fell down and couldn't get up. My platoon medical orderly gave me a shot of morphia, applied a rifle splint and found my flask in my hip pocket. I always claim that I lasted 25 minutes in action, but I really cannot be sure how long it was.

With the bridges in Allied hands, Major Howard and his band dug in to await reinforcements from Brigadier Nigel Poett's 5th Parachute Brigade and the arrival sometime after dawn of Lord Lovat's 1st Commando Brigade, which would come ashore on *Sword* beach, six miles away and make a fighting advance to join them.

Brigadier Poett hit the ground twenty minutes after midnight, but his brigade was well scattered by strong westerly winds then stirring up the Channel waves. This wind had carried 5th Parachute Brigade's pathfinders well away from their designated DZs and with no time to march back they set up their beacons where they were. The result was that the brigade landed well to the east and were unable to get back to the bridges before German infantry with armoured support began to probe Major Howard's defences. By 0300 hours the battalion detailed to reinforce Howard's group, the 7th Parachute Battalion, could muster only 300 men. This was just enough and as the night wore on more 7th Battalion paratroopers arrived, trickling in alone or in small groups, obeying the old military dictum: 'When in doubt, head for the sound of the gunfire.'

One of those to drop with the 7th Battalion was Private Bill Elvin:

My D-Day started in the afternoon of 5 June, when we boarded trucks at our concentration area on Salisbury Plain and drove to the airfield. As our convoy passed through the villages, groups of people waved us farewell; some of the women were in tears for they had guessed that something big was about to begin. We arrived at Fairford in the early evening and were taken to our planes, which were four-engined Stirlings, twenty Paras to each plane.

We then had parachutes issued and looked like a lot of little Michelin men, parachutes on our backs, all our weapons and gear on our fronts. Being only 5 foot 4 inches I was as broad as I was long, carrying as much equipment as I weighed myself. With our faces blackened we settled down on the floor of the plane for the trip to France. If an officer had said to me, 'You cannot go', I would have cried my eyes out, and so would many of my mates. We were all green, having never been in action before, but we all wanted to have a go.

Another member of this 7 Para company was Sergeant Bob Tanner:

I joined the Parachute Regiment from the Royal Tank Regiment. An officer came round and explained what joining the Paras entailed, the hardships, training and relentless exercises but I did not care. First and foremost was a desire to get away from Catterick Camp. My whole tank crew volunteered, and as far as I know, only two of us survived the war. I realised that I would be losing the protection of all that armour plating, but the horrors of seeing burned tanks and crews in Normandy made me realise how lucky I was.

Then came D-Day. The airfield, fitting chutes, checking equipment, last-minute instructions, the talk by our CO, Lt-Colonel Pine-Coffin, going to the toilets – which did a roaring trade. As you know, some of us in B Company carried rubber dinghies for crossing the Caen Canal in the event of the bridge being blown. Last minutes to blacken faces and then emplane . . . just thinking about it all still gives me the willies! Engines started and finally we began to move. The plane seemed to be taking a long time before we lifted off. There was not much to see inside a darkened aircraft fuselage, and each man had his own thoughts. I remember deciding that I was going to come back. Although thoughts of death and injury cropped up, I made my mind up. I was coming back.

The majority of 7 Para was flown to France in converted Stirling bombers, and Private Elvin recalls his first operational jump:

Stirlings were large planes and it was just like riding in a double-decker bus, only not so comfortable. To get out of the plane we had to waddle to the rear of the fuselage and drop out of a large hole shaped like a coffin. There was plenty of back-chat early on and we all had something to say – excitement and nervous tension, I guess.

When we got near the dropping zone it was a case of 'Red Light on; Hook up; Get ready to jump.' The engines throttled back and it was Green Light on 'Go' and we were out and floating down over France. It was so silent, only the noises of the plane's engines going away from us. Where was the war? Where were the

Germans? We saw aircraft coned by searchlights and going down in flames, and this heavy flak, combined with the high winds, dispersed the aircraft and gave many of the paratroopers a scattered drop. Then I looked down and wondered, where was the land? All I could see was water and with a splash I was in it and being dragged along by my chute. Eventually I found my feet in waist-deep water and was able to stand up – I had landed in the flooded Dives valley.

The 5th Brigade suffered nearly 100 casualties in the drop alone, and over 400 men were still missing when they assembled next day, though most of the missing trailed in later.

While 7 Para were mustering at the Orne and Canal bridges, 13 Para began clearing the drop zone of obstacles ready for the arrival of the Airlanding Brigade. They also cleared the enemy out of Ranville while 12 Para, though fifty per cent under strength, made for the brigade concentration area, the high ground south of Ranville, where they dug in to await the inevitable German counter-attack.

George Price, now a lance-corporal, jumped with the 12th (Yorkshire) Parachute Battalion:

I was a member of the anti-tank section of Headquarters Company, but had been attached to C Company for D-Day. My weapon was the 'Projector Infantry, Anti-Tank', or 'PIAT'. This was a heavy, spring-operated weapon, firing a hollow-charge round. It was very heavy, and cumbersome. Like many others in the brigade, I landed in the wrong place. Suddenly, here I was, lying on my back in a field in Normandy, with only a couple of hand grenades in my belt. I had lost all my equipment in the drop; my rifle and ammunition, my PIAT and food, were somewhere in the orchard behind me – and I was lost.

I scrambled out of my harness, got to my feet and took stock of my surroundings. Although it was dark the sky to the west was aglow with light from the fires in the coastal towns that were being bombed by the RAF. I could see the orchard a short distance away and thought of my kit bag. I could see figures all around me and they all seemed to be going in the same direction, so I joined them, hoping that I would eventually reach my allotted position. Dawn was just breaking when we approached Ranville, having been dropped some four miles from the intended DZ.

Another soldier jumping with C Company, 12th Parachute Battalion that night was Ron Dixon of the Signal Platoon:

I dropped on the right drop zone at Ranville, but I appeared to be the only person on it. Luckily, I linked up with our company commander, Major Stephens, and within minutes we arrived at the battalion rendezvous. We moved off some time later with only half the battalion, the remainder having dropped some distance away. We reached our objective, the Bas de Ranville, around dawn, and an elderly French lady came from her farmhouse, on the land where we were digging in, to see what was going on. I could only guess that she was asking who we were and what we were doing. I told her that we were British and this was the invasion. She went back into her house and minutes later came out with a jug of milk and some bread. I had a block of chocolate in my camouflaged denison smock, which I gave to her.

The original rendezvous for the 12th Parachute Battalion was a quarry on the Cabourg–Caen road. Those who got there found that very few of the battalion had arrived and the commanding officer ordered those who were there to start out for their first objective, the village of Le Bas de Ranville.

At 0330 hours Divisional Headquarters came in by glider, bringing Major-General Gale, more ammunition and the all-important anti-tank guns. The German defenders were by now fully aware that a major parachute assault was taking place and had begun to send out fighting patrols and armoured cars towards the Canal and the bridges. Colonel Hans Von Luck of the 125th Panzer Grenadier Regiment recalls that night:

Our position lay east of the River Orme and the Caen Canal. The bridges there were defended by a 'second-rank' company, whose task was to make sure that Commandos or the French Resistance would not blow the bridge. Our division – 21st Panzer – was in reserve with a strict order not to move unless released by Army Group B. However I knew that the way to halt an airborne attack is to drive right on to the dropping zone so I made a counter-attack on my own responsibility to support two companies of my regiment. These were on a night exercise and had only dummy ammunition to use when airborne people dropped on their position. I am quite sure that had we been able to make a counter-attack at once, in the direction of the coast and Pegasus Bridge [the Canal bridge], it would have been successful. On D+2, part of my battle group met with Major John Howard – a very good friend of mine today, incidentally – at Escoville, where he lost quite a large number of his company.

Lieutenant David Wood of the Ox and Bucks recalls one of the first German probes:

The enemy sent two armoured half-tracks down to the Canal bridge to find out what was happening; one was knocked out and there was a magnificent firework display as the ammo in it exploded. Seven Para thought we were still having a hell of a battle to capture the bridge and the German commander of the garrison returned across the river bridge in a staff car, which we shot up, and he was wounded and captured. He asked

84

the doctor to finish him off because his honour had been lost, but the MO would not oblige. Finally, the Germans sailed a gunboat down the Canal from Caen, to where it was swiftly despatched by a well-aimed PIAT round.

Meanwhile, the 3rd Parachute Brigade of Brigadier James Hill were getting on with their tasks in spite of the chaos he had so accurately predicted. The first of these tasks, as already related, was to take the Merville Battery. Second, they had to secure the high ground at Le Plein, a task given to the 1st Canadian Parachute Battalion. Third, they had to destroy the four bridges over the River Dives at Troan, Bures, Robehomme and Varaville, a task delegated to men of Alastair Pearson's 8 Para. Having achieved all this the brigade was to concentrate close to Ranville, in the area of the Bois de Bavant.

Among those to drop with 3rd Parachute Brigade HQ, was Gunner David King, a signaller with 53 Airlanding Light Regiment, a unit equipped with 75 mm field guns. Like many others that night, David King had a very wet landing in flooded fields:

My kitbag was whipped away and I landed on my back in a couple of feet of water. I tried to keep my head above water and to release my parachute, and as a result my Sten gun, stuck under my parachute harness, was swept away. So, there I was, a twenty-year-old soldier, behind enemy lines, with eight magazines of Sten ammo in my pouches and no gun, no radio and no food!

After wandering about for what seemed like hours, I heard someone approaching. I was so relieved to hear him say the password for the drop, 'Punch', I quickly replied, 'Judy'. This turned out to be an officer and he had a revolver and a Sten gun so he kindly gave me the Sten. Eventually we met other Paras, some heading for Le Mesnil – my target, which we reached without too much bother. There was no sign of my officer or fellow signaller and I was put as Number Two on a Bren gun.

My officer arrived that afternoon, followed by my fellow signaller, struggling in with two heavy accumulators needed to operate our radio; he wasn't very pleased to discover that I had no radio to attach them to but a supply drop during the evening replaced the radio, and we were back in business.

And so to the Merville Battery which now lies as a museum, amid farmland south of the resort of Franceville-Plage. In June 1944 the concrete casements, six feet thick, enclosed four 155 mm artillery pieces, protected by minefields, barbed wire, and fixed-line machine guns, while the living quarters underground could hold 200 men protected by concrete head cover against bombing.

Lt-Colonel Terence Otway had exercised his battalion endlessly in the assault plan which employed every available means of reducing the garrison. First, the battery would be bombed by a Lancaster force just before the assault. Then, after the minefields, havd been gapped by Royal Engineer sappers, the battery would be assaulted by the entire battalion, less another volunteer force, fifty men in three gliders, who would crash-land right on top of the battery position. Finally, if all else failed, the battery would be engaged by the guns of the Fleet. This was a fine but complicated plan . . . and it went wrong from the start.

The 9th Battalion had a terrible drop, being scattered widely across the flooded valley of the Dives, where many men were drowned. Some men fell as much as thirty miles from their proper drop zone, though Lt-Colonel Otway and his batman landed right by a German headquarters and were almost captured while still in their parachutes. When Otway reached the battalion rendezvous he found he had only 150 men and none of the special equipment he needed, except a few bangalore torpedoes for clearing wire. Even so, the colonel decided to attack the battery immediately.

One of those to jump with 9 Para was Private SF Capon, of 12 Platoon, C Company:

Our drop was set for 0030 hours. It wasn't long before we heard the order: 'We are approaching the coast of France,' and suddenly our aircraft was sent into a turmoil with German anti-aircraft fire raining on us. We were hurled from port to starboard before despatch, when a voice shouted, 'Stand by the doors – Get ready! Red light . . . Green light . . . GO!' I had always jumped to perfection but this time I fell out like a sack of coal. As I jumped I could see the amber glow from the shells exploding around the aircraft. A disastrous exit but I floated down to the best landing I had ever had and took a look around.

About a hundred yards further on a group of about six men, including Lieutenant Mike Dowling of B Company, were lying in a patch of stinging nettles trying to find their bearings. We moved on along a narrow road when a lorry shot past full of Germans, so we laid low. When the lorry had gone we crossed the road to be greeted by a Pathfinder, and we joined the few men who had arrived at the rendezvous. The final number reached 150.

On arriving at the assembly area, Otway found that some of his men had already arrived and had cleared a few tracks through the minefields, crawling out in the dark to dig up the mines with their bayonets – an indication of the fine spirit of this battalion. The attack went in as timed, and the 9th Battalion took the Merville Battery by storm, capturing thirty of the garrison and killing the rest. Private Capon again:

When we arrived at the Merville battery all was very quiet. We advanced to the assembly and lay low, facing the gun emplacements that we could now see. My platoon was to capture the Number One gun. The 32 men under the command of Lieutenant Alan Jefferson, who had trained day and night for this job were now reduced to just seven men – to do the job of 32. This left Mike Dowling with a group to take Number Two gun, and another group to take Number Three, and likewise Number Four. However, all was not lost. We still had three gliders with fifty men of A Company, all parachutists, a *coup de main* force to land on the battery and cause havoc and maybe even take it.

We lay low, awaiting the gliders. The first one appeared, only to land well away from the target. The second glider hovered over the battery, and suddenly the German machine-gun tracer bullets raked it and it veered behind us and landed, never to take part in the attack, though the survivors joined us later. The third glider never arrived at all.

That was it and our colonel couldn't wait any longer. Time was running out and the guns had to be silenced before the seaborne troops arrived. All eyes were facing the guns and awaiting the final words from Otway. He shouted, 'Get in!' and Jefferson blew his little hunting horn, which he always did in training. This time he got off two toots on the horn and fell wounded. I ran with my mates across the uneven ground, zig-zagging and firing as we ran. To my left I heard explosions and shouts of 'Mines!' but I ran to my target. Within seconds I arrived with three others at the rear of the gun. Left standing were Eric Bedford, Harold Walker and Frank Delsignore – my mates, just four of us. Eric was in charge and we threw grenades into the gun emplacement. After the din and gunfire it seemed eerie, but after the exploding grenades, voices could be heard within the emplacement and the German prisoners pushed each other from the left-hand enclosure within the gun, across the corridor and out towards the opposite wing to us, with our guns pointing towards them.

Colonel Otway arrived with some of the men he had kept in reserve and we proceeded out of the battery only to come under enemy fire from a machine-gun on the perimeter. After a few bursts the crew surrendered, and handing over the prisoners to Colonel Otway, we proceeded to pull out our wounded. The badly wounded were put on sledges we found, which I later learned were for pulling ammunition. In this my partner was Sergeant Paddy Jenkins and Frank Delsignore did the same with Harold Walker ... and that's how we took the Merville Battery.

While Lt-Colonel Otway and his men were taking the Merville Battery, Lt-Colonel Alastair Pearson and his men of the 8th Battalion were making for their objectives, the bridges over the River Dives. Transported by C47 aircraft, this battalion was widely scattered by high winds and enemy anti-aircraft fire so Pearson could only muster 150 men and had only one Royal Engineer instead of two troops of sappers to blow the bridges, and it was not until 1000 hours on D-Day that the last bridge at Troarn was put out of commission after a jeep sortie behind enemy lines.

To support the troops of 8th Parachute Battalion, landing by parachute, heavier equipment, including jeeps, had to be flown in by glider. Sergeant Watts of the Glider Pilot Regiment was flying one of them. 'At 2300 hours on 5 June our flight of six gliders took off from Blakehill Farm. A C47 Dakota tug got us to the correct area, but there was no sign of landing lights of the LZ. However, we released and glided down to about thirty feet above the ground and then put the large landing light on to see clearly where the telegraph poles were. We landed safely at 1 am on 6 June, only losing part of a wing. About five minutes later the parachutists landed and escorted the jeep and trailer to Troarn to blow up the bridges.'

After the war Colonel Pearson used to lead battlefield tours to Normandy and show Allied officers attached to NATO what actually happened on D-Day. As these officers came from many countries and Colonel Pearson had a strong Scots accent, his account was sometimes hard to follow – or most of it: 'So the fucking Germuns were here ana fucking Germans were inna box, 'n,ach awa, so I tol the battalion warra gonna do an at the fucking Germans an inna bayonts, n' git some bloody fire doun, and so the fucking Germuns ...' The story goes that, after half an hour or so of this, a nervous Canadian officer plucked a British officer by the sleeve and asked what Colonel Pearson was saying. 'I don't honestly know' was the whispered reply 'but I gather he doesn't like the Germans very much.'

The Canadian Parachute Battalion was also widely scattered in the drop. Of the 35 aircraft lifting this battalion, 16 dropped their parachutists more than two miles away from the planned drop zone and many landed even further afield. The plan for the Canadians on D-Day also involved prior *coup de main* operations mounted by C Company which was to drop ahead of the battalion, to seize and secure the village of Varaville, especially the two pill-boxes and a trench system that overlooked drop zone V, the battalion's main landing area; a 75 mm gun on the far side of the DZ had also to be destroyed. Once this had been done, the company was to then proceed to a bridge over the River Dives and destroy it.

Captain John Madden of C Company relates what actually happened:

In training we had encountered defective hatch catches for the cover of the jump hole on the Albermarle. The doors had a habit of falling shut in mid-stick, so before the 'off' on D-Day, I spoke to the pilot and told him that he must not take any parachutists back to England. If the hatch slammed shut while we were jumping, he was to circle round and drop the rest. Well, after the first six got out, the hatch slammed down. The pilot subsequently dropped the last four of my men, but *twenty miles* from where he dropped me. Of the four, two were killed and two were taken prisoner. At the time I was surprised by our wide dispersal but never mind, enough men landed on target to achieve our objective, and those who dropped astray helped to create confusion in the minds of the enemy.

After C Company had secured the DZ at Varaville, the main battalion drop would take place, and while A

Company were protecting the left flank of the 9th Battalion taking the Merville Battery, B Company would ensure the destruction of the Robehomme bridge and HQ Company would secure the drop zone itself. However, as with the other drops that night, the battalion was widely scattered. To compound their problems, they were dropped at the same time as an RAF bombing force attacked the Merville Battery. These bombers overshot the Merville Battery and dropped their bombs too far inland, the explosions often catching the Canadian paratroopers as they landed. Despite all these setbacks the Canadians managed to complete their tasks before being reinforced by men of the 1st Commando Brigade coming from *Sword* beach.

Captain John Madden again:

As the wind dispersed the early-morning mist, I could see a faint line in the distance, which resolved itself into the Normandy coast. It was 0500 hours and we were a mere 1,200 yards from the beaches. I knew we were caught on the coastal strip being prepared for the seaborne invasion, and could see the flashes of gunfire from the distant warships. Following this came the roar of aircraft, bombs showered in astride and behind us. The entire coastline was blotted out by clouds of smoke and we scratched pitiful little holes in the earth. Five minutes after the bomb line passed inland a new terror threatened. Low-flying fighters strafed our area. One of the men had a bullet pass through the stock of his rifle as he held it between his hands. Branches were cut down all around us, yet we survived.

And so the dawn of D-Day arrived. In the hours of darkness, the men of the Airborne Divisions had completed all their tasks – and this applies to the US Airborne Divisions in the Cotentin Peninsula, who had faced many of the same problems as the battalions of the British 6th Airborne Division. All their objectives had been taken. Now they had to be held.

6

THE BATTLE FOR NORMANDY,
June–September 1944

'What you win by stealth and guile you must hold with guts and tenacity.'

Major-General James Gale commanding
6th Airborne Division, 6 June 1944

While the formed, if much reduced, units of 6th Airborne were completing their tasks, all over the Normandy countryside scattered groups of paratroopers, including many men who were completely on their own, were attempting to find out where they were and get back to their comrades and units. Among these were Ernie Elvin and his pals of 7 Para, who were trying to get to their battalion rendezvous point at dawn, having hidden in a barn all night. Once it was daylight and they could see where they were, Ernie and the other two set off again:

> We could see that each side of the road was flooded, so our only way was to go up the road. So up the road we went, and after about a mile we could hear firing in the distance and knew that a battle was taking place. We then came to a driveway leading to a large house about 400 yards away. At the house we could see what appeared to be German soldiers on guard, so it was

back into the water to make our way past, hoping that we had not been seen. Fortunately nothing happened, so we made our way back to the road.

About five minutes later we came across a Frenchman and his wife coming down the road. The only thing we could understand was that there were no Germans in the direction we were going, so we carried on for a while until we saw men moving in the distance beyond what turned out to be the River Dives. We moved cautiously towards them until we saw that they were Paras. They turned out to be men of the 1st Canadian Para Battalion who were about to withdraw after blowing the Robehomme bridge and using it as a road block. So into the water we went again, and holding on to the debris of the bridge, we crossed to the other side of the river and withdrew with the Canadians.

As we withdrew we could see signs of a battle; some Paras were hanging from the high-tension wires strung from pylon to pylon, their 'chutes caught in the wires from which they had been unable to free themselves, and so there they had died. Late that evening we ended up at the 3rd Para Brigade at Le Mesnil and were put into defence positions around the HQ. It was a very noisy night, and by midnight on D-Day I had still not joined up with my battalion – we were in the 5th Brigade remember, but in the early days in Normandy you fought where you found yourself. On the morning of D + 1 we were loaded on to a Jeep to take a very hairy journey to the 5th Para Brigade HQ. The two brigades had not yet joined up and there were still German positions between the two brigades.

I finally got back to my own unit, 4 Platoon B Company, 7th Parachute Battalion at Ranville at about 1130 hours on D + 1. They were dug-in opposite Ranville church. In the distance I could see the wrecked gliders, and the Germans were beginning to infiltrate them. We were being shelled spasmodically and I shared a trench with Private Bushell, who told me what had happened on the west side of the bridges over the Orne and the Canal. Several men were missing from the platoon, but I was back where I should have been, and I felt safe with my old mates.

The great event of D-Day for the Airborne Division was the link up with the seaborne forces at around 1330 hours, when Lord Lovat's personal piper, Bill Millin, piped the leading troops across what is now Pegasus Bridge over the Caen Canal, an event watched by some of Major John Howard's Ox and Bucks from the Airlanding Brigade, now comfortably ensconced in the Café Gondree, where Madame Gondree had unearthed some long hidden bottles of champagne, to celebrate the liberation of the first bar in France. The next major event was the arrival of the rest of the Airlanding Brigade which came swooping over the bridgehead that evening.

Corporal A Darlington of the Airborne Recce Regiment recalls the hours before embarking for France.

We arrived at the airfield in the morning of 6 June and were given a meal by the Air Force WAAF. We even had sugar in bowls and the best meal in years. This we termed the 'Last Supper', and for many it was. We had been issued with a 48-hour emergency ration which when opened looked more like a child's compendium of games. Creamy-coloured dominoes turned out to be porridge with milk and sugar if reconstituted. The dice were tea, milk and sugar cubes. Then we took off and were towed over the Channel and landed in France.

The landing was a roaring, twisting, bumping, skidding event going from high speed to a dead stop in a few seconds and we were all momentarily knocked out by it. Then the side door opened and the pilot looked in and shouted, 'Sorry for the rough landing, boys.' I unstrapped and dashed out of the door to let the struts down for exit, only to find that the undercarriage no longer existed and parts of the wings were missing. The front was clear and the Bren gun carrier engines were

94

already running. 'All clear for exit, Sir, but the damned anchors are jammed!' These were the anchors that kept the carrier in place in the glider, but I took the escape axe from the wall and after three or four good swipes, the carrier shot forward, the door opened and off they went ... for a few yards. On leaving the glider, the carrier settled down backwards and our jeep anchor ropes were jammed also, so the hatchet came into action once more, but the front edge of the exit had risen some two feet and the tail wheel was also torn off. The jeep's front wheels could not reach the ground and we see-sawed on the edge with the chassis. I got out again, grasped the bumper so that the back wheels would drive the jeep slowly forward, and then the front wheels finally took over. I often wonder how I completed this feat of strength.

The arrival of these gliders was very welcome, for the gliders brought fresh men, a resupply of ammunition and the vital anti-tank guns. The 6th Airborne Division had beaten off an ever-heavier series of attacks by the Germans throughout D-Day and with their anti-tank guns and some help from naval gunfire they were able to hold on and even improve their defences, until joined that evening by two more battalions of their third element, the 6th Airlanding Brigade which had with them a lot more heavy equipment, including light tanks and jeeps.

Not every paratrooper was – or is – an infantryman. Among the Airborne soldiers jumping on were engineers (sappers), signallers, artillerymen (gunners) and medical staff. One of the medics was Lewis 'Jack' Tarr, a member of 195 Parachute Field Ambulance, who jumped into Normandy at 0900 hours on the morning of 6 June, in broad daylight:

We landed near Ranville and what is now Pegasus Bridge in the second wave. We found the glider with our medical jeep and trailer and started out for Longueval and our rendezvous. There were soldiers everywhere and, quite frankly, we were all like a herd of sheep, many lost, milling about, looking for their units. Our main problem was the snipers. We were right in their line of fire. Close by our position an officer was manning a machine gun. He was wounded later and I was one of those who had to go and get him in. All those around him had been killed, picked off by the snipers. There was a wood nearby, giving the snipers really good cover and they came in after dark, moving from tree to tree, well camouflaged. The only way to bring them down was to aim carefully directly at them, which one of our corporals did – shooting a sniper right through the forehead. The sniper was, like us, only about 23 or 24 years old.

The Airlanding gliders brought in extra weapons, including a new PIAT for Ernie Price of the 12th Battalion: 'Thus equipped I was able to rejoin my section and not too soon for we were soon attacked by a German tank, a Tiger or a Mark IV which came rumbling into our position to be greeted with PIAT fire and shells from our 6-pounder anti-tank guns. A great many lads had been killed by then, but so far our section had been lucky.

Sergeant Bill Higgs, a glider pilot, remembers more tank action on D-Day:

I was manning a 6-pounder anti-tank gun and we were dug-in and camouflaged at Ranville by about dawn on D-Day. I kept watching the skyline towards Caen from which we expected the enemy to come and eventually a column of German tanks and half tracks crossed our line of fire, with infantry moving in front of them, in extended order. We held our fire and then, just as if someone had blown a whistle, everyone opened up at the same time. We brewed up a lot of tanks – set them well on fire – and half tracks, and then turned our Brens and MMGs on the German infantry, who went to ground and were soon hitting back at us with mortars.

One of the anti-tank gunners had been hit, and a mate of mine 'Chalky' White got to the gun and knocked a tank out, for which he received the DCM. Poor 'Chalky' was later killed at Arnhem, and I got a Mention-in-Despatches.

This wave of gliders flying in on D-Day to the now-secured landing zones also carried 26 Tetrarch light tanks belonging to the 6th Airborne Reconnaissance Regiment. This was their first operation since formation in 1943, and here again their D-Day task did not go entirely according to plan, as Corporal Charles Sheffield recalls:

We took off in the late afternoon, wondering what we were going to find over there. Most of us landed safely, and on leaving the glider I hitched up the three trailers to my tank. These contained petrol in the wheels and ammo in the large box between the wheels. We had very little opposition, just a few mortars thudding down a short distance away, and I was just gaining speed when, suddenly, the tank stopped. The driver did not know why so I slid out of the turret to the ground and found parachute cord and silk wound tightly round the final drive. It was hard work cutting it off and, on moving forward again, we came across the squadron leader, also stuck with parachute cord having wound around his tank tracks and he had to use a blow-torch to burn it off. You never think of things like that but it brought most of the squadron to a complete halt for some time.

As well as bringing men and heavy equipment, the Airlanding battalions also brought in essential items such as fuel, water and rations. One of the pilots on this main lift was Sergeant Sidney Dodd, flying a 'Hamilcar' glider. 'I was second pilot to Staff Sergeant White in Glider No. LA636. We landed in support of the gliders that had taken the bridges over the Orne and the Caen Canal. We were one of three "Hamilcars" that carried petrol and ammunition, and the glider tails were painted yellow for recognition. We landed safely, though having to cut through poles which the Germans had erected to stop us. We didn't encounter much trouble, joined up at the bridge with other pilots, and when the seaborne troops arrived we were pulled out.' Sidney Dodd went on to fly at both Arnhem and the Rhine Crossing, and says: '. . . of these three operations, D-Day was the least demanding.'

Sergeant Roy Howard, one of the *coup de main* pilots, was relieved to see the Airlanding glider force coming in:

> At 2100 hours on 6 June the main glider force came into the Ranville area – a great sight and the end of our duty. The glider pilot task was complete and early on 7 June we decided to go home. Our orders were to return to the UK as soon as possible so that we would be ready to fly in a further load if necessary. We all said goodbye to Major Howard and his men and walked along the road to Ouistreham, snatching as much sleep as the 15-inch shells which HMS *Warspite* was pumping east into Le Havre would allow. As we arrived at the beach a Ju-88 bomber was shot down, crashing some thirty yards from us, where it continued to explode and burn for some time. Later on that night Lt-Colonel Murray and the glider pilots from the main landing force arrived. We all waded out to the LCIs [landing craft] and arrived back in Newhaven at 0630 hours on 8 June.

In the coming days and weeks the Bren gun carriers and Tetrach tanks of the Airborne Recce Regiment joined the 8th Para Battalion in the Bois de Bavant and set up a series of observation posts (OPs) watching the plain towards Troarn-Caen-Escoville. They also sent bicycle patrols deep into enemy territory where invaluable information was obtained leading to some very successful air strikes and naval bombardments, especially from the cruiser HMS *Mauritius*, which were directed on to enemy vehicle parks and armoured forming-up positions.

As more and more heavy gliders swooped in on the

evening of 6 June, space on the landing zones ran out. Corporal Dartington describes the scene: 'I saw two *"Hamilcars"* heading for the same space, and they had obviously seen each other because they tried to bank away. Sadly one glider's wing tip turned the other over and it crashed sideways into the wood and the Tetrarch tank shot out of the front on impact. There was a mad dash over to it and the tank was upright, although it had somersaulted out of the glider. The crew was unstrapped and dragged out unconscious. They were strapped on the back of a passing tank's engine compartment with camouflage nets and retaining straps and taken off to the aid station.'

The LZ was now a hive of activity as gliders landed and unloaded, and Staff Sergeant Wally Grimshaw was there with 6th Airborne Recce Regiment:

I was then the Troop-Sergeant of Number One Machine Gun Troop in HQ Squadron. I rode a James motorcycle and led the way to the edge of the drop zone, dodging the mortar bombs which had started to fall on the DZ, as well as the odd bursts of MG fire. As we reached the shelter of the wood I saw one of the regiment's DZ party, who told me that the troop were to rendezvous at the sawmills above Ranville.

We duly cut through the woods until we met the main road and stopped there for a quick 'shuftie'. We came across a jeep with four dead gunners and saw they had caught a direct hit from one of the German mortar bombs. Further along the road we met some Airborne medics who had some German medics working with them. I gave them the location of the bombed jeep and a party went off to check. Finally met up with the rest of my troop with the troop corporal and two glider-pilots, both sergeants. I was ordered to put out my guns as local protection, and within a few minutes they had engaged two six-wheeled armoured cars. After a few minutes firing the Germans retired down the hill, followed by one of B Squadron's recce troops. Our new neighbours turned out to be the 1st Canadian Parachute Battalion, and I quickly liaised with them to make sure we did not receive any friendly 'misses'.

An Airborne perimeter was being mapped out and after a few hours I went on a recce to a new position with one of the Para battalions, the 12th I think it was, plus one of the Independent Para companies. I had to select two front-line positions and one to cover the rear in case the position was overrun, because the Paras were a little thin on the ground at the time and we had to hold this particular front at all costs.

We used to have a 'Hate Hitler' session, thirty minutes daily, when we fired all our weapons on our front, promptly receiving a similar load of high explosive back in return. It was during one of these days I was wounded and back-loaded to England, but that is what it was like in the early days in Normandy.

By midnight on D-Day the 6th Airborne Division, reinforced by 1st Commando Brigade, was firmly in control of Ranville and the villages round about. As these accounts have indicated their introduction to Normandy had not been without difficulties. High winds and enemy anti-aircraft fire had broken up their aircraft and glider formations. Seven of the transport aircraft had been shot down, and 22 gliders were missing, some having ditched in the sea. More than a third of the glider pilots had been killed or wounded and a third of the paratroopers were still missing, roaming the countryside looking for their units. It had always been hard for the soldiers to think beyond D-Day, for just getting ashore was such a major task, but 6 June was just the first day of a three-month long battle and the parachute battalions were soon in the thick of it.

Parachute soldiers are not supposed to stay on for long after the initial assault landing, and fight as heavy infantry. This is not to say they are not often obliged to do so, but Second World War airborne battalions were small, with a ration strength of around 600 men. They also lacked heavy equipment, although this deficiency was made up after a fashion by landing artillery, anti-tank guns and engineer stores by glider, or providing support from tactical aircraft, ground-strafing fighter-bombers or naval gunfire – and the airlanding battalions were of course, much stronger.

Even so, the original intention for D-Day was that as soon as enough heavy infantry got ashore, the Commandos and Airborne holding the high ground across the Orne on the left flank of the landing beaches would be withdrawn to the UK and given some other task. This did not happen. The 6th Airborne Division and 1st and 4th Commando Brigades hung on to the heights between Sallenelles and Ranville and stayed there for weeks, beating off a constant series of German attacks on the left flank of the Allied bridgehead. As they hung on, losing men in the fighting, more and more lost men trickled in.

In spite of the scattered drop, which littered parachutists over thirty square miles of Normandy countryside, during 6 June and the following days, more and more men still full of fight, rejoined their units, having made their way alone, or in small groups through enemy infested countryside back to the Allied lines. These men were given a meal and sent back to their old platoons and companies – there was no suggestion that they might be given a rest. The weary men of the Parachute and Commando Brigades were dug-in around Breville and Ranville, another instance – and far from the last as we shall see – of the men in the red and green berets working and fighting together, and they continued to fight as one team until the Normandy battle ended, though every unit had a part to play.

Soon after daylight on 6 June 9 Para withdrew from Merville and marched on its next objective, the village of Le Plein. The strength of the battalion was now only eighty men, rather than the five or six hundred Otway should have had under command, but the scattered drop had decimated the strength of all the parachute battalions and he hoped to find more men as the day wore on. The

Germans in Le Plein were fully alert and swiftly beat off Otway's attack and the 'battalion' had to settle for taking the Chateau d'Amfreville, on the outskirts of the village, and holding that until they were reinforced by 3 Commando under Lt-Colonel Peter Young, which came up in the afternoon. These two units then cleared the Germans out of the village.

On the following day though, it became apparent that the British had not finished with the Merville Battery. The guns began firing again and an urgent order to Brigadier Lord Lovat of 1st Commando Brigade, ordered him to send a strong force against the battery and silence the guns once and for all. Lovat detailed two troops of 3 Commando under Major Pooley, to take on this task and they left Le Plein, assaulted the battery position and, having got into the battery position, killed most of the gunners and garrison by hurling grenades through the gun ports. However, since they had no demolition or explosive charges they were unable to destroy the guns and came under shell fire themselves when nearby German batteries brought down a DF (Defensive Fire) shoot on the battery. This did no harm to the guns or the garrison, but caused many casualties among the Commando soldiers who were out in the open.

That redoubtable officer, Lt-Colonel Alastair Pearson of 8 Para, was also in trouble. To begin with, one of his own men had accidentally discharged his Sten gun and shot him in the hand. Then, as mentioned, Pearson's battalion had had a terrible drop; a later estimate revealed that 8 Para landed on over 450 square miles of Normandy; only four of their 37 aircraft dropping their parachutists in the right place. When Pearson arrived on the DZ he found 30 men there rather than 600 and three hours later his total strength amounted to 160 officers and men, a Bren gun, two PIATs, two jeeps and four radios. Major Roseveare and his sappers, attached to 8 Para and tasked to destroy the Dives bridges, were not to be seen and Pearson did not know that, like many other men that night, Major Roseveare, finding himself with just a few men, had simply gathered them up and got on with his task. Pearson had one sapper sergeant who told him that, with luck, he had enough explosives to at least damage the bridge at Bures, so he was sent there, with some other sappers and a platoon of 8 Para as the protection party. The rest of his scanty force was deployed east of Troarn and there it held on, reinforced after a while by twenty 8 Para soldiers and Roseveare's men, who then went on to blow the bridge in Troarn which, like the Bures bridges, was destroyed just after 0700 hours.

The battalion stayed on, blocking the roads, harassing the Germans and picking up more soldiers until noon on D-Day. During the afternoon Pearson made contact with brigade HQ, had the bullet removed from his hand and was ordered to hold the south end of the Bois de Bavant, which the battalion proceeded to do, sending out fighting patrols and ambushing enemy transport moving on the surrounding roads.

Fighting was also going on around Pegasus Bridge, where all the champagne excavated from the garden of the Café Gondree had been drunk, and where the trenches dug to defend the Ox and Bucks position were filling up with tired and wounded men; the euphoria of the landing had worn off and exhaustion was setting in. The first counter-attack, just before dawn on 6 June, was an assault by a company of Germans supported by three old French tanks with German crews. Howard's men drove these off, but the flares, tracer and burning tanks made the men of 5 Brigade, now marching hard for the bridge, think they were about to become involved in a major battle. As the battalions came together and began to sort themselves out, the soldiers discovered another problem.

Quite apart from a shortage of fighting men, the missing soldiers often carried vital equipment. A signaller might have his radio, but if the man with the batteries was missing the radio was useless. The mortar No. 1 and No. 2 crew members might turn up at the rendezvous, but the third man, carrying the vital tripod, might still be lost and wandering about the area, or lying drowned in the marshes along the Dives. The confusion and loss, if general, was not on the same scale everywhere. More than forty per cent of 7 Para, in 5 Brigade, managed to reach the bridges by 0300 hours, while the main drop of this brigade also went well, with more than 2,000 men being dropped over the DZ – but then they were being blown away to the south and east by the strong winds. The men that landed in Ranville were killed or captured in their parachutes, for the Germans still held Ranville and were not evicted until later that day.

Major-General Gale had now arrived by glider and, having been provided with a 'liberated' horse, was riding about the area, trying to get a grip on his scattered division. He discovered that matters, bad as they seemed, could have been a lot worse. His soldiers had been well briefed and the confusion reigning did not come as a surprise. Indeed, at least one officer, Brigadier James Hill, had warned his men about it and many of the men, from experience in other operations and on exercises, simply picked themselves up and headed for the sound of gunfire. Lost they may have been, downhearted they were not, and as the night and day wore on the division grip on their position east of the Orne began to tighten.

Besides, the Germans were equally confused. News of parachute landings in the Cherbourg Peninsula and along the Orne had been coming into Rommel's HQ but Rommel was not there; he was in Berlin, meeting the *Führer* and giving a birthday party for his wife. Had he been in Normandy and seen those two areas on the east and west of the Calvados coast, from where a steady stream of reports were coming in telling of parachute landings, it is hard to believe that he would not have realised what they were for and that major landings on the intervening coast would begin at daylight. But he was not there, so very little was done to mount a major attack on either the British or the American paratroopers holding the flanks of the new Allied front.

By first light, 0520 hours, 6 June, General Feuchtinger, commanding 21 Panzer, had enough information to know what 6th Airborne were doing along the Ranville heights but when he asked his superiors in Army Group B for permission to move at once to the attack, his request was refused. Two hours later, at 0730 hours, just as the seaborne troops were coming ashore, on *Sword*, he asked again and was allowed to send two infantry battalions to Ranville. Fifteen minutes later General Speidel, commanding at Army Group B in Rommel's absence, released the whole of 21 Panzer and told Feuchtinger to drive hard into the Allied flank and attempt to roll it up.

Unfortunately, this order took some time to implement, since 21 Panzer was already engaged with roving groups of parachutists and it was not until 0930 hours that 21 Panzer rolled forward, sending 120 Mark IV and Tiger tanks to assist 3,000 panzer grenadiers drive the British off the Ranville heights and out of the villages of Ranville, le bas de Ranville and Herouvillette. They might have done it, for the defenders had barely enough men and only nine anti-tank guns to hold these positions, but hardly had the Panzers moved when another order arrived; the seaborne landings had now been detected and 21 Panzer were told to ignore the Airborne and drive instead for *Sword* and *Juno* Beaches.

Order and counter-order inevitably lead to disorder, and so it was here. Feuchtinger tried to divert his division to these new objectives but some went on to Ranville and others went to the Calvados coast; all were instantly attacked by Allied fighters and fighter-bombers and Feuchtinger became further alarmed when the gliders carrying the main wave of the Airlanding Brigade swept over his head that evening to land beside the Orne. Fearing that his division was about to be cut off, he broke off the attack, though his division was already engaged with British troops all over the invasion area; the troops holding the bridges at Benouville reported later that German troops had been 'probing or attacking their positions all day'. This confusion was of immense help to the Allies; had Feuchtinger been able to proceed in strength to even one of these objectives – to overrun

Ranville, reach the invasion beaches, or disrupt the arrival of the Airlanding Brigade, it might have had a decisive effect on the D-Day fighting. As it was, 21 Panzer achieved very little, and the Allied strength on the ground continued to increase.

The decisive moment as far as the Airborne were concerned was the arrival of the Airlanding Brigade. Of the 258 gliders that left England, no less than 248 landed on their correct LZs along the Orne valley, and before the day was out these troops, fresh and unconfused, were filing into the parachute positions, bringing more guns and vital stores and offering the men in the trenches at least the chance of relief and some sleep.

Over the next week, German attacks against the bridgehead intensified. In the 6th Airborne area these were concentrated against the positions in the south of the divisional perimeter, around Herouville and St Honerine, the part held by the Airlanding Brigade and 5th Parachute Brigade. These units held and beat off attack after attack, assisted by the tanks of the 13th/18th Hussars and the guns of the Fleet, but casualties were high and continued to rise. By 14 June, the 12th Parachute Battalion was reduced to six officers and around 150 men while other battalions had been equally reduced.

The division was now holding a perimeter between the villages of Sallenelles and Breville and the small town of Troarn on the River Dives. Their task was to maintain a static defence, to hang on rather than break out, but they had to be aggressive, harass the enemy all the time, keep his forces under pressure and supply the Allied Command with information on what was happening on the left flank. The actual breakout from the beaches would come from the Americans on the right flank while 6th Airborne and the other British and Canadian troops around Caen would act as the 'hinge' in the swinging battle to drive the Germans out of Normandy. The Airborne part in this action was a drive for the River Seine by Brigadier Hill's 3rd Parachute Brigade, which burst out of the bridgehead on 17 August in a move known as Operation *Paddle*.

This advance went well, for the Germans were now pulling back, fearing that if they held on they would be trapped and encircled by the American forces sweeping east from the Cotentin and St Lo. Many Germans were indeed trapped in the Falaise Pocket but those in front of the British Airborne and Commando Brigades were swiftly hustled back to the Seine, pushed across it and driven north in retreat. On 26 August the 5th Parachute Brigade entered Pont Audemer; the division's part in the battle of Normandy was over and, in early September, 6th Airborne returned to England, to rest and refit.

The 6th Airborne had put up a tremendous fight on D-Day and during the Normandy campaign but the cost of those battles had been high. Over 500 officers and men had been killed and the total divisional casualties were 145 officers and 2,550 men, killed, wounded or missing, roughly a third of all those who landed in Normandy on D-Day ten weeks before.

7

OPERATION *MARKET GARDEN*, September 1944

'In attack most daring, in defence most cunning, in endurance most steadfast, they performed a feat of arms which will be remembered and recounted as long as the virtues of courage and resolution have the power to move the hearts of men.'

Prime Minister Winston Churchill on the
1st Airborne Division at Arnhem, September, 1944

The next two chapters cover the Battle of Arnhem, the most controversial parachute operation of the war and one of the memorable battles in the history of the Parachute Regiment. To the British, Arnhem was *the* battle, but the fighting at Arnhem in September 1944, and the destruction of the 1st Airborne Division in nine days of terrible fighting cannot be fully understood or appreciated without an understanding of the plan for the whole operation, codenamed *Market Garden*, which involved two US Parachute Divisions, the Polish Parachute Brigade, Lt-General Horrocks' XXX Corps of the British Second Army, as well as Major-General Urquhart's gallant but ill-fated 1st Airborne Division. Arnhem was the centrepiece of all this, but the setting has to be understood as well.

The last chapter has described the situation in North West Europe in August 1944. All seemed to be going well, the German Army was in full retreat, back towards the frontiers of the Reich, the British and Canadians were forging up to Brussels and the River Scheldt, while Paris had been liberated and the Americans were pressing hard to the east. Then matters started to go awry. The main problem was logistics – the matter of supply. The Allied supply lines, going back to the Normandy beaches, were getting longer and longer and those of the Germans were getting shorter. More and more Allied troops were available – Americans divisions were arriving in Europe at the rate of one a week – but they could not be moved forward to the battle area or kept supplied. The greatest shortage was of petrol – or rather of petrol in sufficient quantities in the right places to move the tanks, guns, trucks, ammunition and food forward, and so keep up the pressure on the enemy . . . and keeping up the pressure was vital or the ever resilient German Army would recover.

This required working ports, but all the ports in Allied hands had been comprehensively destroyed by the Germans. Except the major port of Antwerp, which was virtually intact and in Allied hands. Antwerp, however, was forty miles up the Scheldt Estuary from the North Sea, and the way to it was blocked by the German-held island of Walcheran and the German armies on the north bank of the Estuary. It took over two months to clear the banks of the Scheldt and in an attempt to keep the advance going, the Allied commanders – specifically Field-Marshal Montgomery (who had been promoted on 1 September) – came up with the plan for Operation *Market Garden*.

The aim of Operation *Market Garden* was to drive a pencil-like thrust across the rivers and canals barring the route to Germany, to lay out a carpet of airborne divisions from northern Holland to the German frontier. If this could be done it would create a corridor down which the Allied armies could surge into Germany and perhaps end the war in 1944. On paper this was both a feasible idea and useful employment for the new Allied Airborne Army, of which the 1st Airborne Division formed part, but both the plan and its execution were flawed in a number of ways. The plan to begin with was a larger version of Operation *Comet*, a proposal to drop the three brigades of the British 1st Parachute Division on the same drop zones astride the rivers, but *Market Garden* was a much larger undertaking.

The basic idea put forward by Montgomery was for three Allied airborne divisions, the US 82nd and 101st, and the British 1st, to seize the four river and three canal bridges that lay between the British Second Army on its current position, on the Meuse-Escaut Canal in Holland, and the frontiers of the Reich on the Neder Rijn (Lower Rhine) at Arnhem in Holland.

Though the idea came from Montgomery's head-quarters, the commander of the Allied Airborne Army was an officer of the United States Army Air Force (USAAF), General Brereton. Brereton would be in overall charge of the operation, though the *Market Garden* plan was created by the commander of the Airborne Corps, Lt-General 'Boy' Browning, who had these three airborne divisions under command.

Browning was an interesting man, a professional soldier, one of the first of the parachute generals and rightly regarded as 'the Father of British Airborne Forces'; the present home of the Parachute Regiment is at Browning Barracks, Aldershot. Browning was highly-strung and artistic, the husband of the writer, Daphne du Maurier, and a man who has been credited – or blamed – for much of what happened during the battle of Arnhem. Some parts of the tragedy can be laid at his door but two myths at least can be laid to rest here.

The first is that he ever said 'I think we might be going a bridge too far.' The second is that the portrayal of Browning, as shown in the Richard Attenborough film *A Bridge too Far*, has any validity. Regarding the first point, unless the bridge at Arnhem was taken, the whole operation was pointless, but outside a comment in Urquhart's book on Arnhem, there is no evidence that Browning ever made such a remark anyway. As for that film portrayal; a great deal went wrong on *Market Garden* but to lay the entire blame on General Browning is simply not fair and as for the *Market Garden* plan and execution, let the following tale lay out the true situation.

Since this was a British plan, and they had the outline already in the plan for Operation *Comet*, it was only fair that the British Parachute Division should take on the most difficult task, that of taking and holding the furthest bridge, over the Neder Rijn at Arnhem. The first division into action would be the US 101st Airborne which would take the canal crossings between the towns of Eindhoven and Veghel. North of there the US 82nd Airborne would take the bridges over the Rivers Maas and Waal and the Maas-Waal Canal at Nijmegen, and finally, the British 1st Airborne would take the road bridge at Arnhem and hold it until XXX Corps of Second Army came up to relieve them over the 'carpet' laid out by the two American divisions.

So far, so simple, so what went wrong? Those who have read this book so far will see the first potential problem; what would happen if XXX Corps failed to get through quickly, as the seaborne forces failed to do in Sicily a year before? A great deal went wrong there, and a great deal more went wrong on *Market Garden* – and at almost every level – but perhaps the most fundamental error was to ignore the reaction of the Germans and underestimate the recovery rate of the German Army in the West after their retreat from Normandy. The British had now been fighting the Germans for five years and there is no excuse for either underestimating them as opponents or failing to gauge their probable reaction to any Airborne thrust against the Reich. 'If you have not fought the Germans, you don't know what fighting is', says Commando Brigadier Peter Young, DSO MC**. 'No matter how you batter them or however much pressure they are under, the German soldier will always find something to throw at you.'

This point was made to Browning during the *Market Garden* briefing. General Browning concluded his dissertation by making the usual final remark 'Any questions?', and General Sosabowski, commanding the Polish Parachute Brigade had just one. 'What about the Germans?' The Germans, and their likely reaction to this bold landing behind their lines was an element that seems to have been left out – or grossly underestimated – in the *Market Garden* appreciation, that summation of the situation on which military plans are based.

The planners seem to have assumed that the German Army was in retreat and could be kept retreating, but this was based either on faulty Intelligence or wilful ignorance of the facts. The Germans *had* retreated, certainly, and sustained great losses, but the way to keep them on the run was to stay with them, with increasing power and speed, in order to bring them to battle and beat them again. The snag, as mentioned above, is that logistical problems prevented the Allied armies keeping close on the German heels. As a result the Germans got away, managed to rest and re-equip their forces, more reserves came forward, they had those rivers and canals as defence lines and as the frontiers of Germany drew nearer, an ever more pressing need to make a stand.

This feeling – that the German Army had been fought out in Normandy and was now a spent force – was widely believed at Army Headquarters and even at Supreme Allied HQ. The troops facing the Germans in the field had a different impression. They were tangling with the Germans on a daily basis and were in no doubt that they were still full of fight, and if anything were getting stronger by the day. Moreover, the Germans were well aware that the Allied Airborne Army might be used for just such a thrust as the one proposed in *Market Garden*. The German troops that would stand in the way of it, though poorly equipped and few in number, were of superb quality, well-led and highly motivated. Many of them would also be SS troops and they had both tanks, armoured cars and plenty of artillery, the very weapons an airborne division was ill-equipped to cope with.

The 1st Airborne Division was under no illusions: the Germans were regaining strength; on 10 September, seven days before the division emplaned for Arnhem, a divisional intelligence summary concluded; 'There is no doubt that the enemy has made a remarkable recovery, especially in the 21st Army Group [Field-Marshal Montgomery's command] area . . . the fighting capacity of the new battle groups, now being formed from apparently scattered remnants of a beaten army, seems unimpaired. New divisions are being formed in Germany and Nazi control is such that the Germans will fight to the bitter end.' A copy of this estimate would have gone to Airborne Corps and Airborne Army, but no one seems to have taken its content into account when preparing plans for the *Market Garden* operation.

As far as 1st Airborne were concerned this information was beside the point. It may seen strange to a modern generation, unfamiliar with the profession of arms, but a highly trained, well-disciplined unit, full of *esprit de corps*, is always anxious, even eager, to get into battle and try conclusions with the enemy. Strange it may seem today but that is the way it was in 1944, certainly in the 1st Airborne Division. They had been trained to fight and were thirsty for action and yet month after month had gone by and operation after operation had been cancelled. They had been held back while 6th Airborne won glory in Normandy and now they were desperate for battle. Had they been tasked to jump on Berlin, they would have done so happily, and no German opposition would deter them from the desperate task that was represented by the descent at Arnhem – and certainly not the fear of German resistance.

German forces in Western Holland were organised around Field-Marshal Model's Army Group B, the force formerly commanded by Field-Marshal Rommel. Model had his headquarters in the village of Oosterbeek, a suburb of Arnhem, and many of his troops came from crack SS divisions, including 9 SS Panzer and 10 SS Panzer, two divisions of Lt-General (*Obergruppenfuhrer*)

Bittrich's II SS Panzer Corps. This unit had a growing number of well-rested but battle-hardened panzer grenadier infantry, a number of Tiger and Panther tanks and an artillery battalion, all full of experienced soldiers, and all of it was resting, refitting and training in and around Arnhem and the town of Zutphen, twenty miles away.

To back them up was General Student's First Parachute Army, another formidable fighting force, but the strength of these units was only a small part of the problem. Had they been tackled in strength by the full weight of Allied arms, they would have been forced to give way under the relentless pressure the Allies could exert, but against a single, lightly equipped, parachute division descending in their midst, they were a formidable force indeed. These units, whatever their strength, could be relied on to hurl themselves on the landing forces with the minimum of delay and the greatest possible impact.

To beat them off, the paratroopers of 1st Airborne would need air support and rapid relief: air support from ground-attack fighters and light bombers, rapid reinforcement with men and ammunition from the air, and relief by XXX Corps of Second Army within a matter of days. In the interim between landing and relief they needed whatever assistance could be provided by the Allied Tactical Air Force, the force that had savaged the German tanks and armoured units in the recent Normandy fighting around Falaise. Neither of these two elements, Second Army or the 2nd Tactical Air Force, gave adequate support to the 1st Parachute Division at Arnhem; the first was too slow over the ground, the second was never tasked to intervene against the German forces counter-attacking at Arnhem. In the original plan, Browning told Major General Urquhart that he wanted 1st Airborne to hold Arnhem for two days. Urquhart said that they could probably hold for four. In the end, 1st Airborne held the bridge at Arnhem for nine days; the story of how they did so is the epic of Arnhem.

A study of the planning phase does reveal other

problems. Not least of these was the fact that *Market Garden* was laid on at very short notice, and the commanders of the component parts were never brought together to discuss the situation and the plan in detail. Brereton, Browning and Urquhart were in England, Montgomery, Dempsey, the Second Army Commander, and Horrocks of XXX Corps were in Belgium. The plan was proposed on 10 September and the aircraft took off on Sunday 17 September. This gave little time for planning or the holding of meetings to fix that co-ordination of effort between the Airborne Divisions and Second Army on which the entire operation depended, but 1st Airborne Division were so keyed up for any operation that they would have gone at a day's notice, never mind a week. Since D-Day in June, the division had been ordered out for no less than sixteen operations, all of which had been cancelled, some at the last minute when the men had already emplaned, once when the aircraft had actually been in the air. Though the 1st Parachute Brigade had seen plenty of action in Africa and Sicily, the other two brigades, 4th Parachute and the 1st Airlanding Brigade, were thirsty for action and eager to go.

This may have been one reason why 1st Airborne's commander, General Urquhart, was not more critical of certain parts of the plan. Urquhart had been criticised for his actions at Arnhem and for his lack of airborne experience, but he was an experienced officer, with command and front-line experience in the Western Desert, Sicily and Italy, where he had commanded an infantry brigade. He had no experience of parachute operations and being a large man, had sensibly elected to fly in by glider, but he knew his business and none of his soldiers faults him; 'Urquhart was a good man, make no mistake about it,' said Brigadier 'Shan' Hackett, in conversation with the author, 'We all had the greatest respect for him, as a soldier and as a leader.' As a fighting soldier himself, Urquhart knew that his division needed some action, and would not let a few carping criticisms of the basic plan put this latest chance in jeopardy.

However, some of the criticisms he might have made are far from trifling, including the now familiar chronic problem of aircraft lifts. *Market Garden* required the airlift of *three* divisions, ideally in one day, as on D-Day. It had not been possible to lift three divisions on 6 June and it was still not possible in mid-September. Nothing could be done about providing more aircraft, but something could and should have been done about the flight priority and the selection of dropping zones. There never seemed to be enough aircraft to lift the divisions in one go, which should by now have been seen as vital and should have been a priority – and if that meant more aircraft for the front-line battalions and less for divisional and corps HQs, so be it.

The plan, it will be recalled was 'to roll out an airborne carpet' towards Arnhem and this being so, the American divisions took priority. There were enough aircraft for the US divisions to fly in on one lift, but Urquhart was told that his division would have to go in over *three days* – a fact that gybes with the demand that his division hold the bridge for *two days*, and brings Sosabowski's question into sharp focus. What did the planners think the Germans would be doing in those three days while Urquhart's force was still arriving around Arnhem? When Urquhart saw the loading plans, he promptly requested another forty Dakota C47s. His request was refused, though such aircraft were available; Browning had taken 37 C47s to fly his Corps HQ into their position near Nijmegen and these aircraft would have been far better employed flying more men and ammunition up to 1st Airborne.

The next error in this part of the plan was the decision made by the USAAF Transport Groups, and supported by General Brereton, to fly in the divisions by day; the criticism that had followed the widely scattered drops on the night of 5–6 June had made the USAAF very wary of night operations, and they were even more wary of German night fighters – though darkness would have provided the lightly equipped parachute forces of both surprise and cover, both of which had been a boon on

D-Day. There was simply not enough daylight time for the C47s to make a first drop and return to England, refuel, and reload for a second drop on one day, especially when losses and damage were taken into account. This may be a fact but it is also a fact that the decision to fly in 1st Airborne over three days was a mistake – and an obvious one.

Foreseeable errors continued, with the decisions over the Arnhem and Nijmegen drop zones. As has been shown, the way to take a bridge is to seize both ends at once, but at Nijmegen and Arnhem the decision was made to land the paratroopers on one side of the bridges only. As we shall see, the failure of the 82nd Airborne to seize the Nijmegen bridge quickly was not their fault but entirely due to this decision. The assault on the Nijmegen bridge by the 82nd, which crossed the river in small boats under fire, was a real feat of arms. Even so, the result of the decision to drop on the south side of the bridge alone was a fatal delay in the advance of XXX Corps to Nijmegen, because the small Goatley boats necessary for the 82nd Airborne assault crossing were somewhere in XXX Corps' support convoy and could not be brought forward quickly over heavily congested roads.

Urquhart's plan showed a similar error at Arnhem, for he tasked Lt-Colonel John Frost's veteran 2 Para with the objective of taking the Arnhem bridge, admittedly at both ends. Frost's battalion was to march from their DZ outside Arnhem, along the north bank of the river and then send a force over the railway bridge to move along the south bank and take the south end of the road bridge. This was a reasonable idea, but it would have been far better, both at Nijmegen and at Arnhem, to drop *coup de main* forces at either end of the bridges, thereby ensuring surprise and saving both time and a number of lives. Since Brigadier Sosabowski was tasked to drop on the south side of the bridge three days later there seems to be no reason why one of the British parachute divisions could not have been tasked to do that on the first day aided by the inestimable advantage of surprise. The reason, perhaps, was a need to hold the drop zones for the landing of the third British parachute brigade, Hackett's 4th Brigade, on the second day – but whatever the reason, it was a mistake.

This is not hindsight; long before parachute troops were invented, the idea that the only way to take a bridge was by taking both ends at once was part of basic military lore. The reasons are obvious; if the bridge is vital to the attackers' plan, the defenders will fight to retain it and prepare it for demolition should they be in danger of losing it. Seize one end of a bridge and to take all of it will require an attack across an open roadway swept by fire, with the dire thought that the whole structure will be mined and can go up in your face at any second. Better by far to take both ends at whatever cost and have the bridge secure from the start. The whole purpose of *Market Garden* was to take the bridges, but somehow the basic technique for doing so got lost in the planning.

It is possible to go on picking holes in the *Market Garden* plan but this account has already revealed that the planning was a recipe for a shambles; it is not that errors were made, for errors are always made in all levels of human activity, but some of the errors made here were fundamental. Perhaps the biggest error was an excess of optimism that all would go well on the day, but the final, fatal, quantifiable error – at least at the planning stage – was the choice of drop zones. The Golden Rule – which should surely have been established by now – was that the paratroopers and gliders should land *as close as possible to their objective*. Here again, this is inherent in the very idea of using parachute forces. The parachute gives unit commanders the advantage of surprise – but if it then takes the landed troops hours to get to their objective from the DZ, all that advantage is thrown away – and if more troops have to use that DZ, then troops must be left behind to defend it.

Ideally, 1st Airborne should have landed on the outskirts of Arnhem, which is a fair-sized town, and on the south bank of the Neder Rijn where there were adequate drop and landing zones; indeed this area south of the Arnhem bridge had been selected as the DZ for the support force, Sosabowski's Polish Parachute Brigade. Instead, 1st Airborne elected to land all three brigades on DZs west of Arnhem, well beyond the town and the suburb of Oosterbeek and *eight miles from the bridge*.

There was another possible DZ, four miles from the bridge, but that was deemed too small, and Urquhart was told that the ground he wanted to jump on, close to the bridge, was polderland, reclaimed from the river and too boggy for glider landings; clearly if the brigades could not land together they could land in the same place – and that too was to cause a problem as we shall see. As a result, Urquhart went for the landing and drop zones beyond Oosterbeek, and this was to cause real problems. Even by forced marching, by the time the brigades and battalions had landed, got sorted out and reached the bridge, at least three hours of vital time would have been wasted. That would be the case even if the Germans did not intervene to prevent them – and that was most unlikely.

Since this is such an obvious 'error' it is fair to ask why a sensible officer like Urquhart made it – and the answer lies in those aircraft lifts. His division consisted of two Parachute Brigades, Lathbury's 1st, Hackett's 4th and Hicks's 1st Airlanding Brigade, with Sosabowski's Polish Parachute Brigade attached in support. Urquhart decided that, given the shortage of aircraft, the first troops in would be Hill's 1st Parachute Brigade and the Airlanding Brigade. This was very sensible for the gliders would bring in the strong Airlanding infantry battalions and the heavy stores including the jeeps and the anti-tank guns.

Urquhart was well aware that he must get a strong force of troops to the bridge quickly and his intention was to send units from the Divisional Reconnaissance Regiment racing to the bridge in jeeps and follow up quickly with 2 Para, advancing on foot along the north bank of the Neder Rijn to take the bridge. Meanwhile 3 Para would advance on another, more northerly road, into Arnhem and come down on the road bridge from the north, while the 1st

Battalion would not enter Arnhem but take and hold the high ground – high ground being at a premium in this part of Holland – immediately north of the town. Then the problem of the extended lift arose. Not only must Urquhart seize the Arnhem bridge, he must also hold the DZs beyond Oosterbeek for the arrival of Hackett's 4th Parachute Brigade on the second day. This meant he must split his force in the presence of the enemy, sending Hill's brigade of paratroopers to seize the bridge while leaving the Airlanding Brigade to hold the DZs.

So, thanks to the planning errors and the shortage of aircraft, the fighting strength of 1st Airborne was gradually whittled away. Instead of a full parachute division – some 10,000 men – dropping in to seize and hold a tight perimeter position on and around the Arnhem bridge, it would now be taken and held by possibly one and, at best, two parachute battalions – say 1,200 men at best, for at least a day – or until XXX Corps arrived, or the Germans evicted them.

The flaws in *Market Garden* began at the planning stage. Hindsight is a wonderful gift – and historians would be lost without it – but so much of what went wrong at Arnhem should have been foreseen . . . and the errors were not over.

8

THE BATTLE OF ARNHEM,
17–26 September 1944

*'These men don't ask much; all they ask is something
with which to fight back.'*

Stanley Maxted, Canadian war correspondent,
broadcasting from the 1st Airborne perimeter, Arnhem

There is something terribly British about the fighting
stand of the 1st Airborne Division at Arnhem. After the
first few hours it was clear that their situation was
hopeless, and had been hopeless from the moment soon
after landing when matters began to fall apart – and this
without the help of the failures in the plan itself. And yet,
all of this was to be redeemed by what happened
afterwards, for 1st Airborne did not fail. They had been
asked to hold the Arnhem bridge for two days, remember,
and they held for nine. Nine days for Second Army to get
through, nine days for the Tactical Air Force to occupy
the skies over Arnhem, nine days for fresh troops to come
in, nine days for something to be done. Surely, if this
single, lightly equipped, airborne division could do more
than four times what they were asked to do, some other
element in the Allied armies could have done *something*?
Well, if not, 1st Airborne would fight it out alone.

For the men of 1st Airborne the battle of Arnhem began
early on the morning of Sunday 17 September, when they
filed on board their gliders and transport aircraft at

various airfields in Eastern England. Engines roared, tow ropes tightened, men exchanged grim smiles, and the aircraft and gliders, hundreds of them, rose into the air and set out for the Dutch coast. Leading this air armada were twelve Stirlings, carrying men of the 21st Independent Parachute Company, the Pathfinders for the division, who would drop in first to mark the drop zones for the main force. Their task went well, the Pathfinders went out the door at precisely 1200 hours, there was very little resistance from a surprised and startled enemy, and by 1500 hours the 1st Parachute Brigade and the Airlanding Brigade were on the ground and preparing to march on Arnhem ... and then the first of the snags appeared.

Murphy's Law, the one which dictates that if anything can go wrong, it will, was already starting to operate. Among their other loads the gliders carried the jeeps of the Air Landing Recce Squadron. The men of the Recce Squadron had landed, but among the few gliders that failed to make it to the Arnhem landing zone were the ones carrying their jeeps. This was a blow, for it instantly removed the first stage in Urquhart's plan, a rapid *coup de main* by the Recce Squadron, rushing through Arnhem in jeeps to seize the great road bridge and hold it until Frost's 2nd Parachute battalion arrived. John Frost's 2 Para therefore took over the task of getting to the Arnhem road bridge; now is the time to explain that although the road bridge was the vital target, there were other bridges and all of them were Frost's responsibility. These included a railway bridge, a pontoon bridge, and a ferry across the river to the little town of Driel on the south bank. All these bridges, if still intact, would be vital to Second Army and had to be secured. Frost detailed A Company for the road bridge, B Company to seize the pontoon bridge and C Company to take the railway bridge. The battalion set off on foot towards Arnhem and had got to Heelsum two miles on the way before they encountered any opposition. By then, however, General Urquhart had discovered another problem – his radios did not work.

In 1944 the state of battlefield communications, if greatly improved since the beginning of the war, was still far from perfect. Radios were particularly prone to failure in built-up areas where their signals are muffled by the buildings. The possibility of the radios not working, however, had been anticipated by at least one officer, Major Anthony Deane-Drummond, veteran of the Tragino Aqueduct attack in 1941 and now second-in-command of the Divisional Signals. Deane-Drummond entertained the deepest doubts about the entire Arnhem operation but he was particularly concerned about the radios. While the division had been re-equipping in England, he had indented for more powerful radio sets but his request had been refused. In the final week he had applied again, and again been refused, on the grounds that 1st Airborne would be operating in such a small area that their present sets would be perfectly adequate.

Urquhart had arrived by glider, and while his jeep was being unloaded he went off to watch the drop of the 1st Parachute Brigade on DZ 'X', a few hundred yards to the east. When he came back he found that while his Tactical Headquarters had already been set up his signals officer was looking very anxious. There was no signals contact with the Recce Squadron, nor even any contact with the battalions of the 1st Parachute Brigade just a few hundred yards away – or with the UK. Urquhart and his men had been on the ground perhaps half an hour . . . and were already completely isolated. A general has to know what is going on and be able to communicate with his troops or he cannot exercise his function of command, so Urquhart got into his jeep and set off to make a tour around his positions and assess the situation. He soon caught up with the rear elements of 2 Para, slogging hard into Arnhem and already meeting opposition from mortars, snipers, isolated German platoons and armoured cars. This opposition was not yet heavy but all of it had to be dealt with and dealing with it caused delay.

Leaving Frost to press on to the river, Urquhart then went off to find Brigadier Lathbury of the 1st Brigade, while the signaller in the back of his jeep made continual efforts to raise the other battalions and the Recce Squadron. Urquhart eventually found Lathbury near the Arnhem to Utrecht highway, where he and his staff were inspecting a shot-up German staff car and the bodies of its passengers, which included Major-General Kussin, the commandant of Arnhem. Men of the 3rd Battalion were deployed in the trees, and in no hurry to get on, and Lathbury and Urquhart were soon busy urging them towards Arnhem at all speed.

Another problem was starting to appear, small in itself perhaps, but designed to have an effect on Urquhart's rapidly disintegrating plan. Put simply, the soldiers were not pushing on as fast as they should have done, into the town and towards the bridges. Where there was no sign of the enemy the troops were being greeted and fêted by the Dutch civilians, who came out to talk to them, offer food and drinks and greet their liberators; the soldiers were naturally delighted at all this but it slowed them down. Where there was opposition, the soldiers were going to ground and deploying to mount attacks. Most of these attacks were small-scale and should have been brushed aside; the main task, the only task, was to get to the river and seize the road bridge. One is forced to the conclusion that there was a lack of grip among the junior officers and NCOs, who should have been ordering their men to press on and ignore all events, friendly or hostile, that stopped them getting to their objectives.

The German commanders, Model, Bitterich and Student, and their subordinate commanders were showing no such hesitation. They had seen the aircraft swoop over and the gliders and parachutes come down. They may have been surprised but they were not idle. Already they were summoning men, ordering up tanks, getting mortar and artillery fire down on the likely airborne positions, sending out patrols and snipers; with every minute that passed the strength of the German opposition was mounting. Bitterich had fought the British before and had a shrewd idea of their strength, and weaknesses. He

A section commander leads a small patrol in Cyprus, armed with the SA 80

Top left Returning from the raid on Bruneval, 1942

Bottom left The advance into Arnhem, 1944

Right Paratroopers in action with 3in mortars, Arnhem

Below The Allied Airborne Army land across the Rhine, 1945

Above Ringway airport, near Manchester, 1941

Top left An early example of military parachuting, 1936

Bottom left A parachute exercise, 1959

Right Troops climbing into balloon car with exit aperture in the floor, Ringway, 1942

Above British jungle fort, Kalimantan frontier, Borneo, 1964

Left Parachute soldiers on patrol in Aden Town, 1965

Top right Northern Ireland, 1970s

Bottom right 2 Para move on Stanley, Falklands War, 1982

Parachuting from a Dakota

told his officers, 'We must remember that the British soldier will not act on his own initiative when he is fighting in the town and it is difficult for the officers to exercise control. The British soldier is incredible in defence but we need not be afraid of his offensive capabilities.' Up to a point General Bitterich was right – but he had not previously encountered the men of the Parachute Regiment.

C Company of 2 Para did press on – to no avail. They got to the railway bridge just in time to see it blow up in their faces and, thwarted there, they moved on into Arnhem. B Company discovered that the pontoon bridge had been dismantled, and went on to take some high ground just north of the town and it was not until 2000 hours that evening, seven hours after the landing, that Frost got his first sight of the Arnhem road bridge. Much to his relief, it was still intact.

Urquhart meanwhile had problems of his own. He had spent most of the day with Lathbury, trying to urge the men on into the town and attempting to get in touch with the Airlanding Brigade and the missing Recce Squadron by radio, a task made no easier when a mortar bomb struck his jeep, and badly wounded his signaller. The jeep radio survived but failed to work properly and Lathbury's radio was no better. Urquhart decided he had better return to his own HQ by the landing zone, only to discover that German troops had now closed in behind and cut the road. Urquhart therefore decided that matters had to be left as they were. He would stay with 1st Brigade and press on into the town; the Airlanding Brigade would hang on to the dropping zones as directed, and tomorrow Hackett's 4th Parachute Brigade would arrive, after which both the Airlanding Brigade and Hackett's men could march into town. The communication failure was a nightmare, but all-in-all so far, so good.

For a while that night, matters started to improve, especially when Major Gough and the men of the Recce Squadron, lacking jeeps and out of radio contact, made contact with Frost at the bridge. Like all good soldiers, they had done the best they could, and when their jeeps and equipment failed to arrive they pushed on, on foot and with what they had and added their firepower to Frost's scanty resources, which increased still further when C Company came down to join the rest of the battalion by the bridge. By now 2 Para had occupied buildings on the north bank, overlooking the bridge and as dusk fell the fighting for the bridge got into its stride. It was now that 2 Para tried to rush a party across the bridge, only to have it driven back by fire from an armoured car. When the paratroopers turned a flame-thrower on to some German pillboxes by the bridge they were rewarded by a tremendous explosion, for one of the pillboxes was full of demolition material. By the time it was dark SS infantry held the south side of the bridge in strength, and Frost and his men held the north side. From that time on, the fighting in Arnhem never stopped and soon reached a pitch of terrible intensity, with tank and artillery fire criss-crossing with rifle and machine gun fire, the whole subsumed in the crash of mortar bombs and shell.

On Sunday night 2 Para made two attempts to storm across the Arnhem road bridge but both attacks were beaten back by fire from a pillbox on the far end and from a German armoured car. The explosion of the German demolition stores also started a fire among some trucks on the south end of the bridge and these continued to blaze all night, lighting up the bridge better than any flares could have done, preventing any attempt to cross the bridge under cover of darkness. Nor was it possible to cross the river by boat; 2 Para had no boats and with the pontoon and railway bridges gone, there was no way for the men of 1st Airborne to get across the river and outflank the enemy on the far side of the bridge. All they could do now was hang on and wait for Second Army, which was due to arrive on Tuesday.

Urquhart was still with Lathbury and they moved with the 3rd Battalion, whose regimental sergeant-major, a formidable Grenadier NCO called Lord, appointed himself the general's bodyguard. They set up their HQ in a villa on the outskirts of Oosterbeek and sent a signal to Frost that the other two battalions would not now attempt to reach the bridge until daylight on Monday. Both the 1st and 3rd Battalions were now closely beset by the enemy, which was moving up tanks and field artillery to harass them, and although the 1st Battalion had battered its way into the outskirts of Arnhem by midnight, it had already taken heavy casualties and many men had gone missing – though most of these turned up later or pressed on to join Frost at the bridge.

The 3rd Battalion had come under attack almost as soon as they left the DZ. Men of this battalion had killed General Kussin, but they were soon under heavy fire from mortars, anti-tank guns and on one occasion a German self-propelled gun (S-PG), which trundled into the road ahead of the leading rifle company, swung its gun on them and opened a heavy, close-range fire. The S-PG was well handled; the crew knocked out a British 6-pounder anti-tank gun before it could open fire and then began rolling down the road into the 3 Para position, spraying the hedges on either side of the road with its heavy machine gun. Attempts to knock it out were thwarted when the Germans picked up the wounded of the anti-tank gun crew and laid them across the front of their vehicle. During this engagement, C Company were sent off to contact Frost at the bridge while the rest of the battalion fought their way into Oosterbeek, by midnight reaching the grounds of the Hartenstein Hotel.

It is not hard to imagine the mental agonies Urquhart must have been enduring. In his book on the battle (*Arnhem*, published by Cassell, 1958) he only comments that: 'I have many times gone over in my mind the reasons for the battle of Arnhem going the way it did, the mistakes and misjudgements and inadequacies ... on the first night, as a Divisional commander mixed up in a battalion encounter and personally situated in the middle of the column at that, I was in the worst possible situation to intervene too much.'

At daylight on the 18th Lathbury and Urquhart and their men pushed on again, anxious to have a secure perimeter in the town by the time Hackett's 4th Brigade arrived and, with luck, the 4th and the Airlanding Brigade came in to join the troops by the bridge. Urquhart did not know for certain that Frost had the bridge, but when they reached the lower road into the town they found the rear elements of 2 Para, and were pressing on into the town when they were again halted by heavy German resistance, from tanks and panzer grenadiers. The 3rd Battalion split up into companies, the companies into platoons and sections, fighting became fierce and at close range, and Urquhart and Lathbury became separated from their men.

They took shelter in a house and, by the time they had run upstairs to get a better view of the situation from the bedroom windows, a German tank had rumbled to a stop outside and German infantry were already in the garden. The tank and infantry were engaged by the British officers and men – Brigadier Lathbury doing very good work with a rifle – after which they all made a break for it, sprinting down the street until they came under accurate machine gun fire . . . a burst of which hit Brigadier Lathbury in the stomach. Urquhart and a couple of young officers dragged the brigadier into a house and as they laid him out in the cellar, Urquhart looked up and saw a German soldier staring at them through the window.

General Urquhart promptly shot the German dead with his service revolver and after checking that Lathbury's wounds, if serious, were not fatal, he and his two companions left again, hoping to get back to their own lines. They were again headed off by roving German patrols and again forced to take shelter. So much for the senior commanders in Arnhem, on the second day of the battle. Major-General Urquhart was in hiding, Brigadier Lathbury was in hiding and wounded, and both men were now cut off and in danger of capture.

At first light on Monday 18 September, Frost took stock of his position in the houses at the north end of the bridge. Of his own battalion he had HQ Company and A

Company more or less intact, and two platoons of B Company and some of C Company, though most of that company were holed up somewhere in the town and heavily engaged with SS patrols and snipers. Elements of other battalions and support elements had also arrived in Frost's perimeter overnight and were slotted into position, including the remains of C Company, 3 Para. The total came to around 500 men, with limited quantities of food, ammunition, water and medical supplies. They also had around 100 prisoners.

Clearly, matters had not gone according to plan – to put it mildly. Fortunately, John Frost was a very experienced officer and he knew that things very rarely did go to plan, especially in airborne operations, but if he could hold on there was every hope that the situation could only improve. The British soldier fights well on the defensive and Frost knew that if his men had orders to hang on and hold the north end of the bridge, they would not be easily dislodged.

The Germans had other ideas. Attacks across the bridge, covered by tanks and artillery fire, started soon after dawn and continued at intervals throughout the day. Every German attack was beaten off with loss, and morale among 2 Para soared. Although there was no radio contact with the rest of the brigade, the 2 Para signallers could at least hear radio traffic from the tanks of XXX Corps, an encouraging sign that relief was not far away. The only dark clouds were a growing shortage of ammunition and a growing number of wounded.

To conserve ammunition it was found necessary to stop sniping and tell the men only to open fire with the Brens and mortars when an enemy attack was actually in progress, a move which, though sensible, enabled the enemy in the town to move about more freely and find spots from which more fire could be directed on the 2 Para positions. Sorties against the enemy with the bayonet netted a further bag of prisoners, many of them SS panzer grenadiers and a useful number of German weapons which were brought into play.

Overall, however, the situation of the division was not improving. Urquhart and Lathbury had not reappeared and on the evening of 18 September, the brigade major, or senior staff officer, Major Hibbert, asked Frost to take command of the 1st Parachute Brigade, at least until Lathbury was found, or his fate known. The fate of the other two battalions, 1 and 3 Para, was being brought to Frost by the survivors; it was a sad if gallant tale and gave little encouragement to the men around the bridge.

On the opening day of the battle 3 Para had had a day of mixed fortunes. As recounted, they had begun fighting within half an hour of landing. Half the battalion, including A Company, the Heavy Weapons Platoon with the mortars and medium machine guns, three of the four vital anti-tank guns and both the radio jeeps, one belonging to Brigadier Lathbury and the other to Major-General Urquhart, had got lost in the process.

This was not the worst of it. As with 2 Para, progress towards Arnhem was painfully slow and neither Lathbury nor Urquhart, in spite of constant urging, seemed able to speed things up. The battalions were moving through the houses and gardens of the suburbs and under constant attack from snipers and small pockets of the enemy, and seem to have taken a lot of time to overcome this resistance. They were also being fêted by the Dutch causing further delay, though not as much as that caused by a group of enemy tanks and guns, supported by panzer grenadiers, that the battalion ran into in the outskirts of the town. The parachutists were heavily engaged by these enemy units who soon infiltrated behind them, until they were surrounded and under fire from all sides.

In the middle of the Sunday afternoon, six hours after the landing and when the fight around 3 Para was reaching its climax, elements of Lt-Colonel Dobie's 1 Para, which had been moving into Arnhem on the northern route, also became involved. This battalion had been heading for the bridge, aiming to join forces with Frost. Dobie picked up the HQ Company and Heavy Weapons Platoons of 3 Para on the way and found this useful, for his own heavy weapons – MMG and 3-inch mortar detachments – had been lost. Anti-tank guns were now becoming vital, for German tanks, with their panzer grenadier escorts, were now roaming the streets of Arnhem almost at will, and firing into the houses at point blank range. Undaunted, if delayed, 1 Para continued to press on towards the bridge, losing men with every yard and in an increasingly desperate situation. Two days later the divisional doctor, Lt-Colonel Graham Warrack, drove back down the route into Arnhem used by 1 Para and reported that it was the scene of 'a hell of a battle; wrecked trucks and tanks, overturned guns, bodies, smashed houses – the road for over two miles looked as if it had been hit by a tornado.'

Frost was now in command of the 1st Parachute Brigade and he got a message to the COs of 1 and 3 Para, telling them to hang on where they were and form a defensive perimeter, but to send what men they could spare to the bridge. Chaos was clearly reigning but all they could do was hang on for XXX Corps. Alas, further south, Horrocks' XXX Corps were falling behind schedule and had not yet linked up with General Gavin's 82nd Airborne Division at Nijmegen – if relief came to Arnhem at all, it was clearly going to take longer than two days.

Meanwhile, eight miles to the east, the 1st Airlanding Brigade was hanging on to the DZ, and Brigadier 'Shan' Hackett's 4th Parachute Brigade was champing at the bit in England, their take-off for the battle delayed by the weather. Fears of another cancellation were beginning to grow but finally, around noon on the 18th, the order to emplane was given and the 4th Brigade took off for Arnhem.

Their flight out was not as uneventful as that enjoyed by their comrades on the previous day. The enemy were now fully alert and a large force of German aircraft attempted to break through the fighter screen and get at the transports, but was driven off by the escorting Spitfires and Mustang fighters. Once over the German lines light flak was another hazard that cost the brigade at least one aircraft and twenty soldiers. When the aircraft went in for the actual drop, at around 600 feet, they were low enough to see the German gunners, hemming in the Airlanding perimeter, staring up at them, and firing with everything from flak guns to rifles, unable to miss the aircraft passing overhead. Many aircraft were hit on the run in, but the brigade was taken to its DZ and most of the men landed more or less in the right place. A number were killed though and a larger number wounded either before the drop or while still in their parachutes – and, like their colleagues on the previous day, they still had eight miles to march to get to their objective.

The task of the 4th Parachute Brigade was to seize Arnhem town and support men of 1st Parachute Brigade who, if all had gone well, would have been comfortably settled by the bridge. Shan Hackett though had already told his senior officers that this task was the least of their worries, and that in any case it was probably impossible. Any surprise gained by the previous day's drop would have disappeared long since, and their most difficult task lay between the dropping zone and the bridge.

This proved to be the case. Hackett's brigade was in trouble from the moment it reached the ground. Hackett also soon discovered that the divisional commander had vanished and that Brigadier Hicks, the commander of the Airlanding Brigade, had taken command of the division in Urquhart's absence – though actually exercising any form of command was difficult, since the radios were still only functioning intermittently, and messengers sent between the battalions simply vanished in the fighting. Hicks's assumption of command had been in accordance with Urquhart's orders, issued before the operation started, but Hicks was junior to Hackett, and Hackett, who did not get on well with Hicks anyway, did not like it. He liked it even less when he arrived on the DZ and was met by a staff officer from 1st Airlanding Brigade, who told him that one of his battalions, Lt-Colonel Lea's 11 Para, had already left the DZ and, at Hicks's orders, was marching into

Arnhem with the Airlanding's South Staffordshire battalion, in an attempt to reach 1 Para.

Though Hicks was well within his rights – especially given the situation in Arnhem at the time – Hackett sought him out and told Hicks that he, Hackett, was the senior officer and that he would if necessary take command of the division if only to get 'some proper orders'. News of this disagreement swept through Divisional HQ and Urquhart's senior staff officer, Lt-Colonel Mackenzie, GSO 1 of the division, was roused from sleep and told that 'The brigadiers are having a flaming row.' A form of chaos was certainly reigning at this time, but to have two of the brigadiers quarrelling over seniority while the divisional commander was absent and the Germans were swarming everywhere, seems little short of bizarre.

Hackett decided to take his brigade into Arnhem along an axis north of the railway line, aiming to take the high ground overlooking the town at Koepel and picking up another of the Airlanding battalions, the 7th Kings Own Scottish Borderers, on the way. This was in line with the orders given to him by Urquhart in England, but it took no account of the changed situation. The object now, the only feasible object, was to get as much ammunition and as many men and guns as possible into position around the main objective, the Arnhem bridge, and the only feasible way to get there was on the 'southern' route, along the north bank of the river.

Any attempt to enter the town by either of the two northern roads was simply to have the battalions chopped to pieces on the way – a fact clearly demonstrated by what had already happened to the men of the 1st Brigade. It might also have been possible for Hicks to order Hackett to take his brigade and hold the ground overlooking the Driel ferry, which was still in use, and which might have enabled the division to get a force across the river; but this is speculation. Perhaps because of their dispute, or because Urquhart might have reappeared at any time, no changes were made to the original plan, other than those dictated by circumstances. Some of this may well have been due to Urquhart's absence, but a more likely cause was the complete failure of communications, which meant that plans could not be changed or the people in XXX Corps or the UK kept fully informed about the situation.

Fortunately, Urquhart was able to escape from his hiding place on the evening of the 18th and soon met soldiers of 11 Para and the South Staffordshire Regiment, who told him that Divisonal HQ had moved off the LZ and was now established at the Hartenstein Hotel in Oosterbeek, which he finally reached at 0715 hours on the morning of 19 September, having been away from his HQ for a day and a half. Lt-Colonel Mackenzie was very glad to see him and put him in the picture. Hackett was still trying to get on to his original brigade objective, the ridge north of the town, but Urquhart no longer saw any point in that move. In mid-morning, having rightly assessed the situation – as desperate – he ordered Hackett to disengage from the enemy on the northern ridge and withdraw into the town.

'And now', says Urquhart in his memoirs 'in this fateful afternoon of Tuesday 19 September, everything began to go awry.'

This is a fair summation but nothing could be done about it. The division were completely cut off and surrounded by the enemy, for XXX Corps were stalled by German resistance on the road to Nijmegen. Supplies sent in by air were often dropped on to positions in German hands, for communications were still difficult and signals sent to England, requesting changed dropping points, were not received. As a result, most of the supplies went astray and food, medical supplies and ammunition began to run out.

What did not run out at Arnhem, what never ran out during the days and nights of fighting which followed, was fighting spirit and courage. Eyewitness accounts of Arnhem are full of descriptive tales that can make you want to weep. There was the sight of an RAF C47 Dakota, one wing already on fire, coming across the perimeter to drop its load, with every German flak gun firing on it, as it dropped one load and turned, its starboard wing blazing, and came back yet again to drop the rest. Urquhart writes that from their battered trenches and foxholes hundreds of Airborne soldiers watched the aircraft complete its task and then crash. Only one of the crew survived, and the pilot, Flight-Lieutenant David Lord, was later awarded a posthumous Victoria Cross. Of the 163 aircraft which attempted to drop supplies to 1st Airborne on 19 September, 13 were shot down and 97 others were damaged by anti-aircraft fire . . . yet they still came on, flying into the inferno, determined to give 1st Airborne what help they could.

There was a Dutch woman, Mrs Kate Ter Horst, whom Urquhart describes as 'a tall slim Dutchwoman, with blond hair and calm ice-blue eyes', whose house was taken over by the British as an emergency dressing station for the wounded. Her children were in the house when the medical officers arrived and asked if they could move in. Having moved her children into the basement for what safety it offered, Mrs Ter Horst stayed on, amid the fighting, to help and comfort the wounded who soon occupied all the beds and every inch of floorspace as her home was destroyed around her.

Her home was in ruins and the sights were terrible, but Kate Ter Horst did not flinch. When dressings ran out she tore up her sheets and linen for bandages, she found mattresses and saw them soaked in blood, she carried water and fed the wounded, and when men were distressed or dying she was on hand to comfort them. At night, when German tanks rumbled past or shells and mortar bombs shook the walls, she would, writes Urquhart, 'console the children in the cellar with a fairy story then climb the stairs to inspire and help the wounded, quietly reading them a verse or two from the Bible as shellfire rocked the house: "Thou shall not be afraid, not of any terror by night; nor for the arrow that flieth by day. For the pestilence that walketh in darkness; nor for the sickness that destroyeth in the noon day . . . A thousand shall fall beside thee, and ten thousand on thy right hand; but death shall not come nigh thee. For thou, Lord, are my hope and Thou hath set thy house of defence very high . . ." '

Mrs Ter Horst was a very gallant lady, and the soldiers of 1st Airborne have never forgotten her. Nor will they forget the hundreds of other Dutch people of Arnhem who helped them in the battle, at the risk of their lives, both in the fighting and from subsequent German reprisals.

Then there was Sergeant Bakersfield, an anti-tank gunner of the South Staffordshire Regiment, who stood off three German tanks near Oosterbeek. He knocked out the first tank with his first shot and disabled the second with his second shot. Then, his own gun out of action, he ran to another gun, where the crew had been killed, and brought that back into action, fighting off the third tank until he was hit in the head and killed. Sergeant Bakersfield was also awarded a posthumous VC.

The British soldier fights well in defence and the 1st Airborne soldiers had no intention of giving in. They were tired but they could go without sleep and they were hungry but they could manage without food. If they were defeated they refused to admit it, and they would not run. No one has summed up their state of mind better than one of their own officers, in a short speech made in the church of Oosterbeek at the height of the battle.

Major Dickie Lonsdale of the 3rd Battalion had been ordered to form an ad hoc unit, *Lonsdale Force*, from the remnants of his own 3rd Battalion, the 1st and 11th Parachute Battalions, the South Staffs and some glider pilots, perhaps about 250 men in all. He assembled these remnants in the church at Oosterbeek and took a look at them. These were haggard men, many of them wounded, all weary from days without sleep: 'not in their Sunday best', says Lonsdale, 'but still defiant, still unbroken.' While they were filing in, occupying the pews and starting to clean their weapons, Lonsdale climbed into the minister's pulpit, told them that this was a fight to the last man and the last round, and finished with some words the Parachute Regiment would remember:

> This is by no means the first time we have fought the Germans. We fought the cream of their Army in North Africa, in Sicily and in Italy. We defeated them in those campaigns and now we are up against them again here. Well, they were not good enough for us then – and they are bloody well not good enough for us now.
>
> In one hour's time you will take up defensive positions on the Oosterbeek–Arnhem road. Make certain you are well dug-in. Make certain your weapons and ammunition are in good order. We are getting short of ammunition, so conserve it and, when you shoot, shoot to kill . . . and good luck to you all.

And so they fought on, day after day, using the bayonet a great deal, and German weapons when they could get them. For some it became a game, hunting Tiger tanks among the ruined houses with the hand-held infantry PIAT, sniping at German patrols, charging out with the bayonet on any Germans unwise enough to present a target. They fought hard and tenaciously but slowly their strength ebbed away.

The glider troops of the Polish Brigade arrived on the south bank on 19 September, and the rest of the Polish Parachute Brigade came in on the south bank on the 21st, both units being given a warm reception by the Germans. The Poles had to hold a bridgehead around Driel on the south bank, ready to receive the advance elements of XXX Corps whose guns could now be heard during the lulls in firing within the shrinking 1st Airborne perimeter. A Polish officer swam the river that night and told Urquhart that Sosabowski intended to get his men across the river by dawn, but daylight came with no sign of the Poles. They had enough on their hands holding off the Germans around Driel and so the fight on the north bank went on without them. It was proving impossible to get any reinforcements through to the bridge where Frost and his men were hanging on grimly and so it would remain. The division had been cut to pieces and every unit, company or detachment had to stand and fight where it was.

At midnight on the 21st, Urquhart surveyed the strength returns from his battalions. They made grim reading. 1 Para was down to 116 men, 11 Para to around 150 and the South Staffordshire Regiment to 100; 3 Para was 40 strong, 10 Para, 250 strong and the 156th Parachute Battalion 270. The division had been cut to pieces and there was still no sign of XXX Corps, four days into the fight . . . and the fighting would go on for another five days.

The battle for Arnhem is better imagined than described. Buildings collapsed as tanks knocked away their corners, there was the constant rattle of machine guns, the thump and crash of mortar fire, the ripping-canvas noise of the German Spandau machine gun, the slower beat of the British Bren. Tanks rumbled through the rubble-strewn streets, stopping to fire their heavy guns into the parachute soldiers' positions, blasting away with their machine guns while their supporting infantry tackled the Airborne soldiers with grenades and flame-throwers – and were thrown back time and again by men in camouflaged smocks and faded berets, who came surging down upon them with the bayonet, shouting a strange battlecry from the North African war, 'Whoa Mahommed'!

By now Brigadier Shan Hackett had been wounded twice, and was in hospital with a shell fragment in his stomach, the second of the three brigadiers to be wounded. With the great number of wounded men within the perimeter, Lt-Colonel Warrack, the divisional doctor, made contact with SS General Bitterich, asking for a truce in which the British wounded could be evacuated to hospitals in Arnhem; Bitterich gladly agreed, and the British wounded were ferried through the lines and well-treated in the hospital of the II SS Panzer Corps.

Not all the wounded were evacuated. Lt-Colonel Frost

was wounded in both legs on Wednesday 20 September, and had to hand over command to Major Tatham-Water, but he stayed with the battalion until, refusing to surrender, it was overrun by the SS on Thursday morning. The 2nd Battalion had just 150 men under command when the last assault came in and they fought the Germans from house to house and room to room until their ammunition ran out. The bridge position had been lost but elsewhere the battle raged on.

It was not until six days into the battle, on Saturday 23 September, that the division got the first close support from ground-strafing fighters and fighter-bombers of the 2nd Tactical Air Force, which came in to pound the German positions. On the following day a message reached Urquhart from XXX Corps saying that they were within reach of the river and hoped to put the 130th Infantry Brigade across the river that night. On the following day, Monday 25th, this message was rescinded and replaced with the decision that the 1st Airborne Division would be withdrawn.

To say that this was a blow to the parachute soldiers is to understate the case. They wanted reinforcements, not retreat and they knew that if they left, a lot of their wounded would have to be left behind. Besides, the perimeter still held and they wanted to go on holding it.

Other, perhaps wiser heads, accepted the inevitable, and at 2200 hours that night the division started to pull out under cover of a heavy bombardment from the artillery of XXX Corps, firing across the river. Those too badly wounded to move stayed behind, to fire rifles and machine guns and give the impression that their trenches were still held. By first light the remnants of the British 1st Airborne Division, 2,183 men from the 10,000 that had flown to Arnhem nine days before, had been ferried to the south bank and safety. All the doctors, chaplains and medical orderlies stayed behind with the wounded. Over 1,400 men had been killed and over 6,000, many of them wounded, had been taken prisoner, finishing the 1st Airborne Division as a fighting force. Slowly the firing ceased and the smoke of battle cleared away from the battered streets of Arnhem.

One of the last to leave the north bank was Major-General Urquhart who, having seen the men on their way back through XXX Corps lines, made his way wearily to Browning's HQ. Deciding to 'display a little briskness' when Browning eventually appeared Urquhart saluted and reported, 'The division is nearly all out now. I am sorry we haven't been able to do what we set out to do.'

'Never mind,' said Browning 'You did all you could.'

After the battle, praise poured in on the 1st Airborne Division. General Dwight D Eisenhower, Supreme Commander Allied Expeditionary Force, was just one of many who wrote to Major-General Urquhart. 'Before the world, the proud record that your Division has established needs no embellishment from me . . . Pressed from every side, without relief, reinforcement or respite, they inflicted such losses on the Nazis, that his infantry dared not close with them . . . for nine days they checked the furious assaults of the Nazis and when, on 26 September they were ordered to withdraw across the river they came out a proud and haughty band . . . soldiers all.'

Field-Marshal Montgomery added his congratulations: 'In the annals of the British Army there are many glorious deeds. In our Army we have always drawn great strength and inspiration from past traditions and endeavoured to live up to the high standards of those who have gone before.

'But there are few episodes more glorious than the epic of Arnhem, and those who follow after you will find it hard to live up to the standards you have set. In years to come it will be a great thing for a man to say "I fought at Arnhem."'

9

THE ARDENNES AND THE RHINE CROSSING,
December 1944–March 1945

'The battalion policy was to wear our red berets and when we ran into the Germans we went straight at them.'

Sergeant George Butler, 13 Para, 1945

With the virtual destruction of 1st Airborne at Arnhem, the remaining British Parachute Division, 6th Airborne, of D-Day and Normandy fame, steps back into the limelight. After fighting through D-Day and the Normandy campaign, the 6th Airborne Division had returned to the UK in September 1944, and spent the rest of the autumn and early winter re-equipping and retraining, while absorbing fresh recruits into the depleted ranks of its battalions. This period was suddenly interrupted, in mid-December 1944 when the German Army mounted its last great assault in Western Europe with a thrust through the hills of Luxembourg and the Belgian Ardennes – which began the Battle of the Bulge.

General Eisenhower and his US Army commanders had made the same mistake in October and November as Field-Marshal Montgomery had over *Market Garden* in September; they underestimated the strength, fighting ability and sheer will-power of the enemy. Short of divisions as the Allied front expanded, and having lost some of his finest units in the terrible battle of the Hurtgen Forest, near Aachen in October, a battle little known in British military circles, Eisenhower thinned out his forces along the western edge of the Belgian Ardennes, calculating that if the Germans did mount a counter-attack it would hardly come in this difficult, hilly and forested terrain, in the depth of winter.

He was quite wrong. On 16 December 1944, the Germans came swarming through the Ardennes in great numbers, cut the US First Army in half, completely destroyed the US 106th Division, and drove the Americans back in some confusion for the best part of fifty miles, to Dinant on the River Meuse. It was an armoured thrust which aimed to cut the Allied front in two and reach the port of Antwerp. Bad weather hindered the operations of the Allied air forces, which would have been decisive, and it looked for a while as if the Allied front would crumble. The day was saved by the great stand of the 101st US Airborne Division at Bastogne, but the German advance continued until the head of their Panzer forces were on the banks of the Meuse south of Namur.

The German trucks and tanks were now running short of fuel, but large Allied dumps were now in easy reach, and unless they were stopped or the weather cleared to permit the Allied air forces to play a hand in the game, the Germans looked set to surge west and take Antwerp. At this stage in the war that would only have delayed Germany's now inevitable defeat, but had Antwerp fallen, victory in the West would have been put back some months.

In a situation like this desperate measures were needed, and it is some measure of the desperation that Eisenhower put that highly unpopular officer – at least with the American generals – Field-Marshal Bernard L Mont-gomery, in charge of the US forces north of the Bulge and ordered him to take all necessary steps to stop the German advance. Montgomery's first orders were that XXX Corps should drive in the tip of the German advance at Dinant, and that the 6th Airborne Division should be rushed out from Britain to aid them in the task.

142

Before we continue with this account, it is only fair to mention that the Battle of the Bulge was largely an American affair. The German attack took them off balance and for a while the US armies were in some disarray, but they soon recovered and fought back hard. The bulk of the subsequent fighting to pinch out the Bulge and drive the enemy back was carried out by the Americans and they should have full credit for it. That said, the British contribution was certainly useful at a critical stage, and that of 6th Airborne a fine example of what a well-trained division could do.

The men of 6th Airborne were about to go on Christmas leave when they were held back in barracks and told leave was off. On Christmas Eve, nine days into the Ardennes battle, the men were ordered into their trucks and shipped across the Channel for transport to the Ardennes front, making their way up by road in battalions. It was bitterly cold, with snow flurries drifting across icy roads, and the men in the open trucks suffered severely as the convoys drove hard to the east, with the 5th Parachute Brigade, consisting of 11, 12 and 13 Para, in the lead. Once near Dinant the battalions were deployed in defensive positions, waiting for the enemy to appear. One of the first battalions to get a grip on the enemy was 13 Para which went into action ten days later, on 3 January 1945, when they were ordered to clear the Germans out of the village of Bure, which was believed to be lightly defended. In fact, Bure was held by Tiger tanks and panzer grenadiers of their old enemy, Panzer Lehr, and the fight for Bure became one of the stiffest battalion actions of the war.

Sergeant George Butler of 13 Para, was involved in the fight for Bure, and recalls an unusual incident that gives a glimpse of the occasional chivalry that occurs between fighting men in battle:

I was now a platoon sergeant in A Company. We arrived at Calais on Christmas Eve with no winter clothing, and travelled up through Belgium in open

143

trucks, which was bloody freezing, believe me. Christmas dinner, which consisted of a cheese and a jam sandwich, was eaten on the move. Bure was a stiff fight: of the four sergeants in my company, two were killed and one seriously wounded at Bure. Even the approach march to Bure was hard work. Metal-shed army boots are not the best footwear for walking on icy, snow-covered roads, and of course, being Paras, we carried everything on our backs, rations, ammo, mortar bombs, whatever. Our recce group reported no signs of life in Bure but when we topped the rise above the village I saw blue smoke rising from the centre where there was a fire going, so I knew that was not right. The A Company task was to clear the houses in the centre and we advanced from the right of the road . . . and as we advanced it all started.

B Company caught a salvo of shells, right among them as they topped the rise, and as we ran or slid to the village we saw a tank on the flank which opened up on us with its main weapon and machine guns. A shell exploded on the frozen ground, caught a section on the move, killed three and wounded six instantly. Lieutenant Cavanagh and I decided that being down in the village was safer than on the open ground and we got in among the houses, where we were raked with machine gun fire from a Tiger tank. This kept us pinned down and if anyone ever dictated a battle by just sitting tight, that German tank officer did. His position was protected by high walls and only the gun and a bit of turret was showing, so we could not get at him with the PIAT, so there we were stuck.

However, about noon an ambulance came into the village from our lines and our RAMC sergeant, Jock Scott, DCM of the Royal Army Medical Corps began evacuating the wounded and dead. Jock was a mess mate and he just stopped his ambulance in the centre of the village, with the shooting still going on, and started picking up the lads who had fallen. At this the Tiger tank came to life and advanced slowly up the road until, stopping by the ambulance, the German officer put his head out of the turret and asked our sergeant – in perfect English – what the hell he thought he was doing? Jock replied, 'Evacuating the wounded', and the German said, 'You may fill your ambulance with one load only but if you return I will fire.'

From where I was lying in cover I could see the track of the tank and we could have got a PIAT shot off at it with great accuracy, but owing to the situation with the ambulance it wasn't worth it. My last memory is of the Tiger tank reversing back into its lair, and Jock Scott's ambulance, with Jock sitting on the rear steps, looking back at the tank with total indifference, the boots of the casualties seeming to fill the vehicle to the roof. Unfortunately Jock was killed a few months later, in Germany, just before the war ended.

The fight for Bure went on for three days, the 13th Battalion fighting their way through against Tiger tanks, artillery and German infantry before the village was finally captured. The 13th then withdrew from the area as the Germans also fell back. The battalion had nearly 200 men killed and wounded in what has been described in their Regimental History as, 'one of the toughest little battles of the entire Ardennes campaign'.

Meanwhile the 7th Parachute Battalion were engaged in an almost equally fierce scrap for the village of Wavreille, where a two-company attack by A and B Companies lasted all day and cost the unit many casualties to mines and booby traps hidden in the snow. When the weather cleared, during the second week of January, the Allied Air Forces appeared over the battlefields, the rocket-firing Typhoons doing terrible execution among the German tanks. By the end of the month, the severely mauled German Army was back across the German frontier and in full retreat for the Rhine. Sixth Airborne stayed on in Holland, patrolling along the flooded banks of the River Maas, but by the second week in February the division was back on Salisbury Plain, training hard for its next operation, the Rhine Crossing.

By now the division formed part of the XVIII Allied Airborne Corps, a force commanded by an American officer, Lt-General Matthew B Ridgeway. Major-General 'Windy' Gale had been sent to serve as his second-in-command, the command of 6th Airborne Division passing to Major-General E Bols, DSO. Apart from the losses in 13 Para, casualties had been light and the Ardennes, if chilly and dangerous, had enabled the battalions to absorb their new recruits. This was fortunate, for five weeks after getting back from the Ardennes the division emplaned again to take part in the last Airborne operation of the Second World War, the Rhine Crossing. Operation *Varsity*, which, with the river assault – Operation *Plunder* – put the British Second and the US Ninth Armies across the last physical obstacle to the conquest of Germany.

It should perhaps be pointed out that the Rhine is not the western frontier of Germany at every point, and the river had already been crossed at Remagen by the US First Army. One of the men who went across on *Varsity* was Ron Palmer, serving in the 1st Battalion, Royal Ulster Rifles, part of the 6th Airlanding Brigade, and his account will set the scene.

Having returned from the Ardennes, the battalion had seven days leave and started training once again. It was no surprise that we were ordered into a transit camp about the 21st March and informed that on the 24th we would be on the way again for what came to be known as Operation *Varsity*. The weather in the transit camp was already springlike, sunny and warm, and the divisional commander, Major-General Bols gave a pep talk on how this would be the greatest airborne attack ever launched and there would be no balls-up like Ardennes and on D-Day; we also had a visit from Air Chief Marshal Tedder who was in charge of the Allied Air Forces.

By the time Field-Marshal Montgomery ordered the British Second Army and the US Ninth Army to cross the

Rhine at Wesel, the Rhine had already been crossed in other places, but the Allies had as yet made no major penetration east of the river. The Remagen Bridge had been an opportunistic crossing, when the US troops discovered that the Germans had not yet destroyed a railway bridge over the river, but there was no easy access for armoured troops east of Remagen and a major, set-piece crossing in the north was still necessary, as part of the drive into the Ruhr and then across the North German plain, to Hanover, Hamburg and – perhaps – Berlin.

Montgomery had entrusted the twin tasks of *Plunder* and *Varsity*, to General Dempsey, commanding the British Second Army, and to General Simpson commanding the American Ninth Army. Dempsey had enlisted the help of the XVIII Airborne Corps, which consisted of the British 6th Airborne Division and the as yet untried 17th US Airborne Division.

The lessons of D-Day and Arnhem had finally been absorbed by the Airborne planners. Since only two divisions would be going in, there was an adequate supply of aircraft, and both divisions were to be dropped in one lift and at the same time. They would also be dropped in daylight, and their assault would come *after* the land forces had already launched their attack across the river at dawn – though, since the Rhine at Wesel is very wide, their assault took on all the features of a seaborne landing, complete with Brigadier Mills-Roberts 1st Commando Brigade, Buffalo amphibious half-tracks, and assault landing craft. Take off from the UK was 0700 hours, just before dawn, with 680 aircraft, 240 carrying parachutists and the rest towing gliders, taking 6th Airborne to their drop zones beyond the Rhine. H-Hour was 1000 hours but many aircraft arrived early, and since there was plenty of light flak, no one wanted to hang about. At 0950 hours Brigadier Hill jumped from his C47 and led 3rd Parachute Brigade into battle, with the 6th Airlanding Brigade and the 5th Parachute Brigade coming close on their heels.

Ron Palmer of the Royal Ulster Rifles remembers:

At 0200 hours on the morning of the 24th all hell let loose. We had some type of early breakfast porridge that tasted terrible but nobody was very hungry. I was in C Company and our CO was Major Huw Wheldon MC who later became a very well-known broadcaster at the BBC. I landed with 18 Platoon, C Company; the platoon sergeant was Geordie Redpath. The flight out was uneventful though there were hundreds of gliders and aircraft flying across and at about 1000 hours we landed and the company took up a position along a canal near a main road. We held on there until we were relieved by the 15th Scottish Division, and a man I had served with in the 'Skins' years before, Jimmy Sergeant found me around midnight. We had some stiff fighting that day and at the roll call on the night of the 24th the battalion had lost 16 officers and 243 other ranks.

The gliders were not dropped, as at D-Day or Arnhem, in battalion or a brigade group, but in company sections, the gliders carrying the three platoons in each company coming in to land successively, in convoy. As usual each brigade had a clear task. The Airlanding Brigade had to take the high ground east of the Rhine and certain bridges over the tributary river, the Issel. Hill's 5th Brigade were to land on the northwest corner of a large wood, the Diersfordter Wald, capture a defended feature known as the Schnappenberg and hold the western edge of the Wald until the river crossing units came up. Poett's 3rd Parachute Brigade were to seize the ground around the village of Hamminkeln. The area had been heavily bombed and shelled before the attack, and when the aircraft approached the Rhine the entire area east of the river was obscured by the dust thrown up by the bombardment that had supported the river crossing, and by the smoke screen that had been laid down to protect the assault craft.

However, as the aircraft crossed the river, flying low and in tight formation in order to give their passengers and gliders a close drop, they came under heavy fire from

German flak positions. In spite of this the US pilots of 38 and 46 Groups, RAF and the US 8th Transport Command, pressed on regardless and the drop went well, without that scattering that had disrupted drops in Sicily and Normandy. By 1030 hours both parachute divisions were on the ground, and although more than thirty gliders had been lost from 6th Airborne's contingent alone, mainly through losing their tow ropes and having to ditch in the sea, and many of the C47s had been hit by flak, the Airlanding Brigade was also in the fray; 6th Airborne Division was intact as a fighting formation, and ready to go into action.

The British DZs on *Varsity* lay just north of the major town of Wesel, which had already been entered by the Commando Brigade before the drop. The paratroopers were concentrated around the village of Hamminkeln and north of the Diersfordt Wald. The task of the two airborne divisions, 17th US and 6th Airborne, was similar to those given out on D-Day; basically they were to hold the north flank of the bridgehead that Second British and Ninth US Army had won on the east bank of the Rhine, and hold off any German counter-attacks until the bulk of the Allied forces had got across the river and the bridgehead was secure. After that they would spearhead the breakout from the bridgehead which they would have to do quickly, before the Germans had time to summon more troops to seal off and contain it.

This overall mission was broken down into four separate tasks. The main aim of *Varsity* was to seize the high ground north of Wesel, between the Rivers Rhine and Issel. Second, once that ground had been seized, it had to be held. Third, Ridgeway's men had to patrol aggressively out of the bridgehead and prevent the enemy sealing it off, by forming defensive positions or bringing up reinforcements. Finally, they had to gather their forces quickly and stand by for the order to attack out of the bridgehead and thrust directly to the east, into the heart of Germany. The essence of all this was speed, and although these tasks may seem rather a lot for two airborne divisions, Ridgeway and his men set about them with a will – and with plenty of support. This included rocket-firing Typhoons and Tempest fighters flying close support, and artillery fire from the guns of the British Second Army, firing from positions on the west bank of the Rhine. Forward Observation Officers (FOOs) would jump with the parachute brigades and control the artillery fire, while working with the forward troops.

Ridgeway split his task between the two divisions, allocating the northern half of the bridgehead to 6th Airborne and the southern half, close to Wesel, to the US 17th Airborne. Both formations would be reinforced as soon as possible by the 1st Commando Brigade and the tanks of the 6th Guards Brigade, Guards Armoured Division. Remembering Arnhem, the officers of all these units met before the attack to coordinate their plans and fix workable time schedules. The opposition was known to be weak but had not been underestimated. It consisted of the German 84th Infantry Division and the 7th Parachute Division, both of which had been chivvied back across the Rhine in recent weeks and were well understrength. Nevertheless they were now defending the heart of Hitler's Reich and had plenty of artillery, so a stiff fight was anticipated.

The operation began when the Commando troops crossed before dawn on the 24th. They had fought their way into Wesel by mid-morning when they saw a wonderful sight in the skies to the west. 'Next morning', wrote one Royal Marine Commando, 'there came the drone of aircraft engines and the skies were suddenly filled with the parachutes of the 6th British and the 17th American Airborne Divisions, dropping within our perimeter. My own memory is of a large American paratrooper landing almost on top of me, then looking up and saying "Am I glad to see you!" The Americans all sported at least a week's growth of beard. It seems the first thing they do when ordered into action is to stop shaving, so at least we greeted them as Royal Marines should, with clean shaves.'

Four hours after the Commandos landed, at 0200 hours, the infantry and armoured divisions started across. For 6th Airborne the most welcome of these was the 15th (Scottish) Division of the British XII Corps. The 15th Division landed north of Xanten, where they were met with stiff opposition from the German 84th and 7th Parachute Divisions, while the 30th and 79th US Divisions of the Ninth Army crossed the Rhine south of Wesel against light opposition from the German 180th Infantry and 'Hamburg' Divisions. The Americans beat this off and flung a bridge over the river and had tanks across by mid-morning, but the fight for the Wesel bridgehead was continuing when the glider and parachute forces arrived overhead at around 1000 hours.

The plan called for a massive airborne and river crossing assault and this plan worked. In the 3rd Para Brigade area, 9 Para and the Canadian Parachute Battalion had seized their objective, the Schnappenberg feature, a small hill on the edge of the wood close to the Rhine, and 8 Para were clearing the woods to the east. Brigadier Poett's 5th Parachute Brigade had also done well, though 12 Para, commanded by Lt-Colonel KT ('Katie') Darling, had been dropped wide of their DZ, and had to fight their way back to take a battery of 88 mm guns which were firing on the battalion rendezvous. These guns were eventually taken by a bayonet charge, and 12 Para proceeded to mop up any opposition in the surrounding area, assisted in this task by a platoon of US paratroopers who had dropped in their area and joined the British for a while until they could return to their own units.

One useful refinement in the Airborne plan had been the attachment of two *Horsa* gliders to each parachute battalion, filled with men whose task was to secure the glider LZs and prepare the ground for the gliders bringing in anti-tank guns, jeeps, and ammunition. Two such gliders now came swooping in to join 12 Para but both were hit and destroyed by shell and machine gun fire, all but one of those on board being killed. The German

151

opposition was growing and continued to stiffen and had to be suppressed, so while 7 Para concentrated on holding on to the 5th Parachute Brigade dropping zone, the other two battalions, 12 and 13 Para, began mopping up in the surrounding area, clearing the farmhouses and small hamlets and collecting a good bag of German prisoners. By 1100 hours the main objectives had been taken and the village of Hamminkeln had been captured, though not before the Airlanding Brigade had suffered heavy casualties.

Lt-Colonel Clifford Norbury, MBE, MC, was then on the staff of the 6th Airborne Division and takes up the story: 'We in 6th Airborne reckoned we had nothing to learn from the 1st Airborne Division, as we were better at planning our operations and we always considered it essential to jump or land as close to our objectives as possible. After Normandy we all appreciated that on a night drop a high percentage of kit and troops would inevitably go astray – hence the daylight drop on the Rhine. In fact, there was a lot of smoke over the DZs so visibility was not all that good, but at least we knew roughly where we were, and fortunately we had enough aircraft for us all to go in one lift.'

Gunner Jim Purser, a Royal Artillery soldier, was attached to the 8th Battalion, the Parachute Regiment and recalls the flight out:

We were airborne about 0800 hours and found ourselves part of a vast fleet of aircraft headed towards the Rhine, but the journey was uneventful, no sign of German fighters. There was little conversation, with everyone wrapped in his own thoughts. Once over the Continent we could see our fighter aircraft diving and circling on our flanks. Somewhere over Belgium hundreds of aircraft carrying the 17th United States Airborne Division, which had taken off from bases in France, took up position on our right. The sight of so many aeroplanes, some towing gliders, must have given great joy to onlookers on the ground who had been liberated from Nazi oppression only in the last few months.

With thirty minutes to go it was time to stand up and check our equipment. We were stood up and faced the rear of the aircraft and I watched the American crewman remove the large door near the tail. It was a perfect spring day outside, not a cloud in the sky – and pleasantly warm. Then the Rhine river loomed up, difficult to make out in detail because of the smoke that had been used to cover the ground attack. The red light went on, followed by the order 'Stand in the door!' Only two to three minutes left and it all seemed quiet outside. Perhaps we had taken the Germans by surprise. Someone behind me yelled, 'Here we come, you square-headed bastards!' The green light came on and we staggered towards the exit door – my watch registered four minutes past ten.

Out in the slipstream my parachute snapped open and I felt very vulnerable. My kit bag slipped from me and tumbled to the ground. There seemed to be no Germans beneath me but I was drifting into trees. Pulling hard on my lift-webs I landed on the edge of the wood and dived under some bushes to orientate myself and plan my next move. I had to move back along the drop line until I saw blue smoke – the rallying mark for 8th Parachute Battalion – and then about a dozen Paras came out of the woods. I was glad to see them, and together we made our way quickly and cautiously to the rallying point. One hundred yards to our right was an old farm building – the only building left in sight. I did not seem to be occupied, and we left it alone.

Things were beginning to hot up in the vicinity of the dropping zone, as the Germans started reacting. Eighty-eight millimetre shells were bursting in the trees above us, and we dug for all we were worth into the sandy soil. Captain Jackson's nose began to bleed. He thought that he had been hit but was quickly reassured that it was due to pressure from the bursting shells. Soon news came through that Jarvie had been killed. He has no known grave but there is a plaque bearing his name among the lists of others with no known graves in the Canadian War Cemetery in the Reich Wald Forest. I assume he must have been hit by an 88 mm shell as he was coming down in his parachute.

Sergeant George Butler, last heard of in the fight at Bure, went in with 13 Para: 'Over the drop zone we met intense anti-aircraft fire, which fortunately caused very few casualties. On landing most of us at once swapped our steel helmets for red berets, rallied to the officers blowing the "Tally-ho" on their hunting horns. It went well and we took our objectives and secured the left flank in just over two hours. Having got it, we held it, in spite of German counter-attack and two days later, we struck out for the Baltic. The battalion policy was to wear our red berets and go for the Germans as hard as we could, wherever we found them.'

Lieutenant Peter Elliot Forbes jumped into battle that morning with the 9th Battalion, Parachute Regiment:

I was 28 years old in 1945. We took off from an airfield in East Anglia at about 0730 hours and prior to take-off an American flight engineer took some snapshots of my 'stick' of twelve paratroopers attached to 3rd Para, Brigade HQ. The engineer sent copies of the snaps to my wife, though I didn't see them till after the war. There was a US crew in the Dakota and the Jump Master, who would give us orders for the drop, was an excitable little man in a baseball jacket and flaksuit, who dashed about a great deal after takeoff.

The British half of this airborne armada set course for a drop zone in the Diersfordter Wald, a wood north of Wesel. Over Belgium I opened a bottle of whisky to flavour a half-warm tea canister someone had scrounged. The journey was passed in singing, card games and dice until H-Hour (1000 hours) approached and we prepared to 'Stand-in-the-Door' ready to go; I was second in the queue.

The Red 'Stand-by' light was on and we were waiting for the green 'Go!' when the port engine, only yards away from the door, burst into orange flames and black smoke, probably hit by flak. The Jump Master screamed for us to get back from the door and ran up to the cockpit; fortunately the 'Green Go' light, didn't come on. The aircraft then made a violent bank to the left which almost chucked us out of the door and through the flames. Over the shoulder of 'Number One' I saw the ground getting rapidly nearer but the pilot did an excellent job, flying the machine on one engine. The flames were put out, we scrambled back to our seats and I consumed what was left of my whisky. We landed an hour later at Louvain in Belgium, where I spent some time organising transport to catch up with our division, and we joined the 3rd Parachute Brigade near Hamminkeln on the following day.

Gunner Jim Purser again: 'In the late afternoon the 8th Battalion moved to a position in the woods on some high ground about a mile distant. Our OP [observation] party remained attached to A Company, commanded by Captain Bob Flood. His conduct that day did much to help the morale of those of us who were in action for the first time. Digging-in and lining our trenches with discarded parachutes, we tried to make ourselves comfortable, but the night was very cold and sleep was impossible. At about 0800 hours on the Sunday morning there was the rumble of tanks, and lining the track we cheered as the Second Army tanks came up to us from the Rhine.'

Dixie Dean jumped with 13th Para:

We had American aircraft and therefore American crews. Our Jump Master was a talkative New Yorker and shortly after take off he came round with cigarettes, but finding that few of us smoked, disappeared into the cabin, to come out again and offer us candy – boiled sweets. That was the last we saw of him until he came back into the cabin and announced, 'Twenty minutes to go.' You couldn't criticise these American pilots: their airmanship was first class. We flew in a very tight, battalion 'box' of forty aircraft and the formation they adopted – nine abreast – gave the impression you could almost step from one wing-tip to another. Flak was encountered close to the drop zone though, and instead of descending to a dropping height of 600 feet, with engines throttled back to stalling speed, we raced across the DZ, flat out, at around 1,000 feet but out we went.

On the ground visibility was poor, no more than 200 yards, with smoke drifting across from the burning town of Wesel. There was a certain amount of small-arms fire, and we had a lot of young soldiers in the unit who dived for cover when the first shots were fired. To their credit, it required only a few words of encouragement to get them on their feet again and our battalion sign, a black rectangle with a white border painted on the back of our smocks, concentrated 13th Battalion people in the woods along the road at the edge of the drop zone. As I arrived there, prisoners were already being rounded up and searched and Arthur Higgins, one of the sergeants, was busy disarming a group of twenty or more. 'What'll you have?' he called, 'A Luger or a Schmeisser?' Since I already had a Sten and 9 mm pistol, to say nothing of a fighting knife and several grenades, I settled for a pair of German binoculars, far superior to British Army issue . . . and I still have them.

One of the commanding officers, Lt-Colonel Crookenden gives his account of *Varsity*:

I was CO of the 9th Parachute Battalion in the 3rd Brigade, with the Canadian Parachute Battalion and 8 Para as the other two; our brigadier was James Hill. On 21 March, D minus 1, everybody wrote their so-called 'Last Letters' for posting after the drop. Company officers had the job of censoring the company's mail and the OC of B Company was not amused by one of his lance-corporals, who wrote no less than eleven 'last letters' to eleven different women, swearing undying devotion to each one. I was just getting into my jeep for a final tour of the battalion aircraft, which were lined up round the perimeter track at Weathersfield, when I heard the sound of a shot. Driving down the line I found one of my sergeants lying on the ground, looking ruefully at the ugly mess of his right foot. He was whisked away in a jeep and subsequently faced a court martial for a self-inflicted wound – a sad business as he had done well in Normandy. I later discovered he had done it because his wife threatened to leave him if he ever jumped again.

Then we emplaned, the engines started and we began taxiing towards the runway, a long queue of 36 Dakotas. Our aircraft turned on to the runway, lined up with two others, and all three set off together. Thirteen minutes later all eighty aircraft were in the air and had formed up into their nine aircraft 'elements' – flights of three – a fine piece of flying discipline. The flight was uneventful, a couple of hours, then came the warning order and the usual routine. I was jumping first and I could feel the slipstream and saw the river below us as I stood in the door. Seconds later the 'Green' came on, and out we went.

Once my canopy developed, I could see the DZ looking exactly like the briefing photos. There was a double line of trees along the road to the west and a square wood in the middle. The ground was covered with parachutes of the other battalions and I could see men running towards their objectives. There was a rattle of machine gun fire, the thump of a mortar bomb and the crack and thump of two near-misses. It was a most concentrated and successful drop and I felt a great surge of confidence as I sailed down to earth. In fact, we had reached the Rhine nine minutes early, and the guns firing on the AA [anti-aircraft] defences had to cease fire to let us fly through their trajectories. A good many of our aircraft were hit by 20 mm cannon and machine gun fire, but only the leading aircraft was shot down. Happily all the crew bailed out.

I landed in the middle of the DZ, banged my quick release and stood up. I could see our battalion blue smoke going up at our planned rendezvous in the north east corner of the DZ and a lot of men moving towards it. The wood was the scene of a brisk battle, but my aim was to get to our rendezvous as fast as I could. There was no sign of my batman, Lance-Corporal Wilson, or of CSM [Company Sergeant-Major] Harold, who had jumped after me, but a few minutes later I reached the rendezvous, where RSM Dusty Miller was standing by his blue smoke canister, grinning broadly and guiding men into their positions in a tight circle round the rendezvous.

I wanted to get the mortars' baseplates set as soon as possible and grabbed a passing mortarman, saying 'Any sign of Mr Jefferson!' (the Mortar Platoon commander). 'He's copped it, sir,' came the reply. 'Right through the head, a horrible mess.' Two minutes later, Alan Jefferson came bouncing in – he had been a ballet dancer and walked like one – with a broad smile and a cheerful, 'Good morning, sir.' By 1330 hours we were dug-in our final positions, a picnic compared to Normandy. The next excitement was a counter-attack by a German assault [S-P] gun and a few brave infantry, who came straight up the road through B Company's position; the gun reached B Company's HQ and everyone dived into their slits or the ditch, but the company clerk, Tillotson, jumped up as it passed and banged a Gammon bomb on the engine covers. The S-P gun stopped, a German put his head out of the hatch, Tillotson shot him and the rest surrendered. The S-P gun was still a runner, so two ex-RTR [Royal Tank Regiment] men in the battalion took it over and it rumbled along with us for a week or so as we marched on into Germany.

The Canadian Parachute Battalion succeeded in clearing the south side of the DZ, but they met stiff resistance from men of the German 7th Parachute Division. Their CO, Lt-Colonel Nicklin was killed, still in his parachute, when it caught a tree as he landed. The gamble of dropping on top of the enemy positions still paid off as most of them were too shocked by seeing 2,000 men landing on top of them to cause us any major damage. The brigade loss at the DZ was some eighty killed and wounded. It was in bringing in some of these wounded under fire that the Canadian Corporal FG Topham of the Canadian battalion won the Victoria Cross.

Meanwhile, as at Arnhem and Normandy, the heavy equipment and infantry battalions of the 6th Airlanding Brigade was coming in by glider, and Rifleman Paddy Devlin from Galway, an Irishman serving with the British Army, came in with the 1st Battalion of the Royal Ulster Rifles.

We cast off from the aircaft tug at about 1030 hours and on our own. Fully loaded the glider could only fly a mile for every thousand feet in height. I sat alert and ready, gripping my Bren, intent on getting out fast as soon as the glider landed. The two lads on either side of the door stood up and slid the door into the roof, and I was out that door like a jack rabbit and running to the tail to cover the rear as I had often done in training. As I ran I saw German soldiers in the two-storied farmhouse about fifty or sixty yards away and one of them was firing a Schmeisser sub-machine gun in our direction. I threw myself down, positioning my gun, and brought it into the aim position, at the same time releasing the safety catch. This only took seconds but the Germans nipped back into the house. I put a few quick bursts after them through the door and windows to keep them pinned inside while the platoon got out and unloaded our stores.

I continued firing short bursts through the windows and doors of the house, and as I was changing magazines there was a shout that the Germans were running for the village of Hamminkeln. I looked up and saw about a dozen of them, legging it for cover behind a tall hedge. In my excitement I fired before I was properly on aim and my burst hit the ground in front of me. It was a few seconds before I could aim and fire again and this time I sprayed them as they reached the cover of the hedge, but I could not say if I hit any of them.

As I looked about me at the platoon lying beside the glider, everybody was flat on the ground and I seemed to be the only one firing. Then there was a shout that two German tanks were coming up the road. This road ran north–south and bounded the landing zone, about seventy yards or so away, so I repositioned my Bren so that I could fire at them as they came up opposite the glider. I would only have fired if the tank commander had his head exposed from the turret. In the event they weren't tanks but armoured personnel half-tracks. The Germans were standing up in the first one, shoulder to shoulder. They had obviously packed it as much as possible to get back to their own troops on the other side of the River Issel via the village of Hamminkeln. As they came opposite me I let them have a burst and they all collapsed behind the armoured sides. I couldn't have hit them all but there was a lot of shouting and screaming.

The troops in the second vehicle were concealed behind the armour, and having seen what happened to the first vehicle they were travelling about fifty yards behind it. I sprayed it with a burst anyway, hoping to hit the driver, but both vehicles continued on towards Hamminkeln.

Although the DZs and LZs had been bombed and strafed by Allied aircraft, the aircraft and gliders met fierce anti-aircraft fire as they came across the river. The US Transport Group dropping 6th Airborne lost 47 aircraft shot down or damaged out of the 120 Dakota C47s taking part that morning, and over a quarter of the glider pilots taking part in *Varsity* were killed or wounded. This was

160

rather a hard fate for men who had not wanted to go to war in gliders at all, for many of the *Varsity* glider pilots were RAF officers who had been trained to fly heavy bombers, only to discover, as the war neared its end, that there was a super-abundance of bomber pilots but a dearth of glider pilots. Flying gliders may have been an acceptable role but a glider landing in action is really a controlled crash, and after landing the glider pilots were often obliged to join in the infantry fighting. It is to the great credit of these RAF officers that they did so willingly and well.

Frank Haddock was an RAF pilot who had been moved on to gliders after Arnhem:

At the briefing it sounded so simple. We would be in one large formation with the Ninth US Air Force and 2nd Tactical Air Force giving top cover – flak would be negligible because 2nd TAF would have blasted everything in the area during the previous two weeks. In fact German records show that there were 712 light guns and 103 heavy guns in the landing areas.

We climbed away into a clear blue sky, across the River Orwell. The sight of 120 tugs and *Horsa* gliders was exhilarating, and we saw people in the streets of Herne Bay waving up at us as the aerial armada moved across Kent. We crossed the French coast and later the message came from the Halifax captain that we were within sight of the Rhine ... and at that moment a Stirling bomber came across our formation in a shallow dive, its starboard engines and wing on fire, the crew bailing out in quick succession. We saw five bodies in space before their parachutes developed. It was an awesome sight and we felt that all was not well. The tug pilot called out that we were crossing the river and we were immediately aware of flak bursting around us and the smell of cordite. Any idea of a peaceful landing went out the window.

Another RAF glider pilot was Dickie Taylor:

During the summer of 1944 there were a number of trained RAF pilots in Harrogate, Yorkshire, occupied with various odd-ball postings. I was one of these but the disaster at Arnhem altered all that and we were told we were going to see some action and would be transferred to the Glider Pilot Regiment of 6th Airborne Division!

On the Rhine crossing, our glider was loaded with a jeep, a 75 mm howitzer, ammo trailer, and a gun crew of three. There was thick smoke everywhere and we could hardly see the ground as we went down. The glider was soon unloaded and the gun crew left us by about eleven o'clock in the morning. There was no resistance from the enemy, though we could hear the chatter of German machine guns around us and learnt later that a good many of the airborne troops had run into opposition. We also learnt that our flight commander, Captain Strathern, had been killed soon after landing . . .

There was heavy fighting all around the DZs and in Wesel, but by the end of the day, the 6th Airborne Division had taken all its objectives in return for about 1,400 casualties among the 7,220 men who dropped that morning. They had linked up with the 15th (Scottish) Division advancing from the river, and the landing and drop zones were secure. The US 17th Airborne Division, landing 9,650-strong, had about 1,300 casualties; 21 parachute or tug aircraft had been shot down and 60 more were damaged over the drop zones. The two airborne divisions took 3,500 prisoners, and by the end of the day both divisions had linked up with the ground forces all around their perimeters and were holding them.

By that evening, Ridgeway and his divisional commanders had every reason to feel satisfied. They had seized all their objectives and had held on to them. All the support arrangements had worked. Aircraft had formed a cab rank in the sky over the bridgehead and Tempests and Typhoons had come swooping down to blast any recalcitrant German defenders. The artillery fire control arrangements had also worked well, the artillery (observation officers) getting a grip of the gunfire within half an hour of landing, and bringing heavy and accurate fire against German positions all around the bridgehead. There had been losses, but this had been a well-handled parachute operation. The next task was to break out and push on into Germany.

The fierce German resistance at the Rhine Crossing had removed the notion that the German Army was ready to capitulate. A good indication of the severity of the fighting around Wesel comes from that day's casualty figures. Total 21st Army Group casualties for *Plunder* and *Varsity* – British, Canadian and American – came to 6,781 men killed, wounded or missing. This can be compared with the 10,000 men killed or wounded landing on a fifty-mile front on D-Day in Normandy, just nine months before. Clearly, the war might be ending but some stiff fighting lay ahead.

Gunner Jim Purser again: 'From now on events began to move fast. The chase was on. In order to keep up the momentum of the advance into Hitler's Reich the 6th Airborne Division commandeered just about any vehicle that could be pressed into service. In addition to riding on the backs of tanks and in service vehicles, horse-drawn carts, steam rollers and fire engines could also be seen among the long convoy of transport. The Germans were still full of fight and were able to mount local counter-attacks.'

The move out of the bridgehead began on 27 March and made good progress, 6th Airborne advancing with Poett's 5th Parachute Brigade in the van. Their first objective, the town of Bruen, was found abandoned, having been flattened by the RAF; hardly one brick stood on another and the tanks rumbled over the debris and pushed on with the paratroopers riding on top, to the town of Erle, where the Germans put up a stiff fight before pulling back. From 27 March until their war ended on the Baltic on 2 May, the Airborne Division acted in effect as a normal infantry division, and gradually acquired all the essential extra elements including tanks, artillery and air support from a cab rank of fighter-bombers. Thus aided, their advance continued but not without loss.

On 8 April 1945, forward elements of Second Army crossed the River Leine and reached the River Weser, after an advance of 180 miles from the Rhine bridgehead. Lieutenant Gush, of 7th Battalion, the Parachute Regiment, gives an account of what happened to his men on the advance into Neustadt:

About 1800 hours on the evening of 7 April, I was told to leave my platoon position and go to Neustadt. As it was getting dark, the battalion halted along the road about two miles south of Neustadt, where orders were given out. The three platoon commanders at that time were Captain Woodman commanding 4th Platoon, myself with 5th Platoon, and Sergeant Keilly, 6th Platoon. Briefly, our orders were that the battalion was going to move into Neustadt and capture the bridge over the River Leine. B Company's particular job was the bridge. While A and C Companies moved off up the road towards Neustadt, B Company was to move off the road, march across country to the river and then follow it to Neustadt, enter the town near the bridge, then cross and hold it.

It was a fairly dark night but the going was easy and we had no difficulty finding the river, and we began to follow it into the town. There were many small streams and large patches of water and we had to take a very winding course, but at last we could make out the shapes of the houses ahead and we could hear Germans walking about and shouting on the other side of the river. It sounded as if they were pulling out.

We found our way between some houses and gardens and filed out into the main street. We followed this in the direction of the bridge, moving in single file as quietly as we could, but there seemed to be an awful lot of people about. No one could see who they were and we hoped they were all civilians. Since we did not know where we were, the map was not much help, so Captain Woodman and Major Reid asked some civilians where the bridge was.

We were shown the way and told that German soldiers had been preparing the bridge for demolition, but had left without blowing it up. When we were certain we were close to the bridge, Major Reid called Captain Woodman and me, and pointed out that the best plan would be to rush the bridge with 4th Platoon on the left and my platoon slightly behind to the right. I told my three PIAT men, Privates Lloyd, Jones and Lees, that because of the weight of the PIAT and its bombs they had better wait and come over when we had consolidated. The men knew that the bridge might blow up at any moment and no one knew whether there were Germans on the bridge or on the other side, but there was a shout from Captain Woodman and 4th Platoon set off at full speed. My platoon followed and we quickly came to the bridge and crossed it, running as hard as we could go. There were no signs of any charges and no one firing at us.

Then I heard Captain Woodman shouting that there was another, bigger bridge ahead. Once more we ran forward and immediately came on to a large concrete bridge, definitely prepared for demolition. I ran into a wide wall of explosive laid across the bridge and up the sides and immediately beyond this wall of explosives was a second one. We ran so fast that as we reached the other side of the bridge, we had caught up with 4th Platoon and at this moment we were checked. The leading men of 4th Platoon had been fired on and were firing back with their Sten guns. One man had crossed the road and was in front of me, firing into a house on the right. Then there was the most terrific cough and rush of air and many thousand coloured lights – the bridge had exploded . . .

It occurred to me that we were all being killed. I remember hearing a voice, the exact words were 'Come on, B Company!' The voice sounded distant and rather feeble, but I recognised it as Captain Woodman's. I thought what a very peculiar thing to say, when it was obvious that most of B Company were blown to pieces. I got up and went over and found that Captain Woodman was hit in the knee. I was hit in the middle of my back and behind my left knee. However, we could both walk.

We looked around on a scene of utter devastation: small fires, bits of wood and even corpses were burning, which gave out a flickering light. Then some men appeared – Privates Crofts, Wylie and Elliott I remember – there were about two more, but I cannot remember their names. There seemed to be no Germans about but it didn't matter much to us now, whether there were or there weren't. Captain Woodman recce'd a house a few yards from the remains of the bridge which was badly knocked about but we decided to carry the wounded men in. How many were wounded and how many were dead we did not know. I asked if any of the unwounded men could take a message back and Private Crofts volunteered and swam back across the river with a message for the company commander, Major Reid.

The rest of the night was such appalling chaos that it is impossible to describe. We sorted the wounded from the dead, carried them into the house, dressed their wounds as well as we could and injected morphia into the ones in great pain. We knew that the people on the other side of the river would be making repeated efforts to get over to us, but we found it hard to understand why they couldn't get across. After a while we found we could spare two men to act as sentries in case we were attacked. The other men acted as medical orderlies and attended the wounded. I can only remember Privates Wylie and Elliott. There were about two more and all these men did extremely well.

Other bridges over other rivers went up in the faces of the advancing troops, but none caused as many casualties as the demolition over the Leine; 22 men of B Company were killed in that one incident and many more were wounded.

By the evening of 7 April the 5th Parachute Brigade were leading the eastward dash of 21st Army Group and there the Airborne Division stayed until, on 30 April the division crossed the River Elbe and stood at last at Wismar on the shores of the Baltic Sea, where they met the Russians coming from the east. They could go no further, and having landed in Normandy ten months before, it is fitting that this division, 6th Airborne, that had spearheaded the invasion of Hitler's Europe on D-Day, should be the one that reached the Baltic and cut the Nazi armies in two. A week later, on 8 May 1945, the war in Europe ended and the Airborne soldiers were there in Germany, ready to celebrate their well-earned and hard-won victory.

10

KEEPING THE PEACE,
1945–50

*'There was no ceremony. We in the 12th Battalion
paraded with all our kit, the trucks lined up and the
order was given "12 Para, to your vehicles, Dismiss"
. . . and that was it, a very sad day.'*

Major Sim, on 12 Para's disbandment, July 1946

The end of the war in Europe in May 1945 did not mean
the end of the Second World War, which still had another
three months to run in the Far East before the two atomic
bombs on Hiroshima and Nagasaki finally convinced the
Japanese that their future would be bleak if they continued
fighting. Besides, this account of the Second World War
in Europe cannot end without considering the actions of
the 2nd Parachute Brigade, which stayed behind in Italy
after the 1st Parachute Division left for the UK in 1943.
This brigade, consisting of the 4th, 5th and 7th
Battalions, The Parachute Regiment, under the command
of Brigadier CHV Pritchard, was to see a lot of serious
fighting, both on the Italian mainland and around the
Balkans and in Greece before the war finally ended.

After the 1st Airborne Division left for home, the 2nd
Brigade found itself homeless for a while before it came
under the parental control of the 2nd New Zealand
Division, a unit that had done outstandingly well in the
Western Desert and was to enhance that reputation still

further at the battle of Cassino in 1944. The Parachute Brigade began recruiting men, and soon established great rapport with the aircrew of the US 51st Troop Carrier Wing, which helped in the training at the brigade base at Lido di Roma, and stood by to drop the brigade on any parachute operation. Such operations were not immediately forthcoming, and for a while the brigade was used as regular infantry, going into action in November 1943 on the River Sangro where 5 Para were deployed to fill in the gap between the New Zealanders on the plain and the nearby mountains.

The battalion pushed ahead until it was relieved in terrible winter weather by the 4th Battalion. The brigade stayed in the mountains, in freezing conditions swept by snow and sleet, throughout January and February 1944, patrolling hard and trying to take prisoners for interrogation, since the Allied Command were very anxious to find out what the Germans were up to after the collapse of their Italian allies in September 1943. At the end of March, with the Allied armies stalled at Cassino, at Anzio and in the mountains, the 2nd Battalion were taken out of the line and sent back to Naples for a rest before moving up to the Rapido River and taking part in the battle for the monastery at Cassino.

The brigade was tasked with patrolling the slopes of Monastery Hill, above the shattered town of Cassino, and after a few weeks there were again moved into the mountains, this time north of Cassino, where they were so far into the hills that their supplies of ammunition and food had to be brought up at night by mule. There they stayed throughout a wet spring, and in June 1944, after the Cassino position and the city of Rome finally fell into Allied hands, they were pulled back to Salerno and told to train for an airborne operation at an unspecified location but which turned out to be in Southern France.

The 2nd Brigade landing, near Frejus on the south coast of France was part of Operation *Anvil*, the 'other' Allied invasion of Continental Europe, which took place on 15 August 1944. This was a daylight drop and just for once all went well. The aircraft took off on time and the green light came on to the minute, 76 of the 126 sticks landing on the right DZ and the rest landing nearby; Brigadier Pritchard actually landed within fifteen yards of the main force DZ designation beacon, an all-time record. Once assembled, the brigade advanced north into the hills of Provence, pushing the German forces ahead of them and making contact with the French Resistance fighters, the *Maquis*, who were more than glad to join up with the *berets rouge*.

This enjoyable campaign was all too short, and by the first week of September the brigade was back in Italy, preparing for a drop into Greece – Operation *Manna*, an airborne landing to seize Athens before the Germans could destroy it and the nearby port of Piraeus. This operation was to bring the 2nd Parachute Brigade into conflict with some erstwhile allies, the ELAS fighters of the Greek Communist Party, who wanted to take over Greece once peace had been declared.

Peace is a delicate creature, and the disruption of war could not be easily healed, for a great many problems were starting to surface as the war drew to a close, many of them created by the rise of Communism which, in the form of Communist-led resistance movements, was hogging the credit for the defeat of Germany and was intent on replacing domination from Berlin with domination from Moscow. In many countries the Communists were now in arms, ready and willing to replace Hitler's Nazis with another form of totalitarian regime, and even before the war in Europe ended, the soldiers of the 2nd Parachute Brigade were engaged in quelling a Communist-inspired insurrection in Athens against the government of newly liberated Greece. Thus began a series of peace keeping, or police actions 'in aid of the civil power' that would keep the Parachute Regiment fully occupied for the next twenty years. Before that though, the 2nd Parachute Brigade had to help get the Germans out of the Balkans.

By the end of 1944 the Germans were being forced out

of Greece by a combination of Allied pressure in the Balkans and the actions of Greek and Yugoslav guerrilla bands, many of them Communist under the direct influence of Moscow. The aim of these nascent Communist Parties, in Greece, Yugoslavia, and elsewhere in the Balkans, was to take over the liberated countries as the Germans were driven out. In most of these countries – Yugoslavia, Bulgaria, Albania, Hungary and Czechoslovakia – the Communists succeeded in their aim, seizing power, murdering anyone who stood in their way and imposing a totalitarian rule that lasted for over fifty years until the collapse of the Soviet regime. The Communists might have done the same in Greece, but here the Western Allies decided to make a stand. British troops were on hand and they were soon tasked to support the Royalist Government against the insurrection inspired by ELAS.

This intervention began in October 1944, when the 4th Battalion of the Parachute Regiment, under Lt-Colonel Coxon, part of the 2nd Parachute Brigade, was parachuted on to Magara airfield near Athens. There it linked up with a force of SBS and RAF Regiment troops, under Lt-Colonel Earl Jellicoe, DSO, MC, who had been trying to persuade the local German garrisons to surrender – which they were unwilling to do, fearing massacre at the hands of the ELAS partisans. Jellicoe urgently needed reinforcements and in spite of high winds the drop went ahead, though nearly fifty parachutists were injured, some of them fatally. The rest of the brigade then arrived and having chivvied the Germans across the mountains as far as the Yugoslav frontier, where Tito's Communist partisans declined their assistance and refused them entry, the brigade marched on Athens where they were well received by a jubilant crowd – at least for a while.

The Germans having departed, the Communists made their bid for power. ELAS fighters, well armed and truculent, were soon swaggering round the town, shooting anyone they identified as bourgeois. Disputes soon arose between the Parachute Regiment soldiers, who had been charged with security in the city, and ELAS guerrillas, who were clearly looking for trouble and soon found it. Fighting also broke out between ELAS and the Royalist party, EAM, and in their bid to keep the peace until the legitimate government could take over, the British soldiers soon came under attack. ELAS clearly regarded the British as intruders in their private quarrel and when the 5th Battalion was sent to take over the northern Greek port of Salonika which had just been captured from the Germans by an SBS patrol commanded by that redoubtable Dane, Anders Lassen, the ELAS fighters gave them a frosty reception. So the tension mounted until the end of November 1944, when newly liberated Greece exploded into civil war.

All the battalions of the 2nd Parachute Brigade were recalled to Athens, for if Athens and the port of Piraeus fell, Greece was lost. By this time more British troops had arrived and the parachutists were joined in their new role by the 3rd Armoured Brigade, with Sherman tanks and armoured cars. The armour proved useful, for the British troops were greeted with sniper fire. The shooting increased until a full scale war was raging in the streets of the city, bringing the British soldiers under attack from people who, until a few weeks before, had been their allies. The Greek Government formally declared war on ELAS on 7 December, and fighting then became widespread. An attempt by ELAS to infiltrate through the sewers and blow up the British headquarters was only narrowly averted, and the parachutists even had to send out small parties armed with PIAT anti-tank weapons, to take out ELAS sniper positions on the rooftops overlooking the main streets and boulevards.

Matters were further complicated by the presence of US soldiers in the city, for the United States had declined to support the Greek Government and their representatives in the city were badgering the British not to do so either. Since they were under attack and taking casualites, the British decided to ignore this advice and took the

Communists on, with all the power at their disposal. Sniping, machine gun and tank fire, the crash of mortar bombs and the whine of bullets soon dominated the city and as the days went by and the fighting intensified.

After a few days fighting, a combined force – *Arkforce* – consisting of the 2nd Parachute Brigade and the 3rd Armoured Brigade, was put together in mid-December, and given the task of driving the Communists out of the city. This was getting back to the sort of war the British soldier understood and they proceeded to drive across the city, clearing ELAs out, house by house and street by street. The fighting was severe and many parachute and armoured brigade soldiers were killed or wounded, either in the fighting or in attempts to evacuate the wounded or civilians from the battle area; the 5th Battalion alone lost over 100 men, killed or wounded, including all the company commanders.

ELAS fighters paid no attention to the rules; they advanced or retreated behind a screen of women and children, fired on ambulances, and shot at the wounded lying in the streets. Tempers were not improved by reports appearing in the left wing British press, including papers that should have known better, claiming that British soldiers were killing 'the workers' in the interests of Greek capitalist businessmen. The British Government eventually flew out a trades union leader, Lord Citrine, head of a delegation from the Trades Union Congress, to see the situation for himself and meet the soldiers. When he addressed an audience of soldiers in an Athens cinema, they told him exactly what they thought and sent him home, a sadder if not wiser man, and he had the decency to tell his members that the 2nd Parachute Brigade were doing a good job and deserved the support of the British public.

The 4th Parachute Brigade stayed in Greece until February 1945, by which time the Greek Army had established a measure of control and could take over the struggle against ELAS, though the Greek Civil War was an extremely vicious affair and went on for some years before the Communists were defeated; one of the final acts in this bloody conflict was the public execution by firing squad, in an Athens square, of fifty ELAS leaders, captured by the Greek Army.

On leaving Greece the brigade returned to Italy, where it was kept ready for further operations against the retreating Germans in the north, and it was standing by for a parachute operation in the Austrian passes, when the war in Europe came to an end in May 1945. The brigade returned to Britain the same month and became part of the 6th Airborne Division, sailing with that division for Palestine, where more trouble was brewing. The League of Nations Mandate in that country, held by the British, was due to draw to a close between 1946 and 1948, and the Jews and Arabs had started to fight for the territory – as they have done at intervals ever since.

Another part of 6th Airborne Division, the 5th Parachute Brigade, was also tasked with an end of war aid to the Civil Power role, this time in the Far East, in the Dutch territory of Java. After returning to Britain from Germany in May 1945, 6th Airborne was ordered to prepare for the war against the Japanese. The 5th Parachute Brigade was the first to go east of Suez, arriving in Bombay just two weeks before the dropping of the atomic bombs on Hiroshima and Nagasaki. As in Europe, however, there were some immediate post-war problems around, especially on the island of Java where the Indonesian population were determined that their former colonial masters, the Dutch, would not regain control after the Japanese left.

The 5th Parachute Brigade first sailed for Malaya, where they had some encounters with Communist guerrillas of the MPAJA – the Malayan People's Anti-Japanese Army. The MPAJA, like their comrades in far-away Greece, were not pleased to see the British return and were anxious to take control of the Malayan Peninsula in the name of Communist China before democratic control could be re-established. For the moment though, they held their fire, waiting for the

British to leave, and in December 1945, the 5th Parachute Brigade was despatched to Batavia in Java, to help contain a growing insurrection against the Dutch.

In August 1945, the Japanese Army in Indonesia surrendered, not to the Dutch people held in their prison camps, but to the Indonesians who, arming themselves with Japanese weapons, formed guerrilla bands and started to take a terrible revenge on any Dutch they could find, including those just released from Japanese prisons. Dutch civilians were chopped to pieces, hanged, burnt, raped and tortured. The Dutch had no regular units in the islands and the British inevitably became involved, to save lives and to restore law and order. The parachutists arriving in Batavia got off the ship into the middle of a civil war but lost no time in quelling the more excited spirits among the Indonesian population and soon had the situation under control. That done in Batavia, they moved to the north of Java, to the town of Semarang, and repeated the process there.

The situation in Semarang was, to say the least, bizarre, for the only force capable of maintaining order after the war ended was a battalion of Japanese troops under a Major Kido. This battalion had obeyed the order to hand over their arms but when the Indonesians had used them to shoot Japanese prisoners and had hacked Japanese soldiers to death with machetes, the Japanese decided to rearm themselves, give the Indonesians a drubbing and await the arrival of the British. When Brigadier Poett arrived he accepted Major Kido's surrender – and then discovered that the only way to keep control of the deteriorating situation in Semarang was to recruit the Japanese soldiers as part of his peace-keeping force. The Japanese were duly employed as armed guards and eventually even found themselves mounting guard on the British brigadier's bungalow.

The brigade stayed in Semarang for three months, keeping the peace, restoring public services, calming the situation down and becoming very popular with the local people in the process. When the Dutch Army finally arrived to take over, evacuating Major Kido and his helpful troops, the local people did not want the British soldiers to leave. The 5th Parachute Brigade, however, had already been tasked for the Middle East and duly sailed for Palestine where it rejoined 6th Airborne Division . . . and found itself in the middle of yet another insurrection.

By now – the summer of 1946 – the great armies that had fought and won the Second World War had already shrunk considerably as soldiers were demobilised – demobbed – and returned to civilian life. The 1st Airborne Division had never properly reformed after Arnhem and was finally disbanded in September 1945, just a year after the Arnhem battle. The Canadian Parachute Battalion which had served with 6th Airborne in Normandy and the Rhine had gone home, and was replaced by the 3rd Battalion, the Parachute Regiment. It had also been decided that the glider brigades would go and that parachute divisions would be all-parachute formations, so the 6th Airlanding Brigade became the 31st Infantry Brigade and was replaced in the 6th Airborne Division by 5th Parachute Brigade.

The problems of Palestine continue to this day, so it would be as well to know how they began. To do that it is necessary to go back to the end of the First World War and the breakup of the Turkish Empire. In 1917, the British prime minister, Arthur Balfour, said that the British Government would look with favour at the idea of establishing a national home for the Jewish people in Palestine, the ancient country of Israel, from which the Jews had been expelled by the Romans nearly 1,500 years before. When the war ended and many parts of the Turkish Empire claimed their independence, The League of Nations, a forerunner of the UN set up to reshape the post-Great War world, took Balfour at his word and, as a result, Britain was given a 25-year Mandate to create this home for the Jews. A thankless task indeed, for the Mandate overlooked the fact that Palestine was already home to a considerable number of Arabs who did not take kindly to a new nation being formed in their midst. This was the crux of the problem; Mr Balfour had proposed a *home*, but the Jews of the world had another idea, Zionism, and they wanted to create a Jewish *nation state*.

There always had been a strong Jewish presence in Palestine, ever since the time of the Crusades and, by and large, the Jews and the Arabs had lived peaceably together. This peace was about to be jeopardised by the Balfour Declaration and by the rising tide of Jewish immigration that followed it, a tide that grew when the Nazis took power in Germany and began to drive their Jewish citizens out. The Arabs first began to murmur, then they began to riot, and finally a small scale war broke out between the Arabs and the Jews which was already under way when the Second World War broke out in 1939.

After the war, and the revelation of the Holocaust – the murder of six million Jews by the Germans – the need for a secure place for the Jews of the world, their own country, Israel, was an unstoppable idea – but the Arabs of Palestine saw no reason why it should be established in their homeland, or that the Europeans should salve their consciences over the Holocaust at their expense. So the brew began to simmer and into this desperate situation stepped the British Army, to be abused and attacked by both sides, as the League of Nations Mandate began to run out and more and more shiploads of Jewish immigrants, many from the concentration camps of Germany and Poland, began to arrive off shore and demand admittance – an admittance that could only exacerbate an already dangerous situation with the resentful Arabs.

Sixth Airborne were tasked to control the area around Gaza on the Mediterranean coast and were soon under attack from both Jews and Arabs, seeking to obtain weapons, kill British soldiers, and make the British position in Palestine untenable. Rioting was one method commonly employed and a serious riot broke out in Tel Aviv in November 1945, a violent affair that was finally brought under control by 8 Para of the 3rd Parachute Brigade. An uneasy peace then simmered through the winter until April 1946 when a group of Jewish killers, the Stern Gang, murdered seven unarmed soldiers from the 5th Battalion who were guarding a car park. When two captured Jewish terrorists were tried and hanged for murder, two British Army sergeants were kidnapped and hanged by the Jewish *Irgun* organisation; the bodies of these men were then hung in an orange grove opposite a British Army camp and when they were cut down a violent explosion injured several more; the bodies had been booby trapped.

Internal security duties – IS – duties 'in aid of the Civil Power' – would form a major part of the British Army's activities for the next twenty years, so it would be as well to know how it worked. The aim was to keep the peace and let normal life go on, as far as possible, until the politicians sorted things out and the Army could withdraw. IS duties were a hard and thankless task, with little sleep, any amount of verbal and physical abuse and not a little danger from ambush, bomb and grenade attacks. To find arms and arrest terrorists the soldiers set up road blocks and conducted house searches in the towns and villages and 'cordon-and-search' operations in the countryside, usually in conjunction with the police and civil authorities. The trick was to keep everything under control and for the individual soldier not to lose his temper, however constant the provocation, for this is what the enemy wanted.

In November 1947, having brooded over the Palestine situation for months and spent a great deal of time blaming the British, who only wanted to leave, the United Nations came up with a solution – Partition. The result within hours was violent attacks on the British troops and inter-communal rioting, as Jews and Palestinians fought each other to grab as much territory as possible before the Partition commissioners moved in to decide where the boundaries should be. This situation, growing in violence, went on until 13 May 1948 when the last British soldier left Palestine. The State of Israel came into existence on the following day and the first Arab–Israeli War broke out the day after that.

By the time it left Palestine, 6th Airborne had been greatly reduced in strength; the 3rd Parachute Brigade had been disbanded and the 2nd Parachute Brigade had been withdrawn to Britain. The two and a half years in Palestine had cost the division 58 men killed and 236 wounded. The 6th Airborne Division had done its last service and on return to the UK would be disbanded. Like the 1st Airborne Division, it had done sterling service but the day of the big divisions was over. Peacetime problems would need smaller but equally active units and these were now being formed in Britain for the difficult years that lay ahead.

11

CYPRUS AND SUEZ,
1955–56

*'The drop was spot-on; I landed in a soft patch of sand
and knew from the sound of small arms fire that this was
not an exercise.'*

Captain Mike Walsh, 1 Para, Port Said, 1956

The 6th Airborne Division finally left Palestine in early
March 1948; just two months before the British Mandate
expired and the State of Israel came into existence. It had
not been a happy time for the division, which was losing
men all the time as their periods of service expired, but
the troubles in Palestine had not been without loss and
now the division was about to disappear entirely.

Palestine was the last campaign of that famous wartime
airborne division, for, on its return to the UK in April, the
6th Airborne was disbanded. Like the rest of Britain's
armed forces, the Army was shrinking to a peacetime level
and the 'brigade' was replacing the 'division' as the most
common large unit among special forces, though the
infantry and armoured corps retained divisions in
Germany and the UK for some time to come. To
commemorate the two British airborne divisions of the
Second World War, the newly formed parachute brigade
became the 16th Parachute Brigade Group, made up of
the three battalions of the Parachute Regiment, 1, 2 and
3 Para, and the usual brigade elements of artillery,

signallers, sappers and transport. The 16th Parachute Brigade numbered about 6,000 men, with all its ancillary units, but the three battalions of the Parachute Regiment remained the core of the brigade.

Various other wartime battalions and parachute units became Territorial units – 10 Para in London and 15 Para in Scotland, for example, and the parachute artillery and engineers also remained in a Territorial form. The 16th Independent Parachute Brigade was formally established on 1 April 1949 and was joined shortly afterwards by a special company, raised from the Brigade of Guards for the Pathfinding role, which became known as the 1st Guards Independent Parachute Company.

As a mobile brigade group, 16th Independent Parachute Brigade was soon employed in various parts of the world, suppressing dissent and aiding Britain's allies in or around the periphery of the shrinking British Empire. In 1952 the brigade, now commanded by Brigadier KT Darling, was rushed to Egypt, following the Egyptian Army coup that toppled the then ruler of Egypt, King Farouk. They then spent the next two years on internal security operations in the Suez Canal Zone, a dreary strip of land on the West Bank of the Suez Canal, but a place that then contained Britain's largest strategic military base in the Middle East. The Egyptians, having got rid of their king, were now even more anxious to get rid of the British, who had virtually ruled Egypt since 1882. To this end they mounted a sporadic guerrilla campaign against the British bases in the Canal Zone in which a considerable number of men were killed or wounded.

This campaign did not persuade the British to abandon the Zone, but a new base was being established on the island of Cyprus and in 1954 Britain concluded an agreement with the Egyptian Government, by which Britain and France retained control of the Suez Canal and Britain had the right to use the Canal Zone bases in case of need. With that much established by a formal treaty, the British left Egypt, but within months of Britain leaving the Canal Zone, Egypt broke both these undertakings.

The background to what followed is political and financial rather than military. Egypt was anxious to industrialise and needed to build a dam across the Nile at Aswan to provide hydro-electric power to its factories. This project was to be funded by the USA and a consortium of European nations led by Britain, but the Egyptians were also dealing with the Russians, and after various arguments the Americans pulled out. As a reprisal, and to fund the project, Colonel Nasser, the new leader of Egypt, nationalised the Suez Canal, seizing it from the French and British shareholders, which started a process that led to the Port Said landings – Operation *Musketeer* – of November 1956. Long before that brief and bungled affair though, Britain's soldiers had more trouble to cope with, in the beautiful island of Cyprus.

Like the troubles in Palestine, the problems of Cyprus are still with us and date back to the period of British colonial rule. Britain had leased Cyprus from the Turkish Sultan in the 1880s and annexed it during the 1914–18 War, when Turkey was an ally of Germany. Cyprus had belonged to Turkey since the fifteenth century when the Turks had seized it from the Venetian Republic, and before that it had belonged to the Lusignan crusading dynasty. It is important to understand that although many Greeks lived in Cyprus, the island had never been part of Greece, but in 1922 the Turks rose against the Greeks who lived in Turkey and forced them to flee, many from the port of Smyrna – the present Izmir. These homeless Greeks were offered protection by the British, and many settled in Cyprus, which also had a large Turkish community. What followed proves the truth of the old saying that 'a good deed never goes unpunished'.

Gradually, over the next thirty years the Greek percentage of the population increased until Cyprus was seventy per cent Greek and thirty per cent Turkish – and then, in the early 1960s as elsewhere in the British Empire at that time, there came the demand for independence.

The British Empire was not built to endure. The policy that drove it was trade, and the long term aim was to create a trading block of independent friendly nations, the colonies, protectorates, territories and settlements of the empire reaching that state through a process of internal self-government and dominion status before full independence. Running the empire was expensive and after the Second World War Britain was broke and tired. The British had set about dismantling their Empire by the mid-1950s and most of it would be gone by 1960s, but some places were hard to dispose of, largely because of ethnic conflicts.

Having a viable economy and a literate population, Cyprus could have had her independence without much trouble – provided Britain could retain a base there – but in Cyprus there was a particular problem that would prove hard to resolve. First of all, the Turkish part of the population were not particularly interested in independence. Then it transpired that the Greeks, who were *very* keen on independence, had not one aim in their independence 'struggle' but two. First, they wanted to get rid of British rule. Then they wanted *enosis*, the union of Cyprus with mainland Greece, the motherland. But the Turks, both in Turkey and in Cyprus itself, would not hear of it. Conflict was inevitable, and before long the brew began to bubble.

Quite apart from the on-going antipathy between the two communities in Cyprus, the island lies only fifty miles from the south coast of Turkey. Turkey had no intention of letting her countrymen in Cyprus be shanghaied into the Greek State – which certainly would not treat them well – had no intention whatsoever of letting the Greeks grab a major strategic base fifty miles off their southern shore. This opposition had not been considered by the Greeks and when the British, facing this problem, declined to give the Greek Cypriots what they wanted, the Greek Cypriots, or part of them, took up arms in an attempt to throw the British out. This struggle was led by a Cypriot, a former officer in the Greek Army, Colonel Grivas, who set up a terrorist organisation, EOKA. EOKA took up the struggle in the summer of 1954 and it was six long years before peace returned to Cyprus.

The first troops to arrive in Cyprus, when trouble erupted in September 1955, were the 3rd Commando Brigade, Royal Marines, who arrived from Malta and were deployed in the Kyrenia mountains in the north of the island, and in the town of Limassol. The Parachute Brigade arrived in early 1956, after two battalions had been sent hurriedly to Jordan in January where King Hussein had requested British help to head off a coup by pro-Nasser forces there. The Jordan crisis died down and in March the paratroopers were sent to Cyprus, where they were deployed in the Troodos Mountains in the centre of the island and around the town of Paphos, where they were soon involved in operations and sweeps against EOKA bands and civilian rioters.

The two parachute battalions, 1 and 3 Para, had some early successes, capturing three terrorists in the first month. They were then taken from the hills and sent to the cities, including the capital, Nicosia, where shooting and grenade throwing attacks on British Army patrols were a daily occurrence, and where the schoolchildren came out of school every afternoon and spent some time taunting the British soldiery and throwing bricks. It was not a happy time, and it could be dangerous. In mid-June 1956 the battalions were withdrawn and with the Commando Brigade began a series of sweeps in the mountains, trying to flush out the EOKA bands.

These 'cordon and search' operations began with Operation *Lucky Alphonse*, in the Paphos Forest, an operation that went tragically awry, when, probably because of mortar fire from 45 Commando, the tinder dry woods caught fire and a huge blaze swept across the mountains; the total death toll was 21 British soldiers, mostly from the Gordon Highlanders who were forming the cordon for this operation, as well as some members of the Parachute Regiment. This was bad enough, but Grivas, who was in the Paphos Forest at the time got away. A patrol from C Company, 3 Para, actually ran into Grivas's band resting in a gully, but though they opened fire, all the terrorists got away. The only benefit was that they left behind documents proving that the Greek Cypriots, political leader, Archbishop Makarios, was hand-in-glove with the terrorists and aiding their campaign.

This sporadic mountain warfare was good training and got many young soldiers used to the idea of going about with a loaded rifle, ten rounds in the magazine and 'one up the spout'. Alan Staff, of C Company, 2 Para, remembers an unusual incident during one tour in Cyprus:

It was in 1956, during a sweep called *Sparrowhawk One* around Paphos, a popular holiday resort today, but a fishing village back in the 50s. We were at a farmhouse near Trapeza, using that as our base while we searched the area, when one of the lads poking about in the barn saw a face staring at him – through a hole in the wall. He nearly jumped out of his skin, then yanked out his 9 mm pistol and fired at it. This produced no less than five terrorists, who came crawling out from a hide under the floor. We searched the barn and found a great hoard of gear: shotguns, gas piping for bombs, explosives, ammo, even a watch – which I pinched but was obliged to give back.

The police came up and identified the blokes and it turned out they were all wanted with prices of £5,000 a man on their heads – none of which came to us, I might add. Then the Special Branch coppers arrived, and started to beat these guys up – which did not go down at all well with the soldiers. We did not like that sort of thing at all but I have to admit that the terrorists talked and said there was another cache of weapons and explosives nearby. We went off and found it, a great steel drum, filled with arms and explosives. I have been back since and that drum, a bit rusty now, is still where we left it, forty years ago.

In spite of a great deal of provocation, the soldiers in Cyprus behaved themselves and usually got on well with the Cypriots, unless there was a riot in progress. This did not prevent the usual visit from a British politician, in this case Barbara Castle MP, who arrived on the island in 1957 and returned home to condemn the brutality of British troops.

Tom Godwin, then a sergeant in 1 Para recalls his time in Cyprus:

The battalion had its share of casualties, some of which lie in those carefully tended graves in the Wayne's Keep War Graves Cemetery which now – [1998] – lies in the buffer zone of now-divided Cyprus. I recall a lance-corporal in our battalion who put a bullet between his feet, having forgotten to take the magazine out before cleaning his pistol. That might not be worth mentioning but he had just survived a month in hospital and in detention for having fired a bullet through his hand. He was a good machine gunner but was the sort of bloke who should never have been given a personal weapon.

There were also accidents. During one cordon and search we did on the village of Agios Ambrosias, we were part of the cordon and in position before first light. It is difficult to set up an effective cordon in the dark and at first light there is a bit of movement as you shift about to plug the gaps.

Anyway, during this phase a guy broke cover and legged it through a gap in the cordon and set off down the mountain. Those who could see him were all yelling the required challenge 'Halt . . . *Stammata -Dur*', the only phrase in Greek and Turkish that most of us knew, telling him to stop, but he sprinted on, and appeared to be carrying a rucksack and a weapon. He refused to stop and our platoon sergeant dropped him with a bullet through the head at 200 yards. At the subsequent inquiry which followed all shooting incidents, it turned out that the man was a deaf-mute shepherd who was probably just frightened . . . and the sergeant's back-sight had been set at 400 yards, so the shot should have gone well over his head.

Jerry Bastin, who also served with 1 Para in Cyprus remembers some of his experiences:

I was young, just eighteen, and it was all an adventure. I am sure many ex-Servicemen, NS [National Service] or Regular, have similar tales to mine, but life was very different in the 1950s and 60s. I have shared accommodation with a pig, slept in a chicken house and in a vineyard on an incline of about 45 degrees, even in a dried-up river bed that turned out to be infested with snakes. I have never regretted my National Service, though I know that a lot of people hated every second of it. As far as I am concerned it was a great adventure, a time when I grew up – and it gave me good friends that I still have forty years later and laughs we still remember.

I remember we used to keep the fuel for our pressure lamps in a fire bucket, with the inevitable result that one day there was a tent fire and some bright spark threw our paraffin on to the blaze. Another time our section sergeant saw a fox and popped off a few rounds at it and just as he stopped firing a very upper-class voice shouted from the opposite hill, 'I say, you there, would you kindly stop shooting; this is a patrol of the ... Regiment!' We had no idea any other troops were in the area but the sergeant's rounds were bouncing off the rocks all around them and sending the Toms diving for cover. I was more miffed than they were because the sergeant had used my rifle and he handed it back to me saying, 'Don't forget to clean it.'

In July 1956, the rest of 16th Independent Parachute Brigade – 2 Para and Brigade Headquarters, arrived on the island just in time to take part in yet another operation. On 26 July 1956, the Egyptian Government of Colonel Nasser broke the agreement with Britain and France and nationalised the Suez Canal.

There was a considerable international outcry, but when the British and French declared that they would take the Canal back, by force if necessary, international opinion, in the Third World and at the United Nations, but especially in the United States, rapidly turned against them. The Russians became threatening, the US Government refused all support – not least because it was an election year and the US President, Dwight D Eisenhower, wished to present himself to the American people as a man of peace, and the so-called Non-aligned Nations – who were all firmly on the side of anyone who was against the West – set up a great shrieking and wailing in the United Nations against what they described as unprovoked aggression against a weak nation. Which rather overlooked the fact that Egypt had violated an international treaty, freely entered into, and seized the territory of two friendly powers without apology or compensation.

The result of all this uproar was that the instant move to retake the Canal came to a stop as various negotiators tried to find a solution. This was never really on the cards and by now, flushed with this success in seeing off two 'Imperialist Powers', Colonel Nasser had another idea – to unite the Arab nations under his banner and lead them against Israel, which had defeated the Arabs in the first war in 1948 and was now a thorn in the side of all the Arab nations.

There was a snag with Colonel Nasser's plan, for Israel was a small country, too small to absorb an attack. If seriously threatened, Israel had no option but to attack first. When she discovered what Nasser was planning, the Israelis prepared to strike first, and this intention proved a godsend to the British and French politicians, who needed an excuse to send troops into the Canal Zone.

Accusations that the British, French and Israelis were in collusion over the Suez operation of 1956 have floated around for years and need no longer be denied. The original plan was hatched by the French and Israelis, but the British came in later and played a full part in the eventual landings. The broad outlines of the plan were that, knowing the Egyptians were moving troops into the

188

Sinai Desert, east of the Canal, the Israelis would launch a pre-emptive strike and bring on a general engagement, close to the Suez Canal. The French and British would then declare that this fighting put the Canal at risk and would order the two sides to stop fighting. Israel, while agreeing to do so, would actually still carry on attacking the Egyptians, who, it was anticipated, would refuse this Anglo-French injunction and yell for help from its Arab neighbours and the UN. The Anglo-French invasion forces would then land in Egypt, ostensibly to protect the Canal from damage, but actually to seize the Canal Zone and topple Colonel Nasser, who, it was anticipated, could not survive such a humiliation.

While this plan was being hatched the invasion forces were mustering: the seaborne forces, the Royal Navy and 3 Commando Brigade in Malta, the parachute troops, British and French, in Cyprus, where the Parachute Regiment battalions got in some long overdue parachute training on the flat plains around Nicosia. All this training had to go on while keeping up the pressure on EOKA. Operations such as *Sparrowhawk One* and *Sparrowhawk Two* which took place in the Kyrenia Mountains in the hot summer months of 1956 proved highly successful; the Parachute Regiment's bag being a very large haul of ammunition, arms and explosives and six long-sought terrorists.

Attempts to find a solution to the Suez crisis occupied the politicians during the summer and autumn of 1956, but the longer they lasted, the more confident of victory Colonel Nasser became. In October there was a further complication, for the people of Hungary rose against their Communist masters. The Soviet Army occupied the country, and heavy fighting broke out in Budapest, with students and citizens taking on Russian tanks and infantry.

The world – or at least the USA and the UN – became more interested in that conflict and increasingly impatient with the colonial powers, Britain and France, who were demanding action to retake a possession they had clearly lost and were not likely to get back. The French were adamant that Colonel Nasser was not going to get away with this theft and although public opinion in Britain was divided, many British people felt the same way. While all that was being sorted out or at least debated, the British military prepared for war.

The plan was for a combined operation to take Port Said, at the northern end of the Canal, with a landing of Parachute and Commando troops from Britain and France, supported by strong naval and air forces. The fiction that this was simply to protect the Canal was maintained but fooled no one, and in mid-September operational orders were prepared and the troops began training for some specific tasks.

The RAF would spend the first week destroying the Egyptian Air Force. Only then would the Fleet close the Egyptian coast and the troops go in. As for the landing plan, the first task, as on D-Day 1944, was to seize the flanks of the landing beaches. The eastern edge was protected by the Suez Canal, and a French Foreign Legion parachute battalion would drop on Port Fuad, east of the Canal, to prevent any Egyptian troops crossing, but it was decided to drop a British parachute battalion, 3 Para, on Gamil Airfield, just west of Port Said, to seize the airfield and stave off any opposition coming in from the Western Desert. The battalion would go in the day before the seaborne landing and hold on for twelve hours until 40 and 42 Royal Marine Commandos landed at dawn on the beaches of Port Said where they would be joined by 45 Commando, coming in by helicopter.

Another parachute battalion, 2 Para, would come in later with the heavy equipment, field artillery, anti-tank guns and trucks and be sent speeding down the Canal to peg out claims as far as possible to the south, well down the Canal at El Cap. All this duly unrolled and on 5 November 1956, 3 Para dropped on Gamil Airfield to start an operation which would mark the end of Great Britain as a Great Power.

The 3rd Battalion flew out from Cyprus at 0400 hours

on 5 November and dropped at about 0730 hours, the first parachute assault since the Rhine Crossing eleven years before. Only one man in the battalion had jumped at Arnhem and most of the troops were going into action for the first time, but the drop went well, with the crackle of firearms from the Egyptian defenders to show this was not another practice jump at Watchfield or Hankley Common.

Corporal John Morrison dropped with A Company:

We jumped in three waves, at various heights and I was in the last wave, jumping at 1,000 feet over the airfield, though all I could see was the sea as we went in and the red light was on. Then the green and out we went. There seemed to be a lot of shooting going on already and a large chunk of steel came up and tore a great big hole in my canopy, increasing my rate of descent remarkably. I tried to get rid of my weapons container to slow my drop but in the end I hit the ground with a hell of a bang and broke my shoulder. We had a bit of a busy day, with a bit of mortaring and machine gunning and we had to put in an assault to clear them out of the cemetery but nothing came down the Western road, the fleet arrived on time and by the afternoon of 6 November, I was on my way back to hospital in Cyprus.

The 3rd Para's task was to hang on and hold the flank and this they did, in the face of slight opposition from the Egyptians and rather more intense opposition from their supposed allies, the French. Two French jet fighters appeared over Gamil Airfield in mid-morning and subjected the battalion to a sustained strafing with machine and cannon fire. At dawn on 6 November the battalion moved into Port Said to join the Marines who were ashore and fighting their way into the city and on the night of 6–7 November US and UN pressure finally took effect. A cease fire signal was sent to the troops in Port Said, and to the men of 2 Para rushing south to El Cap, telling them to hold their position and await further orders.

News of the landings appears to have horrified the United States who had long since abandoned their former allies. The US Secretary of State, Foster Dulles had asked the UN Security Council to demand a withdrawal and impose immediate sanctions on Britain and France if this order was not immediately complied with. President Eisenhower ordered the Federal Reserve Bank to start a run on sterling and destroy the British economy, and US oil exports to the UK were halted at once.

Eisenhower then phoned Anthony Eden, the British prime minister and told him that unless there was an immediate cease fire Britain faced political and economic ruin and the loss of America's friendship – this last being a factor not immediately obvious in the preceding months or indeed at any time when selling a friend 'down the river' was useful to US interests.

Britain was in no position to resist such pressure and the Suez operation was halted, an event marking the end of all imperial pretensions. The assault troops, the Commandos and Paratroopers, were withdrawn from Port Said within a few days and replaced by UN soldiers. The British troops were not unduly dismayed by what had happened on the political front. That was not their concern and from a military point of view the Suez operation had been successful . . . and there was still some soldiering to do, in Cyprus and in the Arabian Peninsula.

12

ADEN AND BORNEO,
1960–67

*'Here the soldiers relearnt the old infantry lessons; fire
discipline, silence on patrols, good weapon handling,
digging in when you stop, patience and persistence.'*

Major-General Julian Thompson, CB, OBE,
Ready for Anything, 1989

The trouble in Cyprus was over by 1960 but there was no
rest for the crack troops of the British Army. By 1960 they
were deployed again, this time in one of the most
inhospitable corners of the old Empire, the Crown Colony
of Aden and the Aden Protectorate, at the foot of the
Arabian Gulf.

Britain had acquired Aden in the nineteenth century,
seizing it after a local sultan had annoyed the Admiralty by
attacking East India merchantmen sailing to and from
India. Once ashore and established, the British stayed, and
when the Suez Canal opened at the end of the century,
Aden grew in importance. To begin with it was a coaling
station, but it became more important when oil replaced
coal between the two World Wars. A refinery was built at
Little Aden, a garrison was installed to protect it and Aden
gradually became one of the links in the long chain of
bases holding the British Empire together – though it was
one of the least desirable postings to which a soldier could
be sent, being humid, dusty, squalid, and miserable.

By the 1960s Aden could be roughly divided into two parts, the Colony and the surrounding Protectorate, which lay north of the Colony and jutted into the Yemen. The Colony was quite small and consisted of Aden, Little Aden and the suburbs of Ma'lla and Crater – Aden harbour occupies the crater of an extinct volcano, as does Crater itself, a district largely occupied by Arab traders and their shops. There was the oil refinery, several Army camps with barracks for the soldiers and their married quarters, and the great airbase at Khormaksar, from which British aircraft patrolled the Protectorate, the Gulf and the Indian Ocean.

From Aden a road ran north through the Protectorate to Dhala, on the borders of the Yemen. The Protectorate contained a number of wild tribes, who were now more or less peaceful having been quelled over the years, and who were now kept in line by a force of local volunteers, the Aden Protectorate Levies, a force commanded by officers from the RAF Regiment. Aden and the Protectorate is best regarded as an Arabian extension of the North-West Frontier of India, and the guerrilla war that took place there in the 1960s has many similarities with those supposedly romantic campaigns against the wily Pathan, in the old days of the Indian Empire.

Britain was gradually divesting herself of the Empire in the 1960s. The snags in that process usually arose in attempting to replace British rule, which, whatever its faults, gave the local people better justice and more security than they had ever known, with something that was democratic, accountable and – with any luck – friendly to British interests. The fact that these worthy aims were rarely achieved was no excuse for not seeking them.

In Aden, Britain proposed establishing a Federation from the tribes in the Protectorate, and then combining the Protectorate with the Colony of Aden – now called Aden State – and setting up a viable government before departure. By no means all the sheikhs in the Protectorate wanted independence, for they were doing very well under the relaxed British rule, but Britain's politicians were determined that they should have it.

This laudable aim, of granting independence to the 'Federation of South Yemen' faced many snags, but the chief of these was Arab nationalism and the machinations of Britain's most astute and ruthless Middle East enemy, Colonel Nasser of Egypt. Flushed with his political success in seeing off the Suez invasion, Nasser was a hero to the Arabs and was anxious to score another victory over the Western Imperialists in Aden – or South Yemen as it was known to the Arabs. Nasser had the support of anti-Royalist forces in the Kingdom of Yemen (North Yemen), a country which had always lusted after the land occupied by the Protectorate and the fine British-built port in Aden, and of Communist inspired trades union leaders in Aden itself – not to mention the then vocal, anti-Western Third World caucus at the United Nations.

In 1960, when this chapter opens, Aden was defended by the newly established Federal Army, formerly the Protectorate Levies, still British officered but with a growing number of locally recruited officers from the tribes. There were also a number of British Army battalions, quartered in Aden as well as 45 Commando RM, at Little Aden. The Marines later moved up on to the frontier at Dhala, where keeping open the Dhala Road and quelling attempts to run guns into Aden itself took up a lot of their time.

In 1962 this pot began to bubble when the king of the Yemen was overthrown in a Nasser-backed army coup led by a Colonel Sallal. This coup received a lot of support from pro-Nasser revolutionaries in Aden, people kept up to fever pitch by Nasser's anti-Western radio station 'Voice of the Arabs' in Cairo. The trades unions and pro-Nasser factions in Aden were afraid of the sheikhs in the Protectorate, and determined to resist the founding of the Federation, unless and until they gained control of it and could impose their terms on the sheikhs – who, in turn, looked to Britain for protection against their enemies in Aden and in North Yemen. Meanwhile, the Third World caucus at the UN, sensing another opportunity to meddle, were taking an interest in this developing problem. Yet another mess was in the making, and the British Army and Marines had to hold the ring while the politicians attempted to sort it out.

The trouble that began in Aden spilled over from the civil war in the Yemen, which had erupted between Colonel Sallal and the Royalists – the latter backed by some SAS 'volunteers' organised and led by one of David Stirling's original SAS men, Major John Cooper. With their assistance, the Royalists were soon giving Sallal's soldiers and their Egyptian advisers a very hard time indeed, and Nasser became eager to spread the trouble into Aden and thereby take some of the heat off Sallal's hard-pressed forces. His chance came when one of the Protectorate tribes defied their ruler, the Emir of Dhala, who had ordered them to desist from their age-old custom of holding up travellers on the Dhala road and demanding tolls and ransom. Sallal gave these tribesmen weapons and training, the Emir of Dhala called for assistance from the Federation forces, one thing led to another, the fighting escalated and the British Army were called in to add some muscle to the developing struggle.

A force was assembled at Dhala, named *Radforce* and tasked with quelling the dissident tribes. This force contained elements of the Federal Army and all of 45 Commando, but it soon became apparent that it was not sufficient for the job, and in April 1964 the 3rd Battalion of the Parachute Regiment, then in Bahrain in the Persian Gulf, were sent south to take part in the coming campaign. The first company to arrive was B Company and, after a couple of weeks acclimatisation in Little Aden, it was put on standby for a parachute operation in support of a drive into the Radfan mountains which was about to be mounted by 45 Commando advancing from Dhala. The aim of this attack was to cut off the tribes living in the Danaba Basin from supplies of arms and ammunition coming in from the Yemen. The way chosen to do this was to capture and hold the Danaba heights, which controlled both the basin and the road.

The Radfan mountains cover an area of around 400

square miles, and are inhabited by a group of tribes of which the one living in Danaba, the Quteibi, who were known to the Paras and Marines as 'The Red Wolves of the Radfan' were described by one Commando officer as 'a xenophobic lot . . . every man had been brought up from boyhood with a rifle in his hands, knowing how to use it and frequently doing so if any argument could not be settled. The arrival of the British Army was seen as a chance for some target practice.'

The object of the British advance into the Radfan was to pacify this tribe and discourage them from mining the Dhala Road and attempting to cut off the British base at Dhala; if it also served to demonstrate the long arm of the British Raj to the other tribes, so much the better. The task called for the capture of a rocky feature code-named *Cap Badge*, which overlooked the main dissident stronghold, the village of Danaba. Other features on the way in to the Danaba basin were three hills code-named *Rice Bowl*, *Coca-Cola*, and *Sand Fly* all of which would have to be taken on the approach march to Danaba, which was to be made by 45 Commando – about 600 strong – through the rough terrain of the Wadi Boran. The plan required 45 to march in overnight on 29–30 April while 3 Troop of A Squadron, 22 SAS under a Captain Edwards, infiltrated on to *Cap Badge* on the same night and secured a DZ for a parachute drop at dawn by the men of C Company, 3 Para, commanded by Major Walters. The idea was that the SAS should be in hiding on *Cap Badge* before dawn broke and stay there in hiding until dusk, when they would secure the drop zone perimeter and mark it with torches and an Aldis lamp for the parachute drop that night. This part of the operation went wrong from the start and put the C Company part of the plan in jeopardy.

Shortly after dark on 29 April, the ten SAS men led by Captain Robin Edwards, set off in armoured cars for their start line in the Wadi Rabwa. All Edwards' men were tough, experienced soldiers, many having seen action in Borneo and Malaya, the exception being the signaller, a

Royal Engineer soldier named Warburton. After leaving their transport the patrol would have to cover about eight miles on foot over very difficult terrain before arriving at the drop zone. Night infiltration was the only safe way to get about the Radfan, but in this case the darkness did not give sufficient cover and as the armoured cars laboured up the Wadi Rabwa off the Dhala Road, they came under sporadic rifle and machine gun fire from the tribesmen on the nearby heights. The armoured cars could only advance slowly in the dark and it soon appeared that they would have to halt completely and wait for dawn. Therefore, while armoured car gunners gave covering fire, what later came to be called the 'Edwards Patrol', humping their rifles and heavy Bergen rucksacks, crept away into the darkness.

Having lost the advantage of surprise, the patrol made its way slowly up Wadi Rabwa, towards the massive 4,250-foot heights of their objective, Jabal Ashquab. When things go wrong at the start of an operation they often get worse, and so it was here. Signaller Warburton had not been well before the patrol set out and was now suffering from severe stomach cramps, and the patrol had to pause at intervals for him to catch up. This slowed everyone down and it became apparent that he was getting weaker, slower and was struggling to keep going. So, in an effort to stick to their original timing, the patrol split up and started to straggle, some pushing on, others staying to help the unfortunate signaller. Shortly after midnight, realising that they would not reach their objective by daylight, Edwards decided to halt.

They were still a good three miles from *Cap Badge* and any attempt to reach it in daylight was clearly out of the question, so Edwards sensibly decided to take cover, and give Warburton, who was suffering from what seemed to be an attack of food poisoning, but may have been acute appendicitis, time to recover. They radioed their position back to the SAS squadron commander and lay up sucessfully for the rest of the night. Then, some time during the following morning, their presence was detected by the local tribesmen.

Within minutes, armed men were pouring out from a nearby village and were climbing the rocky slope towards the SAS position. The SAS duly opened fire as the tribesmen took cover and began to surround them. Sporadic firing went on for about two hours as the tribesmen worked their way closer and on to a ridge above the SAS position. Edwards had already anticipated this move and managed to make contact with RAF Hunter ground-strafing fighters, who arrived within minutes and flew a contact patrol over Edwards's position. Just as the tribesmen began to assault the SAS from the top of the ridge the first pair of Hunter jets swept down across the hills and racked the advancing tribesmen with cannon fire.

Their airstrike forced the tribesmen to break off their assault but they then took cover close to the 'sangars' built by the SAS – low walls hastily constructed from any handy rocks – and opened a heavy fire. The SAS had no way out and only the Hunters kept the tribesmen at bay – it was stalemate. The tribesmen were firing at anything that moved and they were such good shots that the SAS were completely pinned down. During daylight hours the Hunters continued to circle overhead, sweeping in to chastise the tribesmen at intervals, but the SAS realised that the enemy was being continually reinforced and were moving even closer. They were now under fire from less than fifty yards range and when it grew dark it would be impossible for the Hunters to provide air cover. The tribesmen also knew this and were only waiting for darkness to rush the sangars in force and kill the defenders. What Edwards needed was aid, fast, or he and his men would have to make a break for it in daylight, before they were overrun.

As it grew dark, Edwards was informed over the radio that the C Company parachute drop on *Cap Badge* had been abandoned, since the DZ was swarming with tribesmen, and the SAS were to try and break out just after dark and make their way back towards the Dhala Road from which 45 Commando were currently advancing. Edwards duly requested artillery fire on their position at 1900 hours, hoping they would be able to escape while this barrage kept the enemy's heads down, but meanwhile two of the SAS men had sustained leg injuries, and Signaller Warburton, who had become unconscious during the day, had died.

The artillery fire came down on time, but as the SAS broke from cover a storm of rifle fire swept over them and Captain Edwards was hit several times and fell to the ground. The others continued to run, firing as they went, and as the survivors fled into the valley the enemy continued to fire on their previous position from opposite sides. The SAS realised that two groups of tribesmen were now shooting at each other as, keeping to the high ground, they followed the hillside round the Wadi Rabwa. The artillery barrage was still falling, but the tribesmen had now withdrawn, taking with them the bodies of Edwards and Warburton.

The SAS patrol spent that night struggling up and down the gullies, keeping to the high ground where possible. The wounded men tried to keep up but everyone had to stop time and again while the medical orderly tried to staunch their bleeding wounds. This gave their pursuers time to catch up, but one of the wounded men, straggling in the rear of the patrol, heard the sound of pursuit, set up an ambush and four armed tribesmen walked into it.

As the tribesmen drew near, two SAS soldiers opened fire, shooting all four dead. Then they all moved off again, keeping careful watch to the rear and, within the hour, were once again certain they were being followed. They took cover, waited, and two more dissident groups, descending from the ridge above, walked into the SAS ambush and were killed. Striking back at their pursuers, what was left of the Edwards patrol continued towards the Dhala Road and, some time before dawn, the men were picked up by armoured cars and taken back to base.

The aftermath of this sharp little fight gives some indication of what the Radfan fighting was like. Some days later a report filtered into Aden that the heads of two English soldiers had been displayed, impaled on stakes, in the main square of Taiz, just across the Yemen border. Ten days later an Army patrol reached the area of the SAS position and found two headless bodies buried in a shallow grave. This caused a considerable diplomatic outcry, but the soldiers from 3 Para and 45 Commando, now fighting in the Radfan were not unduly surprised.

The failure of the Edwards patrol to take the DZ had disrupted the parachute drop of 3 Para but meanwhile 45 Commando had been advancing on the Danaba basin and had taken the *Cap Badge* position. B Company then arrived in the basin and after a sharp little engagement took the village of El Naqul.

Radforce intended to stay in the area and give the dissident tribesmen a sharp lesson and more companies of 3 Para arrived from the UK to add their weight to the struggle. They included a Company under Major Mike Walsh and C Company under Major Mike Ward Booth, plus the CO Lt-Colonel Farrar-Hockley, DSO, MC. The battalion were then tasked to move into the next valley, the Wadi Dhubsan, which could best be reached along a rocky escarpment, the Bakri Ridge, which ran for ten miles before descending into the Wadi Dhubsan, and was infested with tribesmen. There was little support or supply, helicopters were in short supply and everything the battalion needed, including water and ammunition, had to be carried. The advance took place at night and soon ran into opposition from tribesmen, who harassed the troops with rifle and machine gun fire before slipping away in the darkness, to fire again from somewhere else. By dawn the battalion were at the foot of the spur that marked the far end of the Bakri Ridge and over the next three days fought its way forward against ever stiffer opposition, to take the village of Quedeishi. So far, so good – and now for the Dhubsan Basin.

It was decided that the Wadi Dhubsan would be attacked by 3 Para, supported by X Company of 45 Commando. Farrar-Hockley decided to enter the wadi by descending directly down the face of the escarpment. This attempt began at dusk on 25 May and by dawn the first company, A Company, were in the valley, awaiting the arrival of X Company, 45 Commando, which was to be flown in by helicopter. Weather grounded the helicopters so X Company followed A Company down the face of the escarpment and were at the bottom by 0630 hours and ready to advance. X Company led the way and were soon engaged with a large force of tribesmen. This battle was still going on when Farrar-Hockley and his intelligence officer, flying up in a Scout helicopter to see what was going on, ran into trouble. The Scout was hit by ground fire and came to earth between X Company and the tribesmen. Fortunately, the Marines were quick to come forward and cover the Scout, and once on the ground Farrar-Hockley had his other companies come up on the flank of X Company and the advance continued, supported now with artillery fire and, as the morning mist lifted, RAF Hunter jets which swept in low overhead to strafe the enemy position. The valley was in British hands by the end of the day and that success marked the effective end of any major resistance in the Radfan. In Aden Colony, however, the struggle continued.

The Parachute Regiment returned to Aden in May 1967, when 1 Para, now commanded by Lt-Colonel Mike Walsh arrived to take charge of the Sheik Othman district, which straddled the Dhala Road, just north of the Colony. The British Government had now decided to pull out of Aden, deeming it no longer a necessary part of the defence requirement, and the Protectorate sheikhs were about to be abandoned to whatever fate the Aden terrorist groups and their allies in the Yemen – and the 70,000 Egyptian troops who supported the Yemen regime – chose to mete out to them after the British had gone.

The British Government, ever hopeful, still wished to establish a Federation, but the two terrorist groups in Aden Colony, The Front for the Liberation of Occupied South Yemen, or FLOSY, and the National Liberation Front, or NLF, while united in their wish to expel the

British and exterminate the Protectorate sheikhs, were also fighting among themselves for control of Aden when the British departed.

In Aden 1 Para were being met with the now common sniping and grenade attacks and after a few days decided to take Sheikh Othman on, sending in fighting patrols to root out the snipers and meeting force with force when rioters took to the streets. This soon had a beneficial effect, but on 1 June a trade union strike in Aden spread to Sheikh Othman and the battalion came under attack from various parts of the town. It was a well-planned attack in which all the battalion OPs (observation posts) came under accurate and heavy rifle and machine gun fire, backed up with grenades and rockets. The battle went on all day and the firing did not die down until well after dark by which time eight terrorists had been killed, three had been wounded and two captured; 1 Para lost one man killed and two wounded.

The battalion stayed in Sheikh Othman for the next four months and the battalion diary records that no less than 800 separate incidents, including sniping, grenade or rocket attacks took place in that time. By September, however, the battalion found itself standing by, ordered not to interfere while FLOSY and the NLF fought it out in the streets. In November the South Arabian Army or SAA, the former Aden Protectorate Levies, now under local officers, declared its support for the NLF and a massacre of FLOSY supporters followed, with truckloads of FLOSY supporters being driven out into the desert in SAA trucks and machine-gunned to death. So, in anarchy and murder did 'freedom' come to South Arabia. British troops were finally withdrawn in November 1967; as the troops left they could hear the sound of firing as the former Colony gave itself over to riot and slaughter. The withdrawal from Empire was generally well handled by the departing British, but Aden was the glaring and shameful exception.

The Borneo Confrontation, which overlapped with the squalid affair in Aden, was much better handled and resulted in a clear victory for the British forces, who were in this case fighting to prevent three former colonies or protectorates, the Sultanate of Brunei, and Sabah and Sarawak, in the north of the island of Borneo being taken over by Indonesia – who called the island of Borneo, Kalimantan. Brunei preferred to remain independent but Sabah and Sarawak opted to join Malaysia on independence, a decision which started a rising among pro-Indonesian rebels in December 1962. This rising was quickly snuffed out by Royal Marines of 42 Commando, who with Highlanders and Gurkhas were flown in from the British base in Singapore. The Indonesians had no intention of giving up that easily and started a guerrilla war along the 1,000-mile Kalimantan frontier, an undeclared conflict which became known as the Borneo Confrontation.

The bulk of the fighting in this vicious little war was carried out by the Gurkha infantry of the 17th Gurkha Division. The Royal Marines of 40 and 42 Commandos though were in there from the start, the SAS arrived to carry out the task of border patrolling and infiltration, and the Parachute Regiment fought one of the most decisive little battles of the entire campaign when a platoon of 2 Para beat off an Indonesian attack on one of the border forts, at a place called Plaman Mapa.

The camp at Plaman Mapa was a typical, rat-infested, border fort, basically a series of concentric trenches dug around a hilltop, with bunkers for the men and stores, the Company HQ and three GPMG (General Purpose Machine Gun) positions. These forts studded the Kalimantan frontier and the idea was that, although they could accommodate a company, two platoons would always be out on patrol and one platoon would be in camp. That meant that these camps were always undermanned and at risk from attack. The garrison at Plaman Mapa at the time it was assailed amounted to just 27 men, an under strength platoon, most of them young soldiers just out of training who had been in Borneo for just a few days and were still finding their feet in the battalion. The company sergeant-major at Plaman Mapa was CSM 'Patch' Williams, B Company, 2 Para, and what happened is very much his story:

I suppose if you had chosen one platoon *not* to have there for an attack, this is the one you would have chosen. They were young lads and they had not got their knees brown yet, but no soldiers could have done better. The Indonesian border overlooked the camp and was only a thousand metres away, so the Indonesians could see the camp quite easily. We were always on the watch, kept our boots and kit on and slept in dugouts just by our stand-to positions, weapons to hand, two mags ready, one round up the spout and safety catches on . . . you know the routine.

Anyway, we were well aware that something was up, for in the two or three weeks prior to the attack our patrols had found prepared artillery and mortar positions and OPs in the jungle around the camp. It was only a matter of time until the balloon went up, which it finally did at around 0400 hours one morning when suddenly all hell was let loose on the camp.

The Indonesians kicked off with everything, using heavy machine guns, mortars and artillery and small arms fire from rifles and light machine guns, all pouring fire into the camp and very accurate it was too, with fire going everywhere. I was in the Company HQ in the middle of the position because most of the camp activity, re-supply, moving in and out on patrol and so on, took place at night, so I tended to sleep in the daytime and spent most nights on the radio. I had a hammock slung in the HQ, which was handy, so I got up and went to see what was going on while the OC got on the radio to battalion and the fire control officer, Captain Webb from the Royal Artillery, got on to the guns at the next base up the line at Gunan and told them to get some fire down around our position. Meanwhile the Indonesians were crossing our wire.

The first attack came in on the north sector of our

position where a fellow called Kelly was manning the GPMG. These Indonesian troops were good soldiers, from one of their TNT Special Force battalions. They put in a company attack, with another company in reserve and about twenty minutes after the firing started, in they came. They attacked in full company strength with three platoons up – about 150 men – we had 27, remember – and they ran up the hill in waves and overran the defences by sheer weight of numbers.

They had got practically to the command post before they were held. They fell back so we stuck in a counter-attack and drove them out again. This took place at night and in the middle of the monsoon, so it was dark as pitch, pouring with rain and a sea of mud underfoot, with us slipping and sliding about in it. Anyway, we pushed them out but then they came in again. We had one man killed and three badly wounded by this time and were back in our southern sector where a young officer, Lieutenant Thompson, was in command. He was from the Gloucester Regiment and not a Parachute officer, who had only just arrived in Borneo and had come up to us to learn the form; I think he learnt more than he bargained for but he did bloody well. Anyway, I told him to take his chaps and counter-attack, straight at them, over the top of the command post, which he was doing when he was wounded by a mortar bomb.

We were getting good support from Mick Baughan, one of the NCOs, who was manning a GPMG in another post. He had about twelve blokes in his sector and he sent some of them over to help cover the north section where the Indonesians were trying to break in. They were trying to break in all along the perimeter so it was a question of finding out what they were doing and putting a stop to it. The entire attack lasted around one and a half to two hours and they put in three major assaults in that time, plus a lot of mortaring, machine gunning and shelling between times.

We were pretty thin on the ground, so I got in the

forward GPMG post and started to fire on them as they came in and that is when I got hit. They came up to within five feet of my position and at least four rounds hit the GPMG; another hit the radio by my head and drove steel splinters and plastic fragments into my left eye – that's why they call me 'Patch', because it blinded me . . . and afterwards I used to wear a patch over the eye.

Anyway, I killed two or three in front of my position and kept on firing. There was a lot of tracer flying around . . . grenades going off . . . a lot of yelling. That went on for quite a while, but it gradually quietened down. When I was sure they had gone or pulled back I went back to the command post to give a Sitrep [situation report], to the OC, who was still trying to rustle up some artillery fire on the radio, but we beat them off without that. When it got light we decided to send out a clearance patrol to search the area . . . and *every one* of the young soldiers volunteered to go on it; they were good lads, like I told you. Another good lad was Corporal Collier, who had been badly wounded in the arm during the action, but he got a brew on and we broke out the G10 rum and shoved a bit of that in the brew. Meanwhile, we reorganised, cleaned the place up, got the bodies out, issued more ammo and grenades and generally got sorted out in case they fancied another go.

I then took a patrol out and we had a good look round the hill and went down into the valley, but they were all gone. We put a bullet into any bodies we found around the position and found plenty of blood trails leading off towards the border, so we definitely hurt them more than they hurt us. Later that day the battalion came back and some Gurkhas arrived, and then helicopters came in and took out the wounded.

By now I seemed to have lost the sight of both eyes, so I went out too, first back to the Base Hospital at Kuching and then to Singapore. They operated on my eyes there and used some kind of giant magnet to draw out the steel splinters, which was fine. Of course the magnet couldn't pull out the plastic bits from the radio and in the end I had five operations on my eyes. They saved them, but the left one does not function . . . and that's about it.

For his leadership and gallantry in the fight at Plaman Mapu, CSM 'Patch' Williams was later awarded a very well-earned Distinguished Conduct Medal. The 2nd Battalion lost two men killed and eight wounded in this fierce little battle in the jungle; Indonesian casualties were estimated at over thirty. The Confrontation with Indonesia lasted for several years but eventually petered out and the three colonies went the way desired by their inhabitants; Sabah and Sarawak to the Malaya Federation, Brunei remaining independent under its own sultan. This sharp little undeclared jungle war gave the British Army some useful lessons in small unit tactics but did little to prepare them for the longest post-war problem, the on-going anti-terrorist campaign in Northern Ireland.

13

NORTHERN IRELAND,
1968–98

'You'll get tired of this before I will, darling.'

A British soldier's reply to abuse from a woman
in the Bogside, Londonderry, 1969

The struggle to find a solution to the problem in Northern Ireland – the current, on-going problem in Northern Ireland – which may have been ended for a while by the Good Friday Agreement of 1998, though a terrible bomb in Omagh some weeks later makes that doubtful – has been going on for thirty years, making it the longest continuous campaign ever fought by the British Army. It is, as the soldiers have pointed out from the first, not the sort of problem that lends itself to a military solution, for the root cause of the problem lies not with the military or even with the politicians, but in the hearts and minds of the citizens of Ulster, Catholic and Protestant, and that minority in each community that hate the guts of people in the other community, and have done so for some 300 years.

To explain a little of the situation confronting the troops in Northern Ireland it is necessary to go back to the reign of Queen Elizabeth I, in the latter years of the sixteenth century, and to that of her successor James I of England in the first half of the seventeenth century. This may seem unlikely, but it happens to be the case. The problem of Northern Ireland is deep rooted, and is not due to the 'oppressive' presence of the British Army, whatever is alleged by the IRA and their dim-witted supporters in the United States of America.

Both Elizabeth I and James I rightly feared an invasion from the Catholic powers of Europe, notably Spain, and regarded Ireland as the 'back door' to England, not least because the population of Ireland was entirely Catholic. These rulers therefore decided to 'plant' first English and later Scots settlers in Ireland, and since it is only twelve miles from the coast of Galloway to the coast of Ulster, in James I's time a great many of these 'planted' settlers came from the Scots Borders and the Lowlands, and settled just across the water, in the province of Ulster. Some of these settlers were sponsored by the Guilds in the City of London, so that, for example, the city of Derry became – and for the Protestants remains – Londonderry. This process of displacing the native Irish continued throughout the seventeenth century and reached a peak under Oliver Cromwell, who sacked the city of Drogheda and drove many Irish people west into Connaught.

Ignoring a lot that follows in the intervening centuries, including various attempts to give Ireland a political voice and the Great Famine of the 1840s – caused not by a British attempt at genocide but by a potato blight brought in from the United States – the scene now shifts to a period just before the Great War, when, after centuries of endeavour, the Catholic Irish finally won their independence from Britain – and the British promptly ran into a problem that was to occur and reoccur frequently during the disengagement from Empire; namely, part of the population, notably the largely Protestant population in the North of Ireland, the descendants of those fifteenth and sixteenth century 'planted' settlers of Ulster who would not consent to live in a Catholic-dominated Ireland. 'Home Rule means Rome rule,' chanted the Protestants of the North, and they were prepared to take up arms to prevent the establishment of an Irish State.

It has to be said that at this time, 1912–14, the Catholic

Church in Ireland had a far more dominant position in Irish society than it enjoys today, with a strong voice in political, public and even family life, but even then there was no likelihood that the Catholics would bring in the Spanish Inquisition, or that the Protestants would stage Cromwellian-style massacres – the root of this hatred was distrust and hatred between the communities, fuelled by centuries of exploitation by the Protestants.

There was therefore an *impasse*. The Protestant leader, Sir Edward Carson, declared that 'Ulster would fight and Ulster would be right', and in the spring of 1914, when the British Government ordered a cavalry brigade stationed at the Curragh outside Dublin to ride into Belfast and coerce the Protestants to accept the new arrangements, the officers threatened to resign *en masse*, declaring, rightly, that it was no part of their duty to drive unwilling British citizens into the arms of another state.

The result of this impasse was Partition. In 1920 the island of Ireland was partitioned into two states, the 'Six Counties' of Ulster becoming the Province of Northern Ireland, and part of the United Kingdom (of Great Britain and Northern Ireland), and the rest becoming the Irish Free State, later Eire and now the Republic of Ireland. The problem in 1920–21 was that some of the people in the Free State did not accept the Anglo-Irish Treaty that set up this situation and codified Partition. A civil war broke out in Ireland, between those who accepted the Treaty and those who did not, the latter banding themselves into a clandestine organisation, the Irish Republican Army, or IRA; the Free State Government had to shoot a large number of IRA men before the Civil War ended, but the problems of Partition – and the reluctance of some Irish people and many politicians to accept it – did not go away. Terrorism and sporadic violence disturbed the peace in Ulster and on the British mainland regularly over the decades from 1920, but came to a head in 1968 when the Catholic population of the North took to the streets under a new banner – Civil Rights.

There can be little doubt that the Catholics of Northern Ireland had every right to take to the streets in 1968, for their grievances were long-standing, deep-rooted and incapable of solution within the democratic process, in so far as that existed in Northern Ireland in 1968. Northern Ireland had its own parliament, Stormont, which was totally controlled by Protestants, many of them members of the Orange Order, a purely Protestant organisation, dedicated to the union with Britain, but strangely ignorant in the matter of those basic rights all British citizens should share. While the Orange Order ran Stormont, the Catholics were barely even second-class citizens; a Catholic could not get a decent job or a decent home or a good education for his children. He would even have difficulty getting justice in the courts. Northern Ireland was a moral and political disgrace and, when the Catholics took to the streets, the public in Britain saw that for themselves, for the largely Protestant police force reserve, the B Specials, attacked the Catholic demonstrators with particular fury, beating men, women and children senseless in the street.

In doing this the B Specials were brutal, and the Stormont Government most unwise. Television was now in every British home and the riots and beatings on the streets of Belfast and Londonderry were relayed back to mainland Britain and then around the world. Questions were soon being asked, in the Press and in the House of Commons, as to what had driven the people on to the streets and produced such a violent reaction from the authorities. When the answers came out, the British public were horrified. Radical reform was demanded and the B Specials were disbanded. This produced another problem, for when the riots continued the Royal Ulster Constabulary (RUC) had no reserves to contain them. And so, once again, for 'actions in aid of the Civil Power', the British Army were deployed in a peace-keeping role on to the streets of Northern Ireland, and have been there ever since.

It seems strange now but when British soldiers first

appeared in the Catholic housing estates they were greeted with smiles, sticky buns and cups of tea. It did not last long but it was nice while it lasted. The soldiers were quite willing to be friendly, but 'hearts and minds' operations, so important if the intolerance so widespread in Northern Ireland was not to spread to another generation, did not stand a chance in Northern Ireland as a Parachute officer, Joe Starling, late of Aden and by now a brigadier recalls:

> Even if the local people were interested in being friendly, and some of them probably were, the IRA soon put a stop to it. The children were being educated in prejudice and violence and with the schools shut and no recreation to keep them busy, had nothing else to do but cause trouble, even when they were not put up to it by their parents and the IRA. The troops would put up play areas and organise canoe trips on the Bann but just as the troops and the kids were getting to know each other, the IRA would spread the word, and the canoes would be smashed up and the play area burnt, anything to spit in our eye. The Provos [Provisional IRA] let it be known that it was dangerous to be too friendly with the Brits, beating, tarring and feathering men and women whom they suspected of even smiling at a soldier. The Catholics soon got the message to 'hate the Brits and to be seen to do so' but the worst of it was the effect on the children which was heartbreaking.

The IRA soon moved on to bombing and sniping attacks against the RUC and the military, and a bombing campaign began. One of the first Parachute officers to arrive in Northern Ireland was Philip Neame, later of 2 Para:

> I was then serving with the RAF Regiment and was sent with a platoon of soldiers to guard some 'stores' on Aldergrove Airport outside Belfast. I was not told what

213

these 'stores' were but on arrival I soon found out. In one of the hangars, crammed in tight, were about 150 Phantom jet fighters, newly purchased from the USA and awaiting conversion to Rolls-Royce engines. Thirty of us, armed with rifles, were to protect the RAF's entire, shiny-new fighter force. As I was taking all this in, a wing-commander appeared and asked me if there was anything I needed. I said, 'How about some machine-guns?' It all fizzled out, of course, and no IRA appeared, but that was my first introduction to the Province. I went back again later when I transferred to 3 Para and that was different . . . very different.

Colin Butcher was a sergeant when he went to Ulster with 2 Para:

The battalion first went there at the start of the Troubles in 1969. I went there on another tour in 1971, when we were based at Magilligan Camp, up on the coast of Antrim, looking across the water to Donegal, which is in the Irish Republic – and north of Northern Ireland if you see what I mean. I was a platoon commander and we did VCPs (Vehicle Control Points – basically road blocks) and mobile patrols, some on foot, some by helicopter. Belfast was hard work, lots of problems. We had a map at HQ, coloured for the Protestant (Orange), Catholic (Green) and 'Mixed' areas; in the 'Green' areas you had to be very careful. We then went to Londonderry to relieve the Anglians [infantry regiment] and were based in the Creggan factory. Colour-Sergeant Danny Poynter and I did our recce tours of the Bogside in Land Rovers with the Anglians' driver trying not to go slower than 50 mph, but when the Para battalion arrived we did our patrols on foot.

Later on, when it was obvious that this sort of thing was going to go on, before we went on a Northern Ireland tour, we had a training course in a mock-Irish village, set up at Lydd in Kent. It was just like the real thing, with a pub and a fish and chip shop, the lot. We would take it in turns to act out all the situations you could face. One company to be the locals or the IRA, the other company to be the Army and we would try to provoke each other. We had WRACs [Women's Royal Army Corps] playing the role of housewives, and the girls really got into it – I never heard such language, but they were right – the Catholic women were the worst of the lot, swearing and spitting and hurling rocks and petrol bombs – and you can't thump women, after all.

It was all right I suppose, but soldiering in Ireland really wasn't much fun. You really had to watch your step, but some amazing things did happen. When we were in Londonderry two of our blokes, the signals sergeant and a signaller, came to check our radios and they *walked*, right across the Catholic Bogside from the Masonic car park to our base. That's indian country, believe me – and a good mile of dangerous ground – and they were in uniform, red berets, the lot. When we realised what they had done we were amazed and told them. 'You must be bloody mad', but all the sergeant said was that he had thought it a bit funny because no one replied when he said 'good morning'. We always tried to be polite but it did no good – all you got in return was a lot of 'effing and blinding about English bastards – often from those happy enough to pick up their British dole money, of course.

The British soldiers who served in Ireland had a lot to put up with from the local population – and it must be remembered that all of them, soldiers and civilians, were fellow countrymen and British citizens. Yet men, women and children on the Catholic estates took delight in spitting and swearing at the British soldiers on foot patrol, as well as throwing stones, bombarding them with bottles full of petrol during riots, and acting as living shields for IRA bombers and snipers at other times. This was not acceptable and was not usually tolerated by the battalions who laboured to get their patch under control and reduce the influence of the terrorist godfathers who held the Catholic estates in fear. Major Philip Neame went to Northern Ireland with 3 Para:

> When I was in the Parachute Regiment I first went to West Belfast with Support Company, 3 Para. Our patch was the Derrybeg Estate, a strongly Republican area, and when we arrived there Derrybeg was said to be a 'No go' area for British troops. We were not having any of that, so Support Company took the Derrybeg Estate on. We had the usual torments at first of course but we stood no nonsense, firm but fair, and in the end it paid off. Everything settled down and life got back to normal, which was good for us and good for the residents, most of whom just wanted to get on with their own lives anyway.

This daily round of abuse and attack should be remembered as background to the daily threat of a bullet in the back or the sudden explosion of a 500-pound bomb, hidden in a culvert, that could blow a personnel carrier and its passengers to pieces. One day perhaps, when these troubles are really over, the Irish people on both sides of the religious and political divide might give a word of thanks to whatever God they believe in that, in spite of the provocation they offered the soldiers, the streets of Northern Ireland were patrolled by men of the British Army, the finest and most long-suffering army on earth. Irish-Americans who doubt that, yelp about British oppression, and fund the IRA, should remember the massacre of innocents by Lieutenant Calley and the troops of the US American Division in a Vietnam village called My-Lai.

With the IRA on the scene from 1969, the situation continued to deteriorate, and before long terrorist attacks and civil disorder problems were not just being found on the streets of the Northern Ireland's towns and cities. The border with the Republic soon became a stalking ground for the 'active service units' – murder gangs – of the IRA, who could withdraw to the safety of the Republic after each attack. In February 1971 the IRA killed their first British soldier, a twenty-year-old member of the Royal Artillery, Gunner Curtis who was hit by a sniper in Belfast.

In August 1971, in response to the rise in violence, the British Government introduced internment: imprisonment without trial. Inevitably, the introduction of internment caused trouble on the streets of Northern Ireland as well as protests in Dublin and the United States, where the pro-IRA lobby was active. It also created heart-searching in Westminster, where the measure, if clearly necessary, was still very unwelcome.

Colin Butcher of 2 Para again:

I remember internment starting. We picked up all the known terrorists still on the loose. It was a Monday morning at about 0400 hours and we had as many detachments as possible out, with lists of 'players' – that's known IRA men – with 'form' for terrorist actions, and we went from house to house, picking them up. They went mad, there is no other word for it, and so did the whole area, kids throwing stones, women out banging dustbin lids, cursing, crying, attacking us. There was a bit of shooting, but not much. Ballymurphy went wild . . . roads blocked with burning cars and so on.

There was the beginnings of a riot so we got stuck in and sorted it out, but don't believe all the stories you hear about violence from the troops. If any soldier got out of order or someone complained about something a soldier had done, the MPs [Military Police] came to interrogate the troops and had to get a report back within 24 hours – all 'hearts and minds' of course. When you got to Ireland you were issued with twenty rounds of 'front line' ammo and if you lost a round you couldn't get another one and got into real trouble. Mind you, I expect some of the old soldiers had a clip or two.

The IRA did not restrict themselves to bombing or shooting. It was equally important to destroy the reputation of the British Army and present the soldiers as aggressive thugs. In this they frequently succeeded. Complaints about the behaviour of the soldiers were made in the Westminster Parliament and the British Press and provided a useful source of propaganda for Sinn Fein and the IRA. A Parachute officer, Brigadier Joe Starling, gives the other side of the story:

> The troops on the streets, most of them young corporals and private soldiers in their late teens or early twenties, always had a hard time. They did not want to be there, they had no axe to grind in this centuries-old, mindless, Catholic–Protestant quarrel that a bunch of bigots lacked the will to settle. Yet they were under constant verbal abuse, spat at, stoned by men, women and kids, all the time, and at risk from snipers and bombs. They saw their friends killed, shot, maimed, blown to pieces . . . and the locals gathering round to watch did not neglect to sneer or cheer when the young British dead were cleared away. This was supposed to be a part of Britain but this was not how decent British people behave . . . or decent Irish people either, come to that.
>
> All the soldiers could do, and what they were ordered to do, was to ignore it. Yes, all right, now and then a few things happened which should not have happened, a fist was swung, a rifle butt deployed, but no one is in any position to point the finger at our soldiers and call them brutes. No other army in the world could have done it. No other soldiers could have resisted the constant provocation to retaliate. We knew, and the troops in the street knew, that retaliation from the troops was just what the Provos wanted.
>
> What upset the troops was not the harassment but the inhumanity of the locals. For example in May 1971 Sergeant Willets of 3 Para was at the Springfield Road Police Station in West Belfast when a terrorist bomb

was dropped into the station, concealed in a suitcase. Before it could go off, Sergeant Willets ushered the people inside, including a local man and woman and their two children, into the street, shielding them with his body as they fled. Just as they reached the street the bomb went off, killing Sergeant Willets instantly . . . and as his body was carried to an ambulance later, the assembled throng outside the wrecked police station sang Republican songs and spat on his body as it lay on a stretcher. They must be proud of themselves.

The story of Northern Ireland is a sad one, since it is all so unnecessary, but the Parachute Regiment were in it from the start and took more than their fair share of both losses and controversy. Chief among the latter was the so-called 'Bloody Sunday' incident on 30 January 1972, when the men of 1 Para were ordered in to back up the police and other soldiers during a riot in Londonderry, caused by about 150 youths in the crowd of over 3,000 demonstrators, hurling stones and petrol bombs at the police during what the organisers claimed was a peaceful procession. The troops were fired on and returned fire and in the shooting 13 'civilians' were killed – though some of them were seen to be armed before the troops opened fire. The soldiers were accused of firing *indiscriminately* into the crowd but if so it is strange that they only shot adult males aged from 18 to 26 years old and not any of the thousands of women and children present. The subsequent inquiry exonerated the soldiers, but as part of the Peace Process yet another inquiry is to be held in 1999, 27 years after the incident took place.

It has been suggested that the British should 'apologise' for Bloody Sunday and it may happen. One might then ask who will apologise for Bloody Sunday, when Lord Louis Mountbatten and members of his family were blown to pieces at Mullaghmore, or for the eighteen soldiers of 2 Para and the Queen's Own Highlanders, blown to pieces at Warrenpoint on the same day. Every day of every week for over thirty years gives someone something to apologise for, if apologies come into fashion, and there seems no reason for the British Government or the British Army to lead the process. Over 3,000 people have been killed in Northern Ireland, by far the majority of them by the Provisional IRA – and that fact ought to be remembered by anyone seeking 'apologies'.

The campaign against the IRA in Northern Ireland has not provided great battles or heroic last stands. This is a campaign where the true glory rests with the soldiers in the streets, who displayed a very British form of courage, the courage to soldier-on, putting up with the long hours, the lack of sleep, the living conditions that a self-respecting vagrant would decline, the constant abuse and the ever-present danger, not for days or weeks or months, but for years and decades, until, perhaps, permanent peace comes at last. They would have done their duty, as soldiers should, perhaps thinking themselves hard done by, but never thinking themselves brave. Their country, and the decent people of Ireland, North and South, all owe them a debt, or at least a word of thanks, for a job well done.

14

THE FALKLANDS WAR: GOOSE GREEN, May 1982

*'Parachute soldiers have, since 1940, been given plans
. . . ranging from the excellent to the abysmal. I know;
I gave 2 Para a rotten task at Goose Green.'*

Brigadier Julian Thompson,
3 Commando Brigade, Royal Marines

Like many post-Second World War crises, the Falklands
emergency of April 1982 came out of a clear blue sky and
caught Britain completely by surprise. There had certainly
been some indications that Argentina, which had been
trying to gain possession of the Falkland Islands – Las
Malvinas – since the early decades of the nineteenth
century, was preparing to take some direct action, but
very little was done to discourage them, probably because
nobody in Downing Street or Whitehall, or at the United
Nations in New York, thought that the Argentine Junta,
the group of generals that then ruled – or rather misruled
– Argentina, would actually be so stupid as to invade the
territory of a friendly power and hope to retain possession.

Anyone who thought that was wrong, for on 2 April
1982, strong Argentine forces came ashore at Port Stanley
in the Falkland Islands and in spite of a brisk response by
the vastly outnumbered Royal Marines of the Falklands

garrison, overran both islands, and the outpost of South Georgia, and declared that both territories would henceforth be an integral part of Argentina.

This announcement did not go down too well in the UK or indeed at the UN, though within days the latter organisation, paralysed with the idea of actually having to take a decision, was wavering over what to do. Speeches were made and resolutions were passed, ordering Argentina to get out, all of which Argentina duly ignored and, as time passed, two things happened. Firstly, the world at large, especially in Latin America and the Third World, began to accept the idea that Argentina would and, indeed, should hang on to the Falklands. Secondly, a British Task Force of some fifty ships, carrying fighting units of Royal Marines Commandos, the Parachute Regiment, the Gurkhas and the Guards, was sent to the Falklands to throw the Argentine Army out if all diplomatic and political persuasion failed. Such persuasion did fail, and on 19 May 1982, six weeks after the Argentine invasion, British forces commanded by Brigadier Julian Thompson, OBE, commander of 3 Commando Brigade, Royal Marines, landed at San Carlos Water in the Falkland Islands and started to move inland.

When Brigadier Thompson was ordered to take his brigade south and evict the Argentine Army, he pointed out that his brigade was too small to carry out such a task. There were about 12,000 Argentine soldiers on the Falkland Islands and, though 3 Commando Brigade is a fully equipped brigade group, with its own Commando-trained artillery, signals, sappers and air squadron, the cutting edge of the brigade is three infantry units, Nos 40, 42 and 45 Commandos, RM. The total strength is around 3,500 men. There is also a Commando Logistic Regiment, usually known as The 'Loggies', and when Brigadier Thompson was asked what extra force he needed he replied that two battalions would do it, since the Commando Logistic Regiment, though tasked to handle three infantry units, could handle five at a pinch.

The Parachute Regiment was very anxious to get in on

this Royal Marine 'show' and, after some sorting out, two battalions, 2 Para commanded by Lt-Colonel 'H' Jones and 3 Para commanded by Lt-Colonel Hew Pike, were transferred from 5 Airborne Brigade and attached to 3 Commando Brigade for the Falklands landing, which had by now acquired a code name: operation *Corporate*.

By the time the Marines and Paras went ashore at San Carlos in mid-May, the Argentine forces that had seized the islands in early April had increased in number and had had time to bring in heavy weapons, including field artillery, and fly in ground-attack fighter aircraft. They had also begun to dig-in, construct bunkers and lay minefields, especially on the hills around the islands' capital, Port Stanley. There were now some 12,000 Argentine soldiers on the island, mostly infantry, but including gunners and air force personnel. They had a quantity of heavy machine guns, 105 and 155 mm artillery pieces, and Pucara ground support aircraft actually on the islands, while flying in from the Argentine mainland, 350 miles away – half an hour in a fast jet – were a large number of first-line combat aircraft, mostly French-built Mirages. Many of them were capable of carrying bombs and some were equipped with Exocet anti-shipping missiles – also supplied by the French.

The British hoped to lever the Argentines out with 5,000 professional soldiers, some 105 mm artillery pieces, a few light tanks, and the eighteen Harrier jump-jets carried on two small aircraft carriers. This task was seen to be a difficult one and the Commando Brigade was due to be reinforced by a second brigade, 5 Airborne (5 Brigade), in which the two parachute battalions now attached to 3 Commando Brigade had been replaced by battalions of the Welsh and Scots Guards. This brigade had not yet arrived when 3 Commando Brigade were ordered to leave their bridgehead in San Carlos and attack the Argentine-held airfield at Goose Green. Brigadier Julian Thompson, who was ordered to send 2 Para against Goose Green, did so much against his will.

The battle at Goose Green was always controversial and

as the years have passed the controversy has grown. To understand the situation it is necessary to understand a little about amphibious warfare, in which 3 Commando Brigade had been specially trained and in which Brigadier Thompson was an expert. Operation *Corporate* was, first and foremost, an amphibious operation, conducted over open beaches 11,000 miles from the UK, against a well-armed enemy who outnumbered the landing force two to one. On the face of it, the British commanders had a stiff task before them, and so it turned out to be.

Given surprise, it is usually possible to carry out an amphibious landing, but it is not always possible to make it stick. What the Argentine forces should have done, as soon as they learnt of the landings, was to move up close to San Carlos, seal off the beaches and the bridgehead, pound the British shipping and the shore positions with their artillery and bombs, and then send in their infantry battalions to drive the British into the sea. Brigadier Thompson had to guard against that, by securing a bridgehead, pegging out claims well inland, building up his supply base, wearing down the enemy with harassing patrols, and holding on until 5 Brigade arrived; then the British would march on Stanley and win the war.

Thompson's first task was to get ashore, which he did on 19 May. His next task was to secure the bridgehead and establish himself inland, towards Stanley, which he was in the process of doing, in spite of heavy Argentine air attacks which sank a number of warships. He was also preparing to move inland towards a central position on Mount Kent when the container ship *Atlantic Conveyor* was hit by an Exocet missile on 25 May and subsequently sank, taking with it a quantity of helicopters, including the large Chinooks. The loss of these helicopters put a crimp in Thompson's plan.

Helicopters are a 'force enhancer', a means of increasing the effectiveness of troops by adding to their mobility, but Thompson was already desperately short of transport and needed helicopters to carry forward not only troops but ammunition and supplies – and ammunition is *heavy*. With the loss of the *Atlantic Conveyor* it became clear that if the British wanted to get to Stanley, fifty miles away across the desolate moors and mountains of the Falkland Islands, they would have to walk and that would take time. Then came the order to attack Goose Green.

While the soldiers had been going ashore, matters had been moving along in Washington, Downing Street and the UN. The US Secretary of State, General Haig, had been shuttling between Buenos Aires, London and New York, trying to find a peaceful solution, and fears were growing in London that a 'compromise' would first be reached and then insisted on by the UN. A 'compromise' that would leave the Argentines on the Falkland Islands, since they flatly refused to get off.

Mrs Margaret Thatcher, the British prime minister, was not interested in compromise; she wanted the invaders off British sovereign territory, *pronto*. If they would not leave willingly then the British Army would make them leave; defending British territory is, after all, what the Armed Forces are for. Her immediate task was to prevent the UN or the USA imposing a 'solution' that would give the Argentine invasion some legitimacy and to do that, to put it bluntly, she needed some blood on the carpet. If British and Argentine troops were already engaged in battle, the time for talk and 'compromise' would be over, so Brigadier Thompson was ordered to attack the Argentine garrison holding the airfield at Goose Green, some miles from the bridgehead and well off the direct route to Stanley.

Even before landing on the islands, Thompson had had his eyes on Goose Green. He knew that Argentine air superiority would be a factor in the fighting and the airfield at Goose Green was known to contain ground-attack Pucara fighters. He had therefore intended to make a battalion raid. 'Nothing terminal,' he told this author: 'Just go in, duff them up, destroy what we could and bugger off, that's all.' Now that the British were ashore though, a raid on Goose Green was irrelevant and the garrison there could be sealed off while the main body of

British troops marched on Stanley. The Argentines had failed to contain the bridgehead or do much to disturb the landing other than from the air; they were dug in around Stanley, where they were busy improving their positions, and Thompson believed, correctly, that the troops at Goose Green could be left to wither away, while he took his brigade up to Stanley and punched a hole in the Argentine defences before they got any stronger.

When the order came to attack Goose Green, Thompson therefore demurred. He also pointed out that, having lost his main helicopters, he had no means of moving up guns to support the single infantry battalion making the attack – and he could only send a single battalion because Goose Green sits on a narrow peninsula and there was no room for more than one battalion to fight there. For all these correct and cogent military reasons, Thompson refused to attack Goose Green. He was then *ordered* to do so, and told that, if he was still reluctant to take on the job, the powers-that-be would find someone to replace him. 'I decided,' he said later, 'that I would win this one for them ... and then I would go.'

Lt-Colonel Jones's 2 Para were detailed for the task and their first job was to collect all the available information on the objective and the Argentine forces in garrison there. Goose Green is a small hamlet with a grass runway airfield, about three miles up the narrow peninsula set between the Choiseul Sound and Brenton Loch. To get to a position ready to attack, 2 Para had to make a night approach march to an assembly area at Camilla Creek House at the head of the peninsula, two miles from the 'start line', the place where the attack would begin on H-Hour. A track up the peninsula from there would provide them with an axis of advance, but the way was barred by a low hill, running halfway across the peninsula, resting on the settlement at Darwin. This ridge was known as the Darwin Heights.

Estimates on the size of the garrison varied. The SAS patrols said the Argentine forces at Goose Green and

Darwin numbered about a company, say 200 men, about right for a battalion attack. Other estimates doubled this amount and added that, in addition to any soldiers, there were also a large number of Argentine Air Force personnel, who might also get involved in the fighting. The garrison certainly had machine guns, some artillery and were dug-in behind minefields which had been laid both around the airfield and on the Darwin Heights.

Thompson said later that when these assessments came in he should have beefed up the plan and gone himself, adding 40 Commando to the attack plus at least one troop of Scimitar light tanks. This may be true, but it is still hard to see where these additional troops could have been deployed. By way of support the battalion would have a section of two 81 mm mortars, each soldier in the assault companies carrying one mortar bomb to drop off on the mortar line, some artillery, three 105 mm howitzers and a supply of shells flown in by Sea King helicopters to Camilla Creek, and naval gunfire from the single 4.5 in gun on the frigate HMS *Arrow*, cruising off the peninsula.

On the night of 27 May 2 Para began the march to their start line and by dawn were in position in and around Camilla Creek House. There they received some disquieting news when, on switching their radios to the BBC Overseas Service they heard an announcer telling the world – and the Argentine forces – that a British battalion, 2 Para, had left the bridgehead and were about to attack Goose Green, while 3 Para and 45 Commando were advancing towards Stanley. 'Within minutes,' says one Parachute officer, 'the buildings at Camilla Creek House were deserted as the battalion scattered and looked for cover, anticipating Argentine recce and air attacks – and there we spent the day, freezing cold, dreaming about what we would do to that BBC reporter when we got our hands on him.'

During the afternoon, Lt-Colonel Jones assembled his company commanders and gave out his orders for the attack. Since the ground around Goose Green was flat and open – it was an airfield, after all – he had elected for a six-stage night attack, to provide the cover of darkness for the attacking troops. His orders having been given, at 0230 hours, the first company of 2 Para, A Company, commanded by Major Dair Farrar-Hockley, whose father had served in the Parachute Regiment in Aden, moved out to attack Goose Green. An account of what happened after that comes from the D Company commander, Major Philip Neame:

As General Thompson has said, the attack on Goose Green originated as a raid, and the idea of a raid on Goose Green was on and off two or three times before we actually went in and did it. During that time the plan seemed to change and we also began to get a better idea of what Argentine forces were based there. In the beginning, from SAS patrol reports, we had the idea that the garrison of Goose Green was two or three hundred, a couple of companies, just about right for a good battalion attack. By the time we attacked, this estimate had grown and we thought there were maybe six or seven hundred there, say the best part of a battalion and in the event there were nearly twice that many, though a lot of them were Argentine Air Force people who took no part in the infantry fighting.

The peninsula containing the settlement at Goose Green is about one mile wide, and some five miles long. The ground is generally flat, or is slightly rolling with shallow valleys, and the most significant feature lies about halfway to Goose Green, where a low rise spans the peninsula between Darwin on the right of the battalion as it advanced, and a ruined cottage called Boca House on the left. This feature contained the main Argentine defensive position before Goose Green. More Argentine troops were dug-in behind Darwin Hill, defending the Goose Green airfield, with others billeted in the settlement buildings or the schoolhouse. There were also a number of minefields and some outlying defensive positions.

Goose Green was defended in depth and the open ground around the airfield gave the defenders a clear field of fire. Lt-Colonel 'H' Jones allocated six hours for his battalion to advance from the start line, penetrate the Argentine defences and be inside Goose Green. After six hours it would be broad daylight and unless this aim was achieved his battalion would be fully exposed on open ground. Given the distance that had to be covered and the enemy that lay in the way, this plan, for six phases in six hours, was highly optimistic.

Major Neame again:

Some people have commented that the plan was unimaginative, the battalion just bashing down the centre of the isthmus into the settlement, but if you have seen the ground you would realise that our options were limited and there was no space for sneaky stuff or flanking attacks. There is precious little room for manoeuvre and a seaborne landing in support was also out of court as the landing craft could not find a decent beach. What we really needed at Goose Green was some effective artillery support. With some guns and the light tanks of the Blues and Royals, which we had later on Wireless Ridge we would have walked it. As it was, it had to be done in the old way, with infantry.

What happened to the gunfire support that was provided will be covered later, but the availability of artillery was limited by Brigadier Thompson's chronic problem, a shortage of helicopters to move the guns and carry the – very heavy – artillery ammunition. Before Goose Green the British forces had not had a major encounter with the Argentine Army and had no idea what they would do, but the general opinion was that if the British gave them a good clout they would fold. That was certainly the view in 2 Para as Major Neame will confirm:

' "H" [Lt-Colonel Jones], our CO, had got the battalion thinking that they could do anything, whatever the situation; the odds did not come into it. We thought that if we hit the Argies hard they would collapse. "H" had inspired that battalion and frankly, if we had had up to fifty per cent casualties, the rest would still have gone on. During the battle it may be that "H" got too close to the action to really see what was going on across the entire area, but . . . such was the man . . .'

The garrison of Goose Green was made up of about 500 infantry soldiers in three companies drawn from two different Argentine regiments. There were also about a thousand Argentine Air Force personnel, whose task was to run the Goose Green airfield and service the Pucara ground-attack fighters that were either based there or flew in from other airfields on Pebble Island or Stanley. The airmen took little part in the fighting and wisely stayed under cover while the battle went on, leaving the soldiers to engage the British infantry. For support the Argentine soldiers had three 105 mm Italian pack howitzers and a number of 30 mm heavy machine guns, weapons intended for defence against air attack, but equally effective against attacking infantry. Though most of the Argentine garrison at Goose Green were not involved in the battle, the advantage still lay with the defenders; the usual attacker-to-defender ratio should be about 3:1; here the odds were about even and it was obvious from the start that Goose Green would be a hard nut to crack.

Philip Neame again:

My company, D Company, was sent to secure Camilla Creek as the assembly area for the battalion before the attack, and the rest of the battalion joined us there after a 20k [kilometre] bash from our position on Sussex Mountain, near San Carlos, where we landed. It was a chilly night and we were on 'light scales', which meant no comforts like sleeping bags. Each man was carrying between 80 and 130 pounds when we moved off for the attack and as you know, 'H''s plan called for a six-phase attack, but since that didn't happen we need not waste too much time on it.

H-Hour, the moment the attack began, was at 0330

hours local time and as we crossed the start line, we were, from the left, A, C and B Company, followed by 'H''s Tactical HQ [Tac HQ], with my D Company in reserve. A Company attacked Burntside House, a position just beyond the start line, which was empty and then moved up the left flank, following along the shore towards Darwin. The rest of us came on a bit later and pushed on until we were driven a bit off track by a minefield . . . and that is when things started to go awry.

A's attack went in OK but B met resistance on the right flank. It was very dark and the men got well scattered as the various rifle sections then found enemy trenches and positions and started to deal with them. Those of us bringing up the rear had overshot the start line and I found that my company was actually ahead of Colonel 'H''s Tac HQ which he took as a personal insult. So 'H' went charging off up the track ahead while D seemed to have nothing to our front. I wanted to push on but was told to wait and then we started getting fire from the right flank, from the B Company area.

Anyway, we duly attacked this position. I had no idea how big it was, but heavy machine guns were firing at us from the flank and it got pretty chaotic – frankly, battle is chaotic. We were concerned that we would hit B Company if we returned fire, we had a platoon pinned down and another one had vanished into the dark. In fact, just like 'B', my sections were being pulled in all directions, seeking out the enemy. Remember it was very dark, low cloud . . . a nightmare. In the end I put up flares to indicate where I was and we eventually overcame the opposition, but we had lost two men killed and two missing. We now had to reorganise and get on.

It took 'B' about an hour to reorganise and us about the same; there is a lot to do after an attack, to round-up blokes, sort out who was who and where everyone was, check the ammo and get organised . . . and that was when I began to realise that 'H''s time-and-space allocation, those precious six hours to get under cover before daylight, was going out the window. Besides, we were clearly not doing a 'phased attack', at all. We were doing an 'advance to contact', pushing on until we bumped something, sorting it out and dealing with it, and then sorting ourselves out, and pushing on again. It certainly works but it takes time. We were not getting any artillery support and were very much on our own.

By now it was becoming clear to all that the battalion plan was coming apart. In the circumstances – pitch dark and plenty of enemy – the battalion did all it could. They were getting negligible support for the mortars had used up all their ammunition in the first couple of hours and the gun on HMS *Arrow* had jammed. So 2 Para pushed on and tackled each obstacle as it appeared, but it is fair to say that at about this time, two hours into the advance, chaos was reigning among the rifle companies. Most of this was due to the dark and the nature of the ground and there was no real cause for concern over the battle. Argentine resistance was not proving excessive but the troops were beginning to slip behind on the timings, which were in any event hopelessly optimistic. Six phases in six hours was simply not on and as a result dawn – and the main Darwin defences – struck the battalion at about the same time.

Major Neame continues:

The situation was that B Company were moving up to attack the Boca House position on the right flank of the high ground, on the crest of the Darwin Hill, such as it is. Boca House itself is a ruin in the lower ground behind the ridge. A Company, with only two platoons up, had run into tough opposition on the left and had come to a complete stop, battering away at the Argentine defenders and losing men in the process. The advance had stopped so 'H' was now up with A Company on the Darwin Hill, where a number of people had been killed, trying to sort things out ... I was listening to all this on the battalion net. Then Argentine artillery started to range on us and I lost another soldier here, Private Meakin, so I moved the company forward into the lee of the hill.

This was interesting, for from this position I could see the coast to my right, and we saw Argentine survivors from the B Company attack on Boca House slipping away along the shore. They were in dead ground and getting clear away, though we fired at them. What they could do, we could do, and if we did that we could outflank the Darwin Hill position at the same time. So I asked 'H' for permission to move forward, but he was still busy on Darwin Hill and told me to stay put ... to keep my nose out ... as he had a battle to fight. It was clearly going to be a long day, so I told the men to get some food inside them and put a brew on. My porridge was just starting to bubble when I heard on the battalion net that 'H' had been killed.

Lt-Colonel Jones had been up with A Company, urging the company commander to put in a frontal attack. The company commander, Farrar-Hockley, pointed out that they had already put in several attacks and lost men on each one, shot as soon as they appeared on the ridge line. Lt-Colonel Jones then rose and, accompanied by his bodyguard, ran off to the flank, perhaps seeking another way into the Darwin Hill position. He was spotted and fired upon by an Argentine machine gunner and died from his wounds a few minutes after being hit.

'How did we react?' says Philip Neame: 'Well, I don't think we were surprised. Given the way "H" was, it was almost to be expected. We certainly were not dismayed. We had now lost five men in D Company, including three killed, but we took it in our stride and got on with it; there is not a lot else we could do. Major Tony Rice, of the Royal Artillery, was at "H"'s Tac HQ and he took over until Major Chris Keeble, the second-in-command, could come up and take over. I never got my porridge because

Keeble ordered me forward to join B Company and take Boca House and suddenly we were moving again.'

B and D Companies attacked the Boca House position with machine guns and Milan anti-tank missiles and as the infantry moved up the Argentine defenders started putting white flags out. D Company moved up along the shoreline to Boca House, pausing there to re-supply with ammo before putting in an attack. B and D Companies overran the company position around Boca House and there were still about forty Argentine soldiers in it when the paratroopers took it; twelve dead and the rest 'wounded or dismayed'.

The rest had already fled as Major Neame recalls: 'From Boca we could see an amazing sight. We had a view right across the airfield to the Goose Green settlement and there were about fifty Argentine soldiers, the remainder of the Boca garrison, running hell-for-leather back towards the settlement, led by an officer *riding on a tractor*. It was like something out of *Monty Python*! It was now about midday, or late morning, and we could see that the main Argentine position had collapsed, for A and C Companies were now coming forward from Darwin.'

The battalion had done very well, but their success so far had not been without loss. They had lost their commanding officer, Lt-Colonel 'H' Jones, and a number of other men had been killed or wounded. They were now in the middle of the Argentine position, there was still a great deal left to do and the Argentine defenders had meanwhile received reinforcements. About the time the Darwin Hill position collapsed, a company of Argentine infantry was flown into the Goose Green settlement by helicopter and more were to arrive later. In the late afternoon a further 150 troops arrived, also by helicopter, having been collected from the Argentine strategic reserve on Mount Kent, a force that arrived just in time to be taken prisoner by 2 Para before they could fire a shot.

The enemy was on the run and the trick now was to keep them on the run, keep the pressure on and prevent them reorganising. Unfortunately, there was the old problem of regrouping after an attack, as Philip Neame explains:

I only had two platoons up – say fifty men. I had left 10 Platoon on Darwin Hill to mop up, under the company second-in-command, and the machine guns had not yet arrived from the beach; I had about fifty blokes with me, so that would have to do and we took off across the airfield after the Argies. We were about a third of the way across the airfield when we saw some trenches and tentage away to our right. I sent 12 Platoon across to check that out and pressed on with the rest towards the Goose Green schoolhouse. There was a minefield to our front, but a very obvious one, and not a problem in itself but one that pushed us away to our left, towards the schoolhouse. I think it was about this time we were joined by the Recce Platoon and the Patrol Platoon from C Company. They had been shelled on Darwin Hill and were a bit shaken and seemed to be under no particular command. When we got into the settlement we fired some rocket rounds into the schoolhouse – or rather we tried to. It actually took four attempts before we got a hit and by that time we were all in hysterics, falling about with laughter after every miss, cheering the eventual hit. Then I got the bad news.

You remember that I had sent 12 Platoon to check out the tentage beyond the minefield. The news was that Jim Barry of 12 Platoon had seen white flags at the tentage, and had decided to go up and take their surrender. We were busy at the schoolhouse and by the time I got back to tell him not to go, or to be bloody careful, he had taken a section of men and advanced towards the Argentine lines. Well, for some reason, they opened up on him and Jim and two NCOs were killed and several more men were wounded.

I didn't think it was a 'false surrender' – to lure my blokes into the open. There was a lot of firing and machine gunning going on, and I think the Argentine soldiers got confused. Neither is it true that afterwards the Argentine defenders at the tentage or at the schoolhouse were massacred in revenge by the Paras. Throughout the entire campaign my men were extremely good and kind to Argentine prisoners and the wounded, as front line soldiers usually are.

Anyway, by the time I got to 12 Platoon, the platoon sergeant, Sergeant Meredith, had neutralised the 'Flagpole' position, by firing into it, which set off a bomb dump inside the Argentine lines. He had also extracted the bodies of Jim and the wounded. My reaction was, 'Then why aren't you going forward?' To which Meredith bluntly replied, 'I would not go any further forward than this.' Since heavy small-arms fire was coming towards us from Goose Green, he was probably right. Anyway, we were scattered and I needed to regroup the company before we went any further, but meanwhile Chris Waddington had stormed through the schoolhouse with grenades, setting it alight. It was now about three o'clock in the afternoon, we had been on the go for twelve solid hours and we were feeling pretty tired so I started mustering the lads and finding out where the rest of the battalion were. They were consolidating on Darwin Hill and D took about an hour to reorganise near the 'Flagpole' position, while being harassed by some artillery fire from guns beyond Goose Green.

Keeble told me he had ordered in an air strike and we were waiting for the Harriers to blast the guns before we moved so when we heard the sound of jet engines we just stood about, looking up for the Harriers . . . and an Argentine aircraft appeared and came diving in on us. It was just like the movies; we were all standing or sitting about in the open, there was no cover, lights were flashing along his wing-tips, cannon fire was stitching up the turf and coming right towards us, closer and closer and then right amongst us . . . and somehow he missed the lot of us . . . a bloody miracle.

Then a Pucara aircraft whistled over us and dropped napalm so we opened up with everything we had and hit him; the pilot ejected and landed nearby and we picked him up. He looked pretty apprehensive, as well he might, for troops are supposed to be very eager to meet any ground-attack pilot who has just dropped napalm on them, but we were not hurt and we sent him back to San Carlos that night, quite undamaged.

It was getting dark and Chris Keeble came on the air again and told me to go firm where I was as 'other things were afoot.' We spent the night huddled together in a minefield; the mines were poorly laid and you could see them quite clearly. We were fully exposed to a counter-attack but I was not worried. I knew that the fight was over and word soon came that the formal surrender of Goose Green would be at dawn. So at dawn we were all sitting up on a bit of high ground and we watched the Argentine troops coming out of Goose Green, hundreds and hundreds of them. It is a good job they jacked it in when they did; we were all knackered, down to our last few rounds of ammunition and right out of food.

What do I remember most about the Goose Green battle? I remember that bloke on the tractor ... hilarious. I remember that we had fifteen killed and eighteen wounded at Goose Green, and I remember watching one of my men die in front of me. I'll always remember that.

Goose Green may have been an unnecessary battle but it was a famous victory and useful politically, which was the object of the exercise in the first place. It also showed the British forces in the Falklands that they could take on the Argentines and win, even against heavy odds. There was a lot of stiff fighting ahead, but after Goose Green the outcome of the Falklands campaign was never in serious doubt.

15

THE FALKLANDS WAR: MOUNT LONGDON AND WIRELESS RIDGE, June 1982

'You say you would be proud if your son died for his country. We all say that, but when the body-bags come home, it's different.'

General Al Haig, US Secretary of State,
to the generals of the Argentine Junta, June, 1982

After the debacle at Fitzroy, when the Welsh Guards took terrible losses in the bombing of the RFA *Sir Galahad*, 2 Para was pulled out of the hills beyond Fitzroy, where they were achieving very little and getting very wet, and were detached from 5 Brigade and sent back to join 3 Commando Brigade. The battalion was now commanded by Lt-Colonel David Chaundler, who had reached the Falklands after parachuting into the sea near the Naval Task Force – the only parachute jump of the Falklands War – and then being flown ashore by helicopter to join the battalion at Fitzroy. Once back under command of 3 Commando Brigade, Brigadier Thompson placed 2 Para in brigade reserve as his other units moved on towards Stanley.

The Commando Brigade, of which the forward elements were now 42 and 45 Commandos and

Lt-Colonel Hew Pike's 3 Para – most of 40 Commando, to their great disgust, having been left to hold the base at San Carlos – was now investing the Argentine positions in the hills around Stanley. Having arrived before the Argentine lines, all the units of the brigade were involved in aggressive recce and fighting patrols, going out each night into the hills, probing the Argentine positions and plotting the location of heavy machine guns, artillery and minefields, ready for the main assault which must soon follow. After Goose Green there was no more talk of a cease-fire, or compromise, or UN intervention; the Falklands War would now be fought to a conclusion and would end when General Menendez, the Argentine commander in Stanley, finally gave up the struggle and surrendered his forces.

At about this time, the end of May, the unit commanders in 3 Commando Brigade were given their objectives for the next phase of the campaign. Their task was to break through the Argentine defences on the hills around Stanley, before making a final assault on the town. This would not be easy and required a coordinated plan, for the Argentine defences interlocked and it would be hard to take on a position unless the other, which supported it, was taken at the same time. The war that had begun so suddenly at the start of April had settled into a grim struggle.

This was no small-scale 'colonial war' operation, involving a company of men and a couple of helicopters. During this campaign in the South Atlantic, ships had been sunk, aircraft shot down, many men had been killed on both sides and a great many more had been wounded. Those soldiers, British or Argentinian, who had rushed off so blithely to do battle in the South Atlantic, now realised what war was really like. The Argentine Junta showed no sign of giving up this struggle, even though by now it must have been clear to them all that the British were going to win and by a large margin. The Junta, those generals oppressing the people of Argentina, also knew that, if they lost this war, they would fall from power, and were urging

Menendez to fight to the end and somehow snatch a victory.

As planned 45 Commando were tasked to attack Two Sisters, 42 Commando were to go against Mount Harriet and 3 Para were to take Mount Longdon. If all went well, and there was enough time left before daylight, two of these units were to move on to their 'exploitation targets', objectives they might hope to take in the aftermath of victory, Tumbledown for 45 Commando, and Wireless Ridge for 3 Para, but these positions were not to be formally attacked, just occupied if the Argentines fled and left them vacant.

If they were still occupied, then 5 Brigade would attack them later, the Scots Guards tasked with taking Tumbledown the following night. Then, if the Argentines had not yet seen that all was hopeless and decided to surrender, 2 Para would come in and take Wireless Ridge, close to Stanley harbour; after that it was only a matter of entering the town and fighting it out, street to street and house to house, though Major-General Jeremy Moore MC*, the Royal Marine officer commanding the land forces, hoped it would not come to that.

The snag for the attacking battalions was that these objectives had interlocking fields of fire; Two Sisters, Longdon and Harriet could all bring fire on to each other's defence lines and Wireless Ridge was commanded by the higher ground on Tumbledown, which would have to be taken before Wireless Ridge was attacked. The whole Argentine defence line around Stanley had been well laid out and well prepared; to take it would take skill, luck and guts. The attacks made by the two Royal Marines Commandos, 45 and 42, on Two Sisters and Harriet were both successful, as was the 3 Para attack on Longdon, where Sergeant McKay won a posthumous Victoria Cross, the second VC for the Parachute Regiment in the Falklands campaign.

Like the other hills around Stanley, Mount Longdon is an open moorland rather than a true mountain, the sides seamed with narrow 'stone runs', with a jumble of much larger rocks on the summit itself. The top of Longdon is actually a narrow ridge, barely large enough for one company to move along at a time. The Argentine defenders on the slopes and summit were well dug-in in trenches and dug-outs hacked out under the rocks, where they were protected from artillery and mortar fire and had a wide field of fire for their .5 inch machine guns. There were also minefields and snipers deployed to cover any of the approaches.

Given the open ground around the objective, a night attack was the best option for all these attacks, and anyway the British Army usually attacks at night. Lt-Colonel Hew Pike therefore selected 2000 hours as H-Hour; this was four hours after dark, and just before moonrise, and his calculation was that 3 Para would have four hours of darkness to reach the start line, and then some moonlight soon after the attack so that the men could see what needed to be done on the objective.

Pike intended to attack with three of his four rifle companies and his Tactical Headquarters up, all coming in from the west to sweep right along the narrow spine on the top of the mountain. The battalion mortars, Milan anti-tank missiles, so useful for knocking out machine-gun nests, and the fourth rifle company, C Company, would form a firm base at the start line – codenamed *Free Kick* – while A and B Companies would get on to the crest and southern slope of the mountain and clear across it, eliminating two Argentine positions, codenamed *Wing Forward* and *Fly Half*, and pressing on to *Full Back*, at the eastern end of the ridge. It was a simple, sensible plan and it worked, though not without difficulty and some loss.

B Company opened the battle when, after getting delayed crossing the Murrell River which lies just west of Longdon, their commander, Major Argue, decided that, rather than carry on with his original intention, which was to have his 6 Platoon clear the northern slope, and his HQ and 4 and 5 Platoons clear the southern one, he would attack from slightly further south, ordering his men to move into the rocks as quickly as possible before the moon

241

rose. Both companies crossed the start line at 2015 hours, just a few minutes late, and the battle began when one of the section commanders of 4 Platoon trod on an anti-personnel mine. The explosion alerted the Argentine defenders and they immediately opened fire, their heavy machine guns firing down the slopes on fixed lines and 3 Para promptly charging into their defences to begin their assault.

A night battle is always confusing, a mixture of shattering noise, yells, gunfire, grenade explosions, flares and tracer, a time when men can lose their bearings and lose touch with their comrades, all in a split second – look away and you can be completely on your own. The commanders, at platoon, company and battalion level, have to try to keep a grip on things, find out what is going on and issue orders if possible, but it really comes down to the soundness of the initial plan and the ability and training of the troops, who have to remember their orders and carry them out, however much noise and confusion surrounds them. It takes an experienced, well-trained and highly disciplined battalion to bring off a night attack successfully – and this battalion, though superbly trained, had never been in action before – and did wonderfully well.

Six Platoon made their way to the crest at the western end of the mountain without firing a shot, although they flung grenades into some bunkers they passed on the way up. Unfortunately, one bunker was missed; it contained a section of the enemy, men who also knew their jobs, for they opened fire into the backs of the British platoon, causing a number of casualties and forcing the para-troopers to go to ground. Six Platoon then found themselves caught in the crossfire between their own 5 Platoon and enemy positions further along the ridge. Four Platoon now came up to join forces with 5 Platoon and, with these two elements, some fifty men, established on the ridge, they began to advance along it towards the eastern summit – and ran at once into heavy machine-gun fire from three guns sited behind the western crest, in a position to rake anyone coming over the rise ahead.

The first burst of fire wounded the 4 Platoon commander, Lieutenant Bickerdike. His platoon sergeant, Sergeant Ian McKay, therefore took command. McKay decided to take out a heavy .5 machine gun which was raking their position from a stone sangar some distance ahead, and rounded up two of his men and a section commander, Corporal Bailey. These men ran in across open ground to assault the sangar. On the way, Corporal Bailey and one of the privates were wounded, and the third man, Private Burt was killed. Sergeant McKay therefore ran on alone, firing his SLR (self-loading rifle), tossing grenades into the sangar, destroying the gun and crew. Then he too was hit and killed, his body falling over the wall into the Argentine sangar . . . but the machine gun had been silenced and his men could move.

The battle on the ridge was now in full swing. Major Argue, hearing that Lieutenant Bickersdike had been wounded and Sergeant McKay killed, sent another NCO, Sergeant Fuller from Company HQ, to take over 4 Platoon. Sergeant Fuller, with the rest of 4 Platoon and with covering fire from a section of 5 Platoon, continued the advance along the ridge. Four Platoon killed more of the enemy but found themselves unable to reach the next machine-gun nest, which was pouring a heavy fire straight along the crest of the ridge which also had to be attacked. These frontal assaults on the machine guns were costing casualties; another five men being hit in Sergeant Fuller's assault, so Major Argue pulled his men back briefly, and had the artillery bring down more fire on the centre and eastern end of the ridge, before moving his men over to the northern slope to put in a flank attack against the Argentine positions there. The paratroopers pulled back while the artillery did its stuff, their retreat covered by fire from Lieutenant Bickerdike and his wounded signaller, who had continued to keep up a steady fire on the Argentine sangars from where they lay on the open hillside.

The B Company attack had stalled and Hew Pike came forward to the company Tac HQ to find out what was going on and see what he could do to help. What was needed, as at Goose Green, was more support and, fortunately, this could be provided by the artillery, naval gunfire and the battalion's own mortars and GPMGs. All these raked the enemy positions with a blanket of fire for some minutes and then 4 and 5 Platoons of B Company, fighting as one, came in again from the flank with bullet, bayonet and grenade, getting among the enemy sangars and clearing the enemy out in a brief burst of savage fighting.

The Argentine soldiers on Longdon were putting up a good fight and were being well handled by their officers. Not only had they stood off B Company, they had found time to bring fire down on A Company attacking the *Wing Forward* position out on the left flank. The Argentines also called down their own artillery and mortars on to A Company, which was forced to go to ground and was unable to fire back because B Company were now entangled in the Argentine positions. Lt-Colonel Pike, seeing this, ordered them to withdraw and pull back to the western end of the ridge and come forward again, this time through B Company, and take the *Full Back* position at the eastern end of the ridge.

Pike was doing his job extremely well, fighting his battalion *as a battalion* and not getting involved in any one company's problems. Under covering fire from the artillery and the GPMGs, the platoons of A Company were soon fighting forward along the ridge, pushing the enemy back steadily, reducing his sangars and trenches with well-directed grenades and bayonet charges. A Company were also well handled, carefully clearing each of the enemy positions before moving on to the next one, leaving no Argentine soldiers alive behind to fire into their backs, using the ground skilfully and taking minimum casualties as they edged along the ridge.

Eventually, after eight or nine hours of hard, close-quarter fighting, the enemy were seen to be pulling out, retreating over the crest of the eastern summit and running off into the valley towards Wireless Ridge, which lies on the far side. This was not the end of 3 Para's problems, however, for as the Argentine infantry pulled out their artillery took up the struggle, firing on pre-set targets – DF tasks – preventing 3 Para exploiting forward on the heels of their retreating foes and taking Wireless Ridge that night. There was also a problem from the flank, for the exploitation target of 45 Commando, Tumbledown, had also not been taken, and for the same reason, lack of time. The Marines of 45 had taken Two Sisters by 0430 hours and the CO, Lt-Colonel Whitehead had radioed to Brigade HQ, telling Thompson that he intended to move on to Tumbledown. Thompson ordered him to hold where he was, since there was fire coming off Tumbledown, where the enemy were clearly on full alert and well dug-in. With dawn only two hours away, Whitehead did not have time to reorganise his Commando after the attack on Two Sisters and put in another major attack before daylight. Fire from Tumbledown was falling on all the brigade positions, and would continue to do so until the Scots Guards took Tumbledown two nights later.

The 3rd Battalion, Parachute Regiment lost seventeen men killed during the battle on Mount Longdon, while another six men were to be lost under the steady rain of shells from the Argentine's 105 and 155 mm guns on Tumbledown over the next day and a half. During that time their forward positions were visited by officers and NCOs from 2 Para who came up to the 3 Para lines on Longdon for a close look at their next objective, Wireless Ridge.

This position was the responsibility of 2 Para, by now the most experienced of all the British battalions on the islands. Philip Neame takes up the tale again:

The battalion was under 3 Commando Brigade and had been moved up behind Mount Longdon and we waited there while 3 Para took it. I can't honestly say that we were thirsting for battle; in fact, far from it. There was no 'gung-ho' spirit left in the battalion and the general feeling was that we had done our bit at Goose Green, so let some other bugger have a go. We were pretty apprehensive about going in again, though once we actually got in, it was all right. We were also a much more experienced, battle-hardened unit, better able to tell what was dangerous and what was only frightening.

Wireless Ridge is actually two hill features; the first is just a low mound and then there is the ridge proper, which actually is a ridge, and quite narrow. This lies south of the mound and overlooks it so again you have two positions which have to be taken together. In addition, the entire Wireless Ridge position was overlooked and commanded by Tumbledown. Therefore, we could not attack the Ridge until the Scots Guards attacked Tumbledown on 13–14 June, so there was a bit of a delay. We used this time to go up and visit 3 Para which was then dug-in on Longdon. While we were there we had a good look at the Wireless Ridge and got the artillery ranged on the enemy. This last was not too easy and we had an argument about one position on the map which 3 Para said was in their lines and we said was held by the Argentines, and in the way of our attack. We settled the argument by shelling the feature and when 3 Para's Toms didn't invade the airwaves to complain we knew we were shelling the enemy.

Wireless Ridge was a strongly held position. The troops holding it were a battalion from the 7th Infantry Regiment, part of which had fought 3 Para so stubbornly on Longdon. This regiment had four full rifle companies on the Wireless Ridge feature, dug-in and well supplied with heavy weapons. Lt-Colonel Chaundler therefore elected for a two-stage attack, with the bulk of the battalion first taking the northern feature, the mound. Three rifle companies would then use that as a fire base to support Major Neame's D Company, which would attack the southern ridge and sweep right along it, rolling up the two main Argentine positions there which had been codenamed *Blueberry Pie* and *Dirty Dozen*.

Lt-Colonel Chaundler had promised 2 Para that this time they would have full support from naval guns, artillery and the light armour and this duly arrived, with the frigate HMS *Ambuscade* and Scorpion light tanks providing useful support to the attacking infantry. The artillery contribution was somewhat less helpful as Major Neame's account shows:

H-Hour for the Wireless Ridge assault was at 0300 hours and at first all went well. We over-ran that outlying position, the one we had shelled from Longdon, and found it deserted. We cleared the trenches carefully, just to be on the safe side, but there was no fighting or coordinated resistance and we moved up to the main, southern ridge. It was a very cold night, bright and clear, with good visibility. We felt all right up on the ridge for we had B Company ready to come in and support us if necessary, but really there was not enough room on the ridge for more than one company, which was pretty standard in all these Falkland battles. There was no opposition on *Blueberry Pie* . . . plenty of signs of recent occupation and rapid evacuation, empty trenches, kit lying about, weapons, including heavy weapons and abandoned ammunition, but no troops. I don't think that the enemy knew we were up there at that time, and we moved on.

We moved on along the top of the ridge until we got somewhere between *Blueberry Pie* and *Dirty Dozen*. I knew that the Argentines had to be around somewhere so I told our FOO [Forward Observation Officer] to put down some fire on *Dirty Dozen* before we attacked and that is when the trouble started.

I should explain that, at least in theory, every assault company should have a FOO, an officer or senior NCO, who travels with the company commander's Tac HQ, to control artillery fire. Unfortunately, there was a shortage of FOOs and we didn't have one – or not a fully qualified one – who could handle radio procedure and read a map and know his job. Instead, we had a signals sergeant and when I told him to call down fire he gave the wrong map reference. As a result, a full artillery battery put down airburst shells . . . right on top of us.

When the shells whistled in we all went to ground but we had one guy killed and another injured. There was no point in having a shouting match in the middle of a battle, so I told this guy to call up the correct reference and get some fire down on *Dirty Dozen*. I don't know what he did, but the shell fire came nowhere near the target and some shells even fell on C Company on the mound. There was then a considerable delay as we tried to get a grip on the gunners, who were sending shells all over the place, including one gun which had its sights right out of alignment and was energetically shelling B Company.

While that was going on Colonel Chaundler came on the air, somewhat irate, to ask what the delay was and why wasn't I sending my Sitrep in the best 'School of Infantry' fashion, every fifteen minutes – I explained that we were rather busy at the moment, and we pressed on.

We finally got four guns firing on *Dirty Dozen* and I said we'll go with that. I should add that the Scorpion light tanks were a terrific help, busy hosing the ridge with fire. This came in useful for diverting the enemy's attention since we were in plain view on the ridge: we could see the Argentines on *Dirty Dozen* clearly and if it had not been for the fire coming in from the northern feature and the Scorpions we would have been in more trouble than we were. Anyway, the time had clearly come for the big push and then, just as we were about to go in, one of the company ran into and set off an illuminating flare . . . and that really blew it.

Thanks to that 'friendly fire' shelling, we had already lost momentum, and a lot of fire came up at us from *Dirty Dozen* and this drove us to ground. Once on the ground the troops were very reluctant to get up again and it all came down to junior leadership. Frankly, I was shit scared – I know I was shouting and swearing, but I don't know what I was saying; everyone else, the officers and NCOs were yelling, 'Come on' and 'Let's go!' with a lot of 'effing and blinding. Anyway, the company got up and we started advancing. As I got up I lost my signaller, who fell into a shell hole; I assumed he had been shot but he was carrying the real link to battalion and was the only signaller we had so I did not want to lose him.

We took the *Dirty Dozen* position at the trot; 10, 11 and 12 Platoons all deployed across the ridge. One of 11 walked into a trip mine but we could see the Argentines running back, so we kept moving. We were very anxious to give them no time to stop, think and fight back. We had been told to stay up on the ridge and not go below the southern ridge line towards Moody Brook or beyond the telegraph wires at the end of the Ridge, as the SAS were having some sort of private party down there on the beach and we were not invited. We got to the end of the ridge and reorganised just as the Argentines put in the first counter-attack.

We had lost our artillery signaller by then but 12 Platoon squashed that attack, though I noticed that there seemed to be a lot of fire following me about as I moved around the ridge. This was probably snipers; the Argentines had very good night sights on their rifles, better than anything we had. When I got up to 10 and 11 Platoons I found that my runner, Private Hanley, had already got a grip on things ... a super chap, Private Hanley. I had time to find my signaller and pacify the colonel who was still demanding Sitreps and we then beat off a second counter-attack. We stayed up there till dawn, when the colonel and Brigadier Thompson came up but by that time we could see the Argentine troops coming out of the hills and flooding into Stanley and it was clear they were jacking it in. The Toms got their berets out and one or two started chucking smoke grenades about, but the sergeant-major soon put a stop to that. Then we moved into Stanley and the war ended that afternoon.

The Falklands victory caused tremendous jubilation in the UK, where the celebrations went on for weeks, reviving every time another ship sailed in loaded with jubilant troops.

'We missed most of that because 2 Para flew home,' says Major Philip Neame, 'though we went back to Ascension [Island] on *Norland*, the ship we had sailed out in. There was a bizarre event some months later, when the battalion got a vast bill from the NAAFI – about £12,000 – for the "comforts", the daily bar of chocolate or packet of fags dished out to the troops in the field. We had assumed it was free. Anyway we had no funds to pay the bill and, when the NAAFI suggested we should levy a charge per head on all the men who had served in the South Atlantic, we pointed out that quite a few had died there.'

Losses in the South Atlantic campaign were significant. The British lost 255 dead and a further 777 were wounded. Four warships were sunk, as well as the merchant ship *Atlantic Conveyor* and the RFA stores ship *Sir Galahad*, lost at Fitzroy. The Fleet Air Arm and RAF lost 34 aircraft, either fighters or helicopters. Argentina had 746 of her young men killed and thousands more were wounded; 12,978 Argentine soldiers and airmen were taken prisoner. Apart from the cruiser *Belgrano*, the submarine *Santa Fe* and several smaller ships sunk, more than 100 Argentine fighter and bomber aircraft were shot down. The Falklands campaign was a nasty little war. Nothing was finally settled, for the Argentines have not accepted the judgement of battle and their insistent claim to 'Las Malvinas' may cause another war some day.

With this account of the regiment in the Falklands War, we can end this story of the Parachute Regiment. In the years since Wireless Ridge, the parachute battalions have served all over the world, and done their full share of tours in Northern Ireland. They remain what they have been since the regiment was formed in the dark days of the Second World War, one of the world's elite fighting forces. The regiment is now part of 5 Airborne Brigade,

itself part of Britain's Rapid Reaction Force, a unit ready
to go into action at short notice anywhere in the world . . .
and wherever they go, the red beret will mark them out as
a regiment to watch . . . and beware of.

SELECT BIBLIOGRAPHY

Cooper, Major John, *One of the Originals*, Pan Books, 1991.

Crookenden, General Sir Napier, *Airborne Operations*, Salamander Books, 1970.

Foxall, Raymond, *The Guinea-Pigs*, Robert Hale, 1983.

Frost, Major-General John, *A Drop Too Many*, Cassell, 1980.

Hastings, Max, and Jenkins, Simon, *The Battle for the Falklands*, Michael Joseph, 1983.

Middlebrook, Martin, *Arnhem, 1944*, Penguin Books, 1995.

Neillands, Robin, *A Fighting Retreat: Campaigns in the British Empire, 1947–97*, Hodder & Stoughton, 1997.

Neillands, Robin, and de Norman, Roderick, *D-Day 1944: Voices from Normandy*, Weidenfeld and Nicolson, 1994.

Norton, GG, *The Red Devils: From Bruneval to the Falklands*, Arrow Books, 1988.

Paget, J, *Last Post: Aden, 1964–67*, Faber, 1969.

Thompson, Major-General Julian, CB, OBE, *Ready for Anything*, Weidenfeld and Nicolson, 1989.

Saunders, Hilary St George, *The Red Beret*, Michael Joseph, 1950.

Sosabowski, Major-General Stanislaw, *Freely I Served*, William Kimber, 1960.

Urquhart, Major-General RE, CB, DSO, *Arnhem*, Cassell, 1958.